Eastern United States

Areas in which this guide is especially useful are shaded.

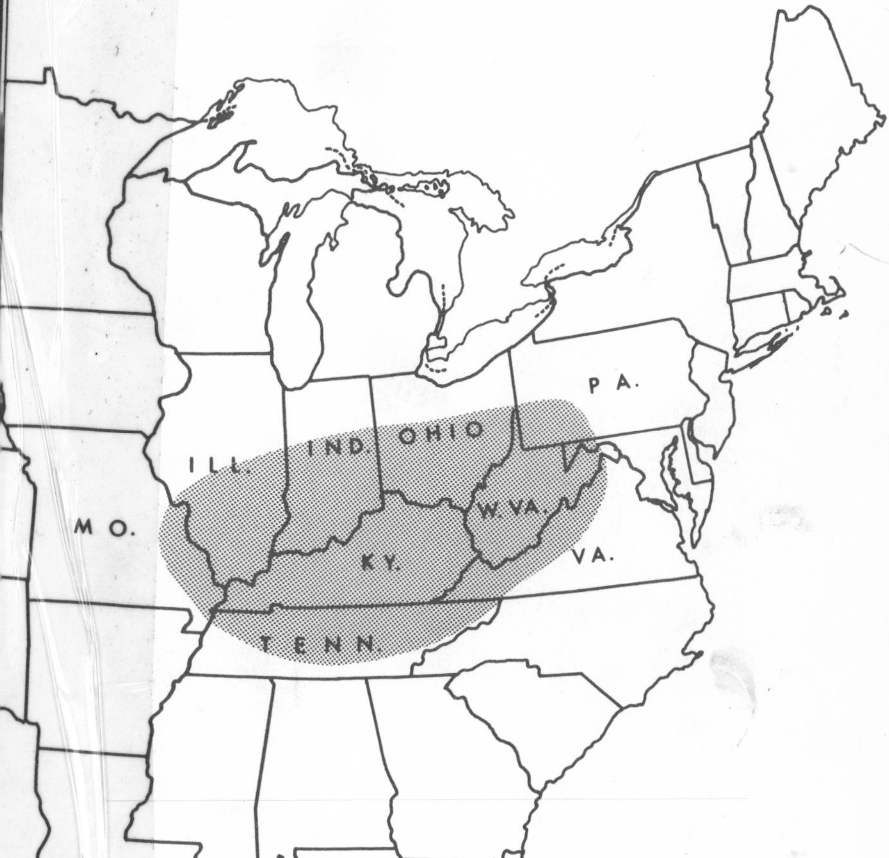

The Wildflowers *and* Ferns of Kentucky

Mary E. Wharton
& Roger W. Barbour

The University Press of Kentucky

ISBN: 0-8131-1234-6

Library of Congress Catalog Card Number: 79-132833

Reprinted with corrections in 1979

Scholarly publisher for the Commonwealth,
serving Berea College, Centre College of Kentucky,
Eastern Kentucky University, The Filson Club,
Georgetown College, Kentucky Historical Society,
Kentucky State University, Morehead State University,
Murray State University, Northern Kentucky University,
Transylvania University, University of Kentucky,
University of Louisville, and Western Kentucky University.

Editorial and Sales Offices: Lexington, Kentucky 40506

Contents

Preface

This venture is an outgrowth of the authors' long-held conviction that any real strides in the conservation of our natural resources must come from the general public, and can be brought about only through increasing awareness of our surroundings.

The text was written by Mary E. Wharton, and reflects her careful study of the flora of Kentucky, extending back over a quarter century. The photographs are largely by Roger W. Barbour, who has been studying and photographing wildlife in Kentucky for some 35 years. Most of the photographs were taken expressly for this volume, and well over 90 percent of them were made in the seasons of 1969 and 1970.

We wish to express our appreciation to the following for the loan of the named photographs necessary to round out this volume:

Austin Peay State University, Department of Biology: *Cheilanthes lanosa* (2) (Series One, no. 3.9); *Hymenocallis occidentalis* (Series Two, no. 1.18); *Hibiscus militaris* (Series Four, no. 1.65); *Gonolobus shortii* (Series Four, no. 1.71); *Eryngium prostratum* (Series Four, no 2.20); *Stachys tenuifolia* (Series Five, no. 2.33); *Aureolaria pedicularia* (Series Five, no. 3.6); *Lythrum lanceolatum* (Series Seven, no. 2.5).

Carol Baskin: *Verbena canadensis* (Series Four, no. 1.75); *Galactia volubis* (Series Five, no. 1.16).

Sylvester Brown: *Hydrophyllum canadensis* (Series Four, no. 1.51); *Oxalis montana* (Series Four, no. 1.92); *Gentiana villosa* (Series Four, no. 1.100); *Baptisia australis* (Series Five, no. 1.4); *Gerardia purpurea* (Series Five, no. 3.34); *Petalostemum purpureum* (Series Five, no. 3.40).

Elwood Carr: *Habenaria flava* (Series Two, no. 2.14); *Myosotis scorpioides* (Series Four, no. 2.19); *Echium vulgare* (Series Five, no. 3.31).

Paul Higgins: *Panax quinquefolium* (Series Four, no. 2.34).

F. G. Irwin: *Calopogon pulchellus* (Series Two, no. 2.11); *Habenaria psycodes* (Series Two, no. 2.13); *Aplectrum hyemale* (flower) (Series Three, no. 3.3).

Kentucky Department of Parks: *Tipularia discolor* (leaf) (Series Three, no. 3.2); *Nelumbo lutea* (Series Four, no. 1.25).

Wendell Kingsolver: *Spiranthes cernua* (Series Two, no. 2.5); *Pachysandra procumbens* (Series Four, no. 2.14).

John A. Patterson III: *Aplectrum hyemale* (leaf) (Series Three, no. 3.3).

Bruce Poundstone: *Spigelia marilandica* (Series Four, no. 1.54).

Oren S. Ryker: *Trichostema dichotomum* (Series Five, no. 3.32).

David Snyder: *Trautvetteria caroliniensis* (Series Four, no. 2.42).

We are indebted to our students and colleagues, past and present, for assistance in many ways. E. C. Hale, Jr., at Eastern Kentucky University, made many of the line drawings. Warren Wagner, Jr., of the University of Michigan, made constructive comments, especially concerning the treatment of ferns and fern allies. The Kentucky Academy of Science and the Research Fund Committee of the University of Kentucky each made a small grant to help defray expenses incurred in preparation of the volume.

We wish finally to express our appreciation to Georgetown College for a reduction of Mary Wharton's teaching duties there during the production of this book.

Part I. Introduction

Purpose

Acquaintance with wildflowers and ferns can be a source of deep enjoyment, a pleasure available to all and not exclusively a privilege of botanists. The mode and tempo of life today accentuate the value of such hobbies as woodland hiking, bird-watching, flower identification, and nature photography. To derive full satisfaction from a walk in the woods one needs appreciation and knowledge of the plants along the way. Appreciation of Kentucky's fast-dwindling wildflower heritage depends upon knowledge concerning it, and widespread knowledge of our wildflowers and ferns depends upon the availability of information that can be followed with ease and pleasure, without technical training.

Therefore this book is designed for the layman. The method for identifying a specimen is to follow a grouping of color photographs, a simpler and less technical means than the use of a dichotomous key. By following the grouping one need not turn through many pages of plates in order to identify an unknown. Technical terms are held at a minimum; the indispensable ones are explained by a glossary and diagrams (pp. 13–18).

Wildflower books covering large areas, such as the northeastern quarter of the United States, are either too large to be carried into the field or, if conveniently small, they omit many species encountered in any one state. Therefore it seems advantageous to concentrate on a smaller geographical area. The need for such a nontechnical work suitable for use in Kentucky has long been evident. The present volume should be useful also in nearby surrounding areas.

Although wildflower books usually do not include ferns, flowers and ferns grow together in many of the same habitats, and naturalists and amateur botanists will also find ferns interesting if information concerning them is readily available. In forests in midsummer ferns are likely to be more prominent than flowers.

Scope

This volume includes color photographs and descriptions of 482 species, plus descriptions of an additional 180 species which are differentiated from the ones illustrated. Out of the total vascular flora of Kentucky, which includes well over 2,000 species of ferns and seed plants, these are the ones most conspicuous, most frequent, or most likely to be encountered because of their location.

Since the authors have in preparation another book on trees and shrubs, these are excluded from the present work with the exception of a few selected small species. Most grasses, sedges, and rushes (approximately 350 species in the state) are omitted because their minute and highly specialized flowers make identification difficult for the layman; a few representatives, however, are included to show the characteristics of these families. Weeds lacking aesthetic qualities are omitted although some "weeds" are included if their flowers are showy enough to attract attention. In some large genera, which are separated into species on the basis of technical characters and therefore are for the specialist, only a few representative species have been chosen.

PLAN AND ARRANGEMENT

Procedure in Identification

In Part II (p. 19) plates are grouped for convenient identification; in Part III (p. 281), however, genera and species are placed in their families, which are described and listed in taxonomic sequence in order to show full relationships.

The plates and descriptions are divided into seven series which are summarized on pages 21–22. After deciding in which series of plates your specimen belongs, turn to that series and select the group, and then the subgroup, with the characteristics of your plant. Check the plates in that subgroup. A tentative identification thus reached may be verified by the description, or the description may differentiate between the species illustrated and one not illustrated to which your specimen might belong. After using the book a few times you will be familiar with the composition of each series and can turn directly to the correct one. When you have identified a plant, turn to Part III and read the account of the family to which it belongs. Characteristics common to all members of a family are not repeated for each species.

So that the illustrations may be interpreted correctly each species description gives at least one measurement: height of plant, dimensions of leaves, or size of flower. An 8-inch measure is shown on the endpaper.

It should be noted that species are perennial unless designated in the description as annual or biennial.

Names Used

Only the common names in widest usage are included although many common names may have been applied to a single species of plant. Calling a plant by a name different from the one given here is therefore not necessarily incorrect. For almost all species the scientific names used follow *Gray's Manual*, Eighth Edition, by M. L. Fernald. If another scientific name is used, the synonym in *Gray's Manual* is given in brackets in Part III.

Frequence and Distribution

The terms denoting abundance and frequence are as follows, in descending order: abundant, common, frequent, infrequent, and rare. "Common" indicates, for example, not only that a plant is frequently found but that it usually occurs in considerable quantity. The frequence rating applies within the habitat; for instance, a species "common" in climax forests and one "common" on roadsides would differ vastly in their overall abundance.

Range of a species is given only for Kentucky. For the total range in the United States consult general manuals. Species distributed throughout the state can be expected also in adjacent states, and species restricted to a particular section may occur in an adjacent portion of another state. The frequency, given only for Kentucky, may vary in other states.

In citing the range of a species in Kentucky, often the physiographic region is mentioned; this can be located on Map 1, p. 7. Often, however, general geographical sections are mentioned, and these are delimited approximately as follows:

Eastern Kentucky: *The Cumberland Plateau, Cumberland Mountains and eastern Knobs*

Southeastern Kentucky:	*Pine Mountain, Cumberland Mountain, Black Mountain, and Log Mountain, which collectively are called the Cumberland Mountains, and adjacent areas*
Western Kentucky:	*The lower two-thirds of the Green River basin northwest to the Ohio River, and westward to the Mississippi River (approximately all the state west of Mammoth Cave)*
Southwestern Kentucky:	*The so-called Jackson Purchase, west of the Tennessee River, and the area between the Tennessee and Cumberland rivers (now impounded lakes)*
Southern Kentucky:	*The basins of the Cumberland and Barren rivers*
Central Kentucky:	*The Bluegrass region, the eastern part of the Mississippian Plateau, and the intervening Knobs*
Northern Kentucky:	*The northern portion of the Outer Bluegrass region*

PRINCIPLES OF NAMING PLANTS

The use of common names for plants leads to confusion and misunderstanding, both because one species may have a host of names and because the same name is often applied to several different plants. Common names are frequently local and vary from place to place. Hence the naturalist or amateur botanist would do well to familiarize himself with scientific nomenclature.

Scientific names are not as difficult as many persons believe and can be learned by anyone seriously interested in plants. The scientific name of a species is a binomial composed of the genus name followed by the species name (specific epithet). A genus is a group of closely related species; therefore the binomial indicates relationship, much as a person's surname, added to his given name, denotes relationship to his brothers or cousins. The words in scientific nomenclature are Latin or latinized, and are adopted throughout the world regardless of spoken language.

There are international rules of botanical nomenclature governing the naming of plants, and no two species in the world

GENERALIZED GEOLOGIC MAP OF KENTUCKY

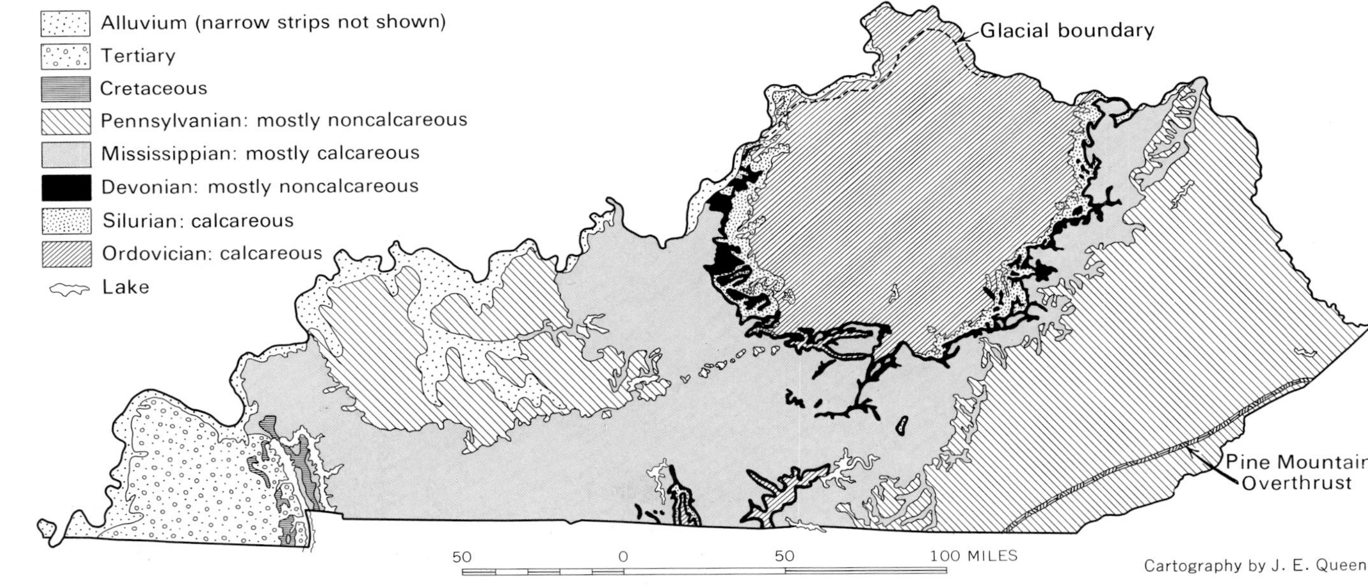

Cartography by J. E. Queen

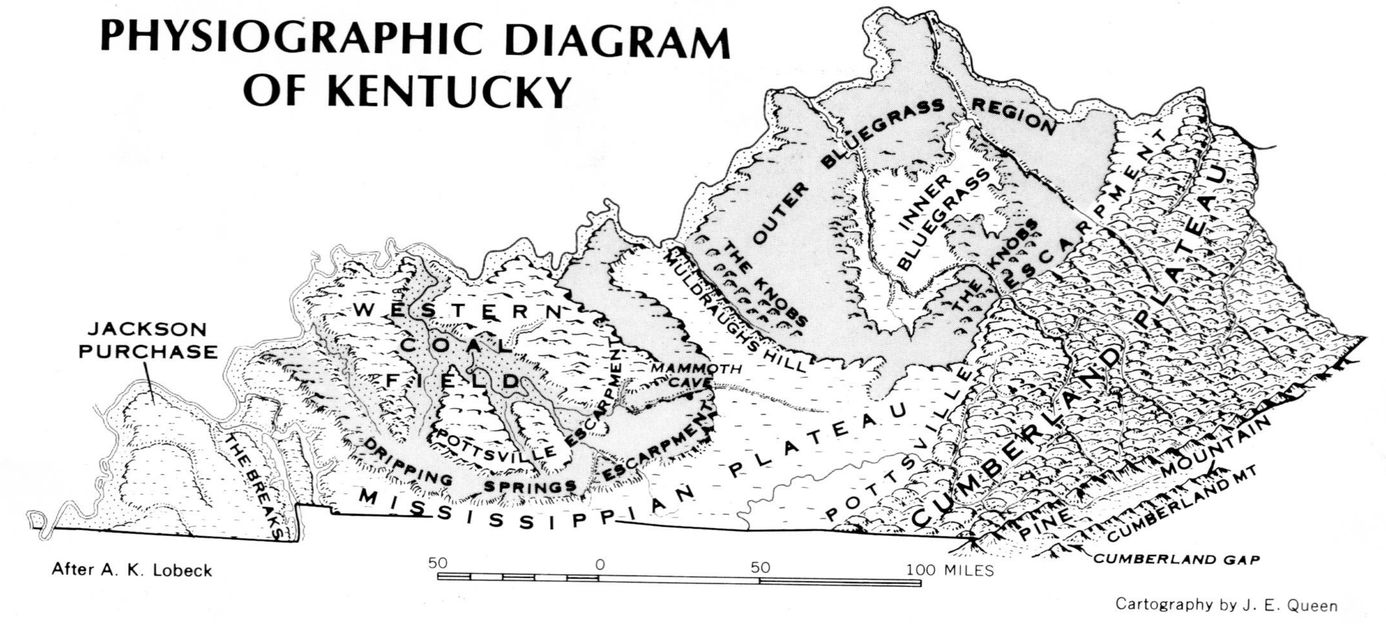
PHYSIOGRAPHIC DIAGRAM
OF KENTUCKY
OUTER BLUEGRASS REGION
INNER BLUEGRASS
THE KNOBS
THE KNOBS
ESCARPMENT
CUMBERLAND PLATEAU
MULDRAUGHS HILL
MAMMOTH CAVE
WESTERN COAL FIELD
POTTSVILLE ESCARPMENT
DRIPPING SPRINGS ESCARPMENT
MISSISSIPPIAN PLATEAU
POTTSVILLE
PINE MOUNTAIN
CUMBERLAND MT
CUMBERLAND GAP
JACKSON PURCHASE
THE BREAKS
50
0
50
100 MILES
After A. K. Lobeck
Cartography by J. E. Queen

RIVERS OF KENTUCKY

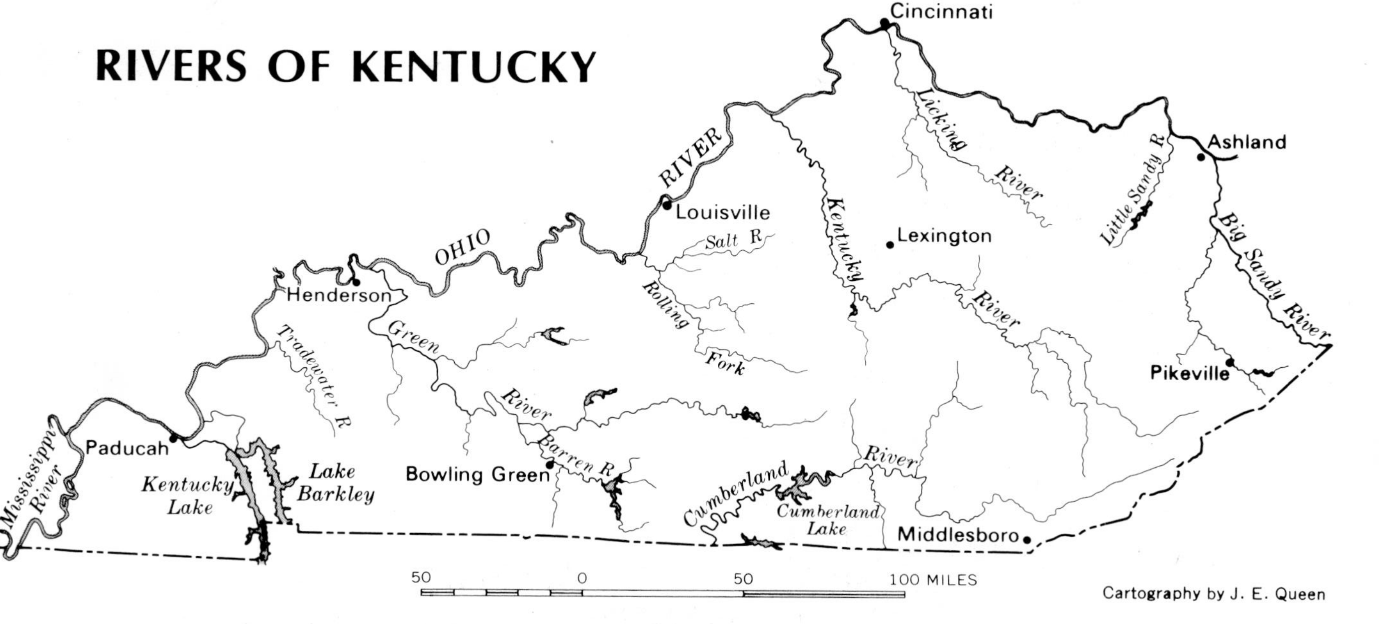

Cartography by J. E. Queen

can have the same binomial, that is, the same combination of genus and species names. According to this code, there would be but one valid name the world over for any single species. However, occasionally there is difference of opinion regarding rank in classification: whether plants with certain characteristics should be considered a separate species or merely a variety within another species, and whether certain species should be grouped with others in a large genus or placed in a separate one by splitting the original genus. Also new knowledge sometimes necessitates some taxonomic revision. Although these situations result in *synonyms* in scientific nomenclature, there is nevertheless no ambiguity as there is with common names.

KENTUCKY AND ITS FLOWERS

Geology and Plant Geography

The flora of Kentucky contains a variety of geographical elements. It has many Appalachian species which are also found in the Appalachian sections of adjacent states; it contains some southern species which extend northward only into our southern tier of counties. Also it contains some northern species occurring at the highest elevations, which have our coolest climates, located in southeast Kentucky, and occurring also in a few other relict colonies left over from the time of Pleistocene glaciation when the southern Appalachians provided a refuge for northern plants. Western Kentucky has some prairie species and also some swamp species characteristic of the Mississippi Embayment. In addition, many species in the Kentucky flora are wide-ranging throughout the eastern half of the United States.

Many factors related to geology affect plant distribution in the state. Geologic structure determines what rock will outcrop in a given area, and the nature of the outcrop affects the physiography, as will be noted in comparing the geologic map and the physiographic diagram. Soil chemistry, especially whether the soil is basic, neutral, or acidic, is often significant, and the location of calcareous and noncalcareous rock can be seen on the geologic map. Topography is important; for example, the same species are not likely to be found on a cliffside and on an alluvial flat. The role of physiography is a complex one which includes past vegetational history and plant migration as related to the physiographic history or the development of the present topography. This is involved in the occurrence of some very ancient, relict Coastal Plain species on the Cumberland Plateau. Geology and physiography also affect the pattern of land use, and this drastically affects our flora.

What Is a Weed?

Since there are some misconceptions concerning what constitutes "weediness," this question deserves consideration. A "weed" produces a large quantity of seeds which have an efficient means of dispersal and a high percentage of germination, or is able to propagate itself vegetatively. Also it establishes itself readily in open situations and grows rapidly and profusely, with the result that it successfully competes with and crowds out more desirable plants. A weed has been incorrectly called "a plant out of place," but it is not a weed unless it has the capacity for "taking over the place."

Most noxious weeds have come from Eurasia and are not part of our indigenous flora, although there are exceptions such as the ragweeds and cockleburs. This does not mean that the Old World flora is more weedy than ours but rather that weeds follow man in his migrations and flourish wherever man breaks into the native vegetation and modifies the environment.

Are Our Choicest Wildflowers Doomed?

A plant does not live unto itself but is part of an organized community. The decimation of the natural communities which had become established here before the first settlers arrived, and which had been only slightly interrupted by the Indians, was inevitable as cities, industries, and farms expanded. Now that our thoroughly mechanized and economically oriented society is in the midst of a population explosion, the appropriation of natural areas for man's immediate use and profit has been accelerated phenomenally, whether it be in highway networks, building developments, dams, or strip mining. We have taken for granted that there will forever be forests of mighty trees with all the lesser dignitaries and diminutive beauties beneath. However, with the continuation of present trends we are destined to lose many of our choicest wildflowers, together with their natural communities, unless precise measures are taken both by government and by individuals.

Some areas need to be set aside as nature sanctuaries. State and national parks and forests, in emphasizing recreation, are not accomplishing adequate protection of fragile ecosystems. When humankind descends on an area for recreation, delicate wildlings are trampled, beaten down, broken off, and wiped out by the masses. Some destruction could be reduced by enforcement of regulations concerning the protection of nature in the parks and forests. However, some natural or semi-natural areas should be acquired, protected, left to nature's management, and set aside for education in addition to those developed for recreational use. Such areas in their tranquility, nevertheless, *re-create* man's emotional, mental, and physical well-being and at the same time constitute a yardstick against which to measure man's modification of the environment.

Individuals should be alerted to the need of being kind to wild plants. "Love 'em and leave 'em" is the recommended substitute for the impulse to pick a bouquet of woodland wildflowers. (However, flowers that grow abundantly in man's fields and pastures, such as the ox-eye daisy, of course can be picked freely.) It is deplorable indeed when endangered species of wildflowers are used in decorative arrangements in resort hotels.

Digging ferns and wildflowers for transplanting into gardens usually contributes more to their destruction than to their conservation. Most transplanted wildflowers do not survive in their new surroundings, and, for the few that do, many are sacrificed. Most of those that appear to survive usually die in a few years because they are adapted for a complex network of environmental factors, not all of which can be duplicated in the new situation. It is better to protect the total environment in which nature grows a garden so that our children and grandchildren may enjoy it. The digging of wild species can be justified if destruction of their own environment is irrevocable, such as in the construction of a highway or a reservoir.

Many wild plants are edible, but whether or not these should be eaten depends on the abundance of the species. If the edible plant in question is a weedy species flourishing in man's fields and waste places, its utilization should be encouraged. But if it is restricted to the woods, the supply of the species is already diminishing with the reduction of forest lands. To gather such plants is justifiable if we are lost in the wilderness and weakened from lack of food; otherwise we are wiser to leave them. Young campers should not be encouraged, for example, to pull up an Indian cucumber-root for a nibble when the plant, now destroyed, had required years to produce that single bite.

Some of the most "unkind" treatment that wildflowers experience from individuals is executed not by the human hand but by the human foot. One person traveling straight downhill can so dislodge loose humus-soil and little roots that the next rain will initiate a gully which subsequent rains will enlarge. The steeper the slope happens to be, the greater is the damage. Youngsters frequently think it is "smart" to rush straight uphill or downhill instead of taking a longer zigzag path; in state and national parks and forests many a switchback on a trail has been by-passed by "short-cutters," and erosion with accompanying loss of plants is the inevitable result. All this occurs because persons do not think of the consequences of their actions and because no one pointed them out.

In summary, while weeds are becoming more abundant, our loveliest wildflowers are in danger and may be doomed without protective measures. Wildflower conservation is one facet of overall environmental conservation.

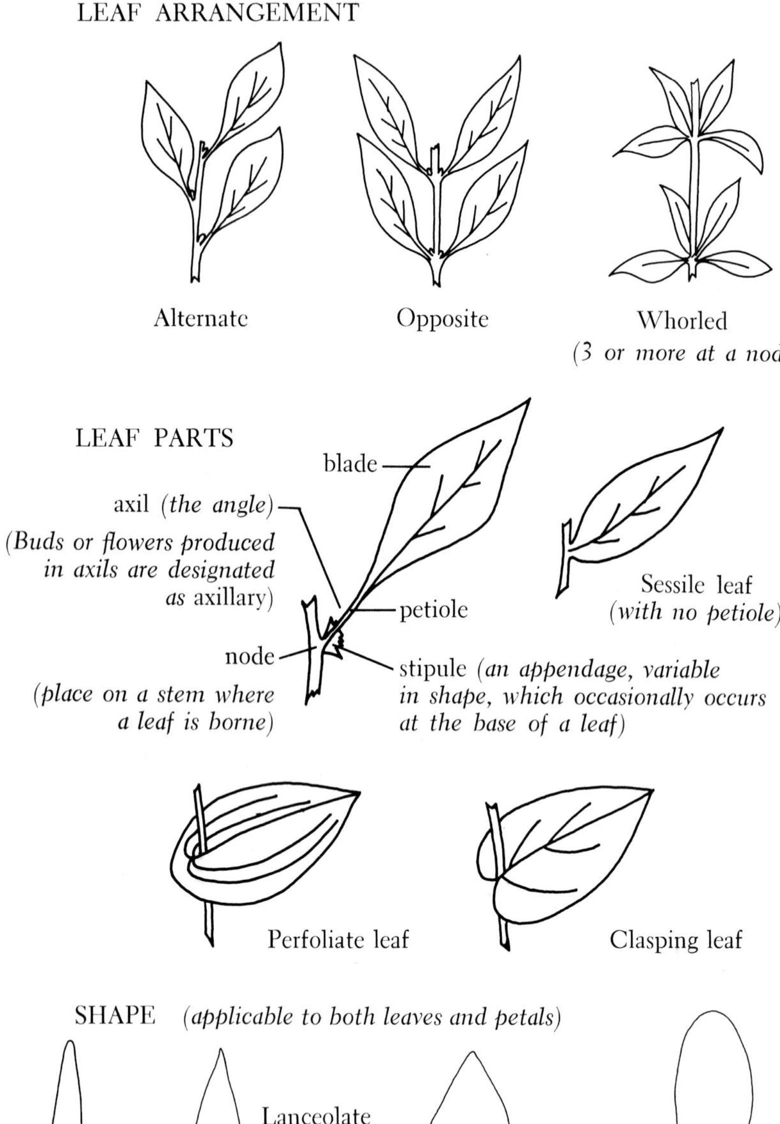

Lanceolate

(lance-shaped)

Linear

Ovate

Oblong

(A combination of two terms indicates a shape between them)

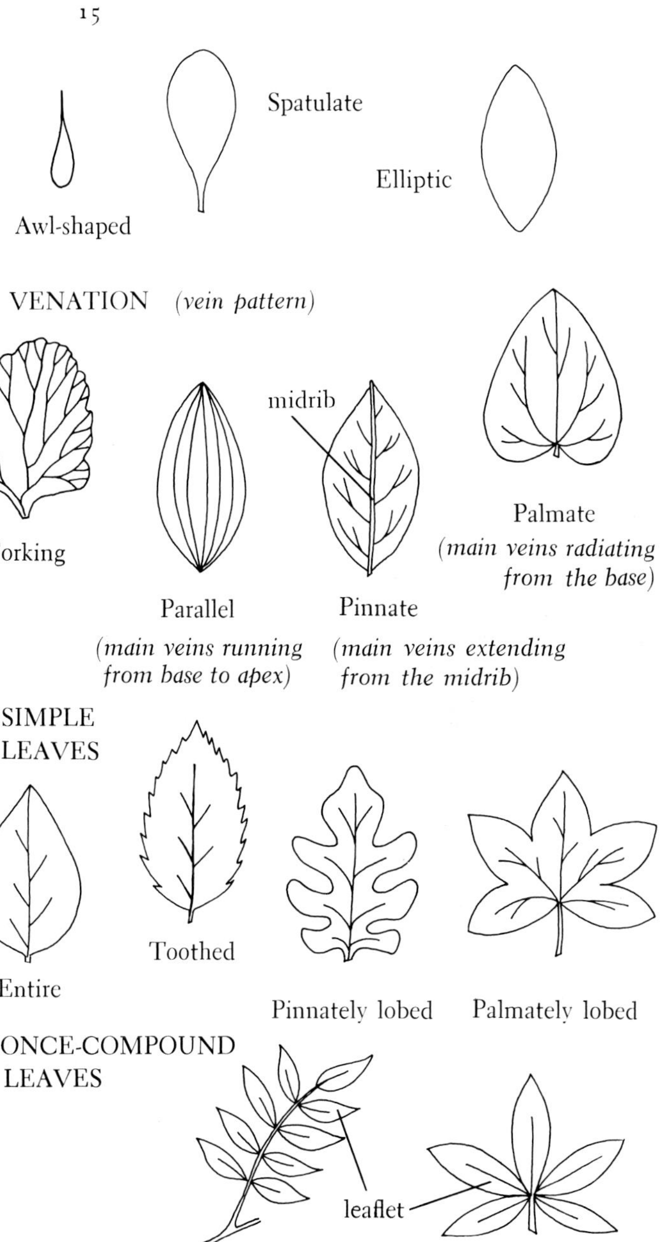
Spatulate
Elliptic
Awl-shaped
VENATION (vein pattern)
midrib
Forking
Palmate
(main veins radiating from the base)
Parallel
(main veins running from base to apex)
Pinnate
(main veins extending from the midrib)
SIMPLE LEAVES
Toothed
Entire
Pinnately lobed
Palmately lobed
ONCE-COMPOUND LEAVES
leaflet
Pinnate
(pinnately compound)
Palmate
(palmately compound)

TWICE-COMPOUND LEAF

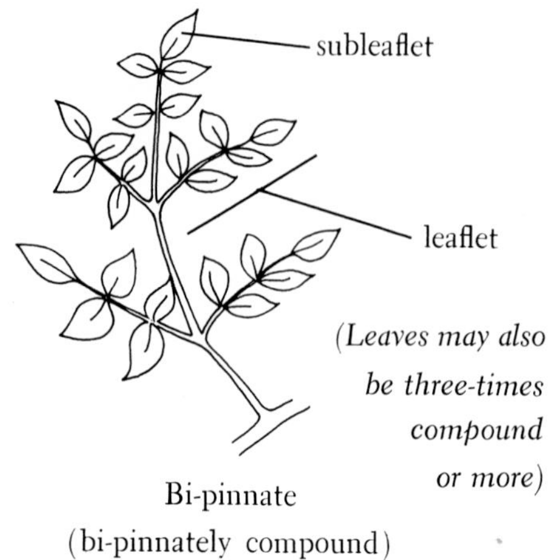

(Leaves may also be three-times compound or more)

Bi-pinnate
(bi-pinnately compound)

STEMS

Arrangement of vascular tissue as seen in cross section

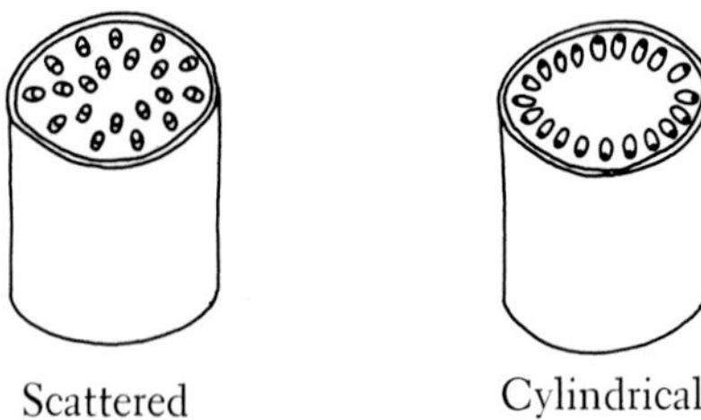

Scattered | Cylindrical

FLOWER SYMMETRY

Radial symmetry

(Can be cut into 2 equal halves in many ways provided the plane of cutting passes through the center)

Bilateral symmetry

(Two-sided. Only 1 plane of cutting will divide it into 2 equal halves)

FLOWER PARTS

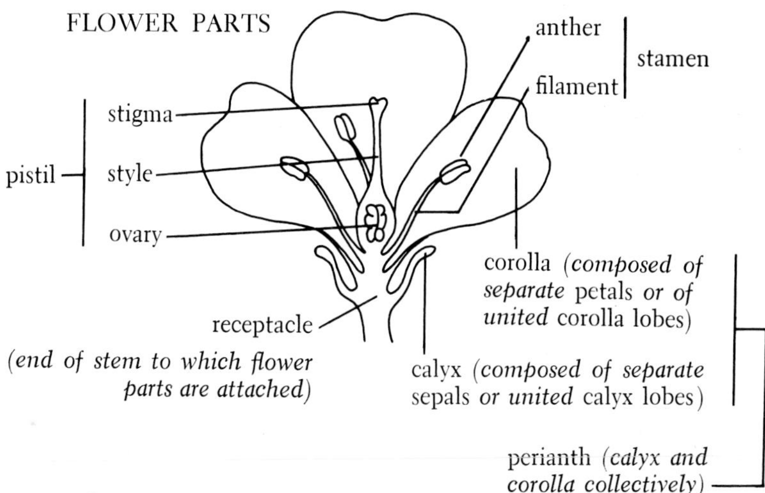

A generalized flower in vertical section

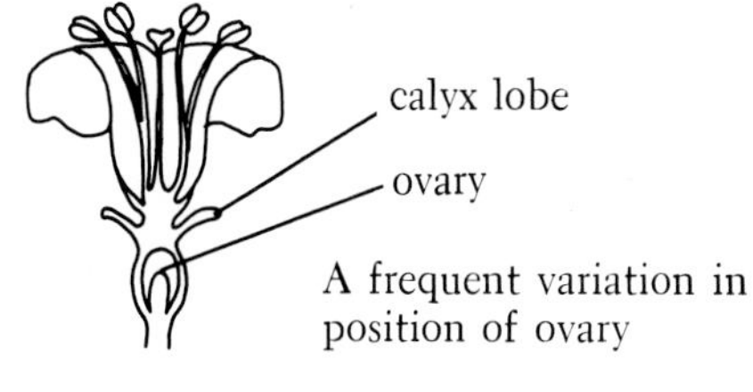

A frequent variation in position of ovary

INFLORESCENCES (*flower clusters*)

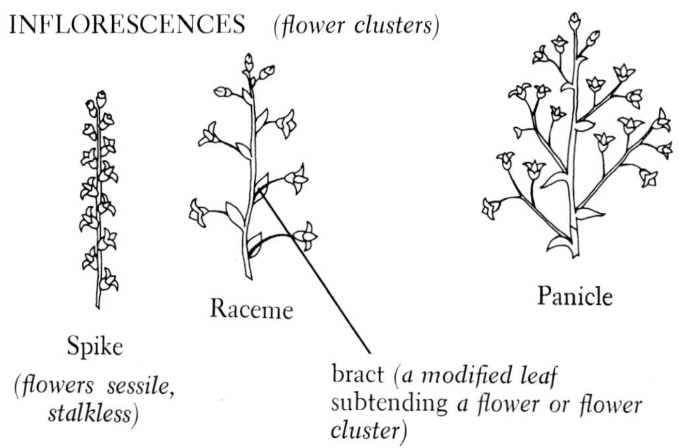

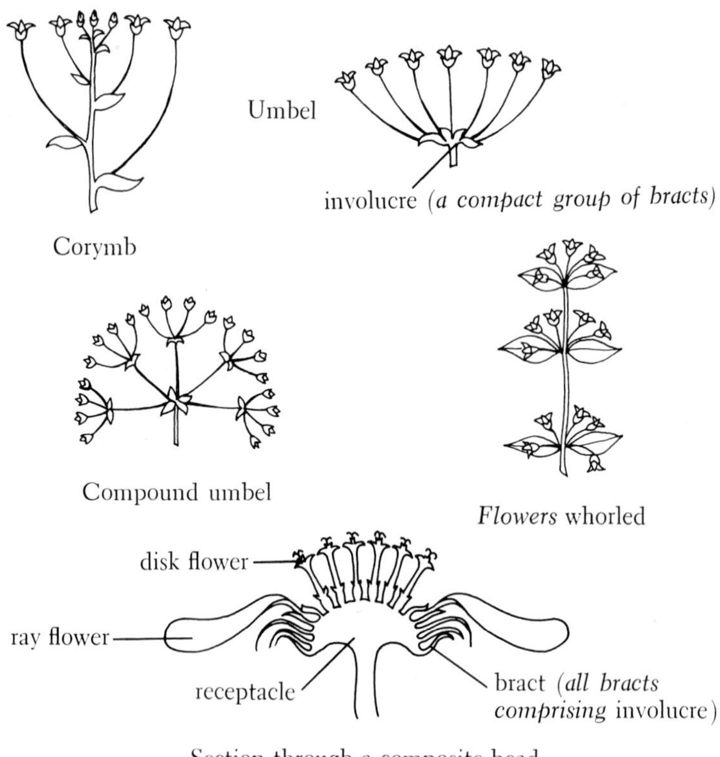

MISCELLANEOUS TERMS USED

(Pertaining to plant surfaces)

Glabrous. *Without hairs*
Glandular. *Having minute, roundish secreting structures, sometimes associated with hairs*
Glaucous. *Having a thin, whitish, powdery coating*

(Pertaining to habitat and nutrition)

Mesic. *Descriptive of a moderately moist habitat*
Mesophytic. *Descriptive of plants or plant communities of medium moisture requirements*
Saprophytic. *Living on dead organic matter*

Part II. Plates & Descriptions

Arrangement of Plates for Identification

FERNS AND FERN ALLIES

Plants reproducing by spores, never by flowers and seeds

[p. 23] Series One: FERNS AND FERN ALLIES

Ferns: Leaves with blades either simple or compound; leaf veins usually forking. Spore-cases either borne in clusters on lower surface or margin of leaf or borne on special branches

Fern allies: Leaves scale-like or awl-shaped or rudimentary. Spore-cases borne in terminal cones or in axils of leaves

MONOCOTYLEDONS

Plants usually with main leaf-veins parallel and perianth-parts in threes and sixes, always with scattered vascular bundles in the stem

[p. 46] Series Two: MONOCOTYLEDONS (1)

Leaves parallel-veined and perianth-parts in threes or sixes

[p. 73] Series Three: MONOCOTYLEDONS (2)

Leaves net-veined or absent, perianth-parts in threes or sixes or absent; or leaves parallel-veined, perianth-parts not in threes or sixes

(Continued on next page)

DICOTYLEDONS

Plants usually with net-veined leaves and perianth-parts in fours or fives, always with a cylindrical arrangement of vascular tissue in the stem

[p. 93] Series Four: DICOTYLEDONS (1)

Those typical herbaceous "dicots," with perianth-parts in fours or fives, which have radially symmetrical flowers

[p. 178] Series Five: DICOTYLEDONS (2)

Those typical herbaceous "dicots," with perianth-parts in fours or fives, which have bilaterally symmetrical flowers

[p. 231] Series Six: DICOTYLEDONS (3), COMPOSITES

Plants, such as the well-known daisy and dandelion, having minute individual flowers inserted on a common receptacle which is subtended by a compact group of many small bracts

[p. 272] Series Seven: DICOTYLEDONS (4)

Exceptional "dicots" with no green leaves, or with distinctly parallel-veined leaves, or with net-veined leaves and a three-parted or six-parted perianth or no perianth

Series One: **Ferns and Fern Allies**

Ferns and their relatives produce spores in spore-cases called sporangia which in the true ferns are borne either in clusters on the lower surface or margin of the leaves, or on special leaflets or special branches. Fern leaves, often called fronds, may be undivided, lobed, or divided into separate leaflets; small veins usually fork.

For positive identification of most ferns it is desirable to have the spore-bearing structures; nevertheless, with caution and close observation one can recognize many species when they are vegetative. Miniature species of ferns, which are only a few inches tall at maturity and which bear sporangia, must be distinguished from young individuals of larger species, which will not have sporangia while they are small.

Many persons think of a fern leaf as being finely divided, but some fern fronds are not divided. Also some flowering plants which have "fern" in their common names, such as the so-called "asparagus fern" of florists and the wild "sweet fern," are not ferns at all.

For the fern allies, the chief claim to renown is in their pedigree. Our living species are small representatives of ancient lines of plants which millions of years ago were both numerous and very large, living in the luxuriant swamp forests which formed our coal. Relatives of *Equisetum* included trees up to 50 feet tall (for example, *Calamites*); relatives of *Lycopodium* (for example, *Lepidodendron* and *Sigillaria*) grew 100 feet high, the tallest trees of the coal-producing swamps.

It should be noted that the ferns and fern allies included in this volume are deciduous unless they are described as being evergreen.

ARRANGEMENT OF PLATES

Group 1. Ferns bearing spore-cases on parts distinct from the green leaf 1.1–1.5

Group 2. Ferns bearing spore-cases on the green leaf, with the fertile leaflets markedly smaller than the sterile leaflets 2.1–2.4

Group 3. Ferns bearing spore-cases on the green leaf, with the fertile leaflets, leaf segments, or leaves approximately the same size as the sterile ones

- Small ferns, usually under 12 inches with a maximum of 18 inches (miniature species illustrated toward the first) 3.1–3.12
- Medium and large ferns 1–3 feet tall, not normally under 12 inches (large species illustrated toward the last) 3.13–3.24

Group 4. Fern allies, having scale-like or awl-shaped evergreen leaves, or rudimentary leaves at the joints of green stems, bearing spore-cases either in terminal cones or in the leaf axils 4.1–4.6

1.1 *Botrychium virginianum*

VIRGINIA GRAPE-FERN, RATTLESNAKE FERN

In the genus *Botrychium* the sporangia resemble a miniature bunch of grapes, accounting for the common name.

The Virginia grape-fern has a thin, finely dissected frond which may be as much as 12 inches across and 18 inches high. In all sections of the state it is frequent in moist rich woods where leafmold is deep, and matures in late May.

Ophioglossaceae (Adder's-tongue family)

1.2 *Botrychium obliquum*

COMMON GRAPE-FERN

The "common" or broad-lobed grape-fern has thick-textured leaflets which are evergreen, though somewhat bronzed in winter, and the frond is rarely over 6 inches across. It is fairly frequent in open woods, woodland borders, thickets, and occasionally old pastures, and is widely distributed. It matures in late September and October.

Ophioglossaceae (Adder's-tongue family)

B. dissectum, the cut-leaf grape-fern, has leaflets of the same texture but more finely cut than those of the common grape-fern.

1.3 *Ophioglossum engelmanni*

ADDER'S-TONGUE FERN

This fascinating little fern does not fit the popular image of a fern. It is inconspicuous and its discovery is always cause for excitement. The leaf (1½–2½ inches long) has a somewhat succulent texture and a different "feel" from that of a flowering plant of the same size and shape. The small veins in the leaf rejoin, forming a network of a very precise pattern. Sporangia, making the "adder's tongue," appear in May. It grows chiefly in calcareous soil, where it may occasionally be found in meadows, open woods, pastures, and other unexpected places.

Ophioglossaceae (Adder's-tongue family)

A similar species, more rare in Kentucky, is *O. vulgatum*, which is slightly larger and which grows in moist noncalcareous areas.

1.4 *Onoclea sensibilis*

SENSITIVE FERN, BEAD-FERN

Usually but inappropriately called "sensitive fern," this species is coarse although only 1–2 feet high. A stalk bearing beadlike spore-cases appears in midsummer and persists through winter. Its habitat is swamps, muddy depressions, and seepage areas in sun or shade; it is frequent in all sections of the state except the Inner Bluegrass.

Polypodiaceae (Fern family)

1.5 *Osmunda cinnamomea*

CINNAMON FERN

This is a stately fern with fronds 3–5 feet tall arranged in a somewhat circular group. The cinnamon-colored, woolly fertile fronds appear in the center of the circle in May and quickly wither after shedding spores. The sterile fronds, green until frost, bear small tufts of cinnamon-brown wool at the leaflet bases and usually some brown wool at the base of the stalk. The cinnamon fern grows in swamps, in wet depressions in woods, and on wooded stream-banks and spring-slopes; it is fairly frequent in most regions of the state except the Bluegrass.
Osmundaceae (Flowering fern family)

2.1 *Osmunda regalis* var. *spectabilis*

ROYAL FERN

The royal fern, 3–5 feet tall, has twice-compound leaves with narrowly oblong leaflets; the fertile portion of the frond is terminal and is present in May and June. It is fairly frequent near springs, in swamps, and in other wet places in most sections of Kentucky except, apparently, the Bluegrass.
Osmundaceae (Flowering fern family)

2.2 *Osmunda claytoniana*
INTERRUPTED FERN

Since the small spore-bearing leaflets are near the middle of the frond, with green lobed leaflets above and below, and since they wither after shedding spores and leave a gap from midsummer on, this fern is aptly called "interrupted." The interrupted fronds, 3–4 feet tall, are encircled by shorter sterile fronds which resemble the sterile fronds of the cinnamon fern (no. 1.5) but lack the tufts of brown wool at the leaflet bases. The interrupted fern grows in moist woods; it is infrequent and less widely distributed than its relatives, the royal and cinnamon ferns.

Osmundaceae (Flowering fern family)

2.3 *Lygodium palmatum*
CLIMBING FERN

Our only species of vine-like fern has very slender wiry stalks which twine around the stems of small shrubs. The leaflets are palmate, usually with 6 finger-like lobes, pale green, thin, and evergreen; the spore-bearing leaflets are terminal, much smaller, and not evergreen. The climbing fern is found in moist acid soil in shade or partial shade in eastern Kentucky; it is infrequent but usually plentiful where established.

Schizaeaceae (Curly-grass family)

2.4 *Polystichum acrostichoides* CHRISTMAS FERN

This evergreen fern has fronds 1–2 feet high, scaly stalks, and firm leaflets, each with a toothed margin and an "ear" at the base. Small fertile leaflets, bearing crowded groups of sporangia on the lower surface, are terminal on the tallest fronds; a mature plant bears some shorter fronds that have only sterile leaflets. Since it is one of the most common ferns in rich woods throughout the state, it adds much to the winter beauty of our woodlands.
Polypodiaceae (Fern family)

3.1 *Polypodium virginianum* POLYPODY, ROCKCAP FERN

Fronds are dark and firm, evergreen, 4–10 inches high, and cut nearly to the midrib, the segments alternating on opposite sides. Sporangia occur in round clusters on the lower surface. A sturdy little fern, the polypody grows on shaded ledges, cliffs, and boulders, especially sandstone, and is fairly frequent in the mountains and hilly sections of the state.

Do not confuse the polypody with young Christmas ferns (no. 2.4), which are more common.
Polypodiaceae (Fern family)

Another species, *P. polypodioides* var. *michauxianum*, the gray polypody or resurrection fern, differs mainly in being smaller, having silvery scales on the lower surface of the leaves, and usually growing on trees.

3.2 *Trichomanes boschianum*

FILMY FERN, BRISTLE-FERN

This is our most fragile and delicate fern. Its fronds are 2–5 inches long; the leaflets, which are cut in a lacy pattern, are only 1 cell in thickness but evergreen notwithstanding, and bear sporangia on marginal bristles. These filmy fronds grow pendent on damp ceilings and walls of overhanging sandstone, far back where light is always dim. This little fern is found in the areas of the Pottsville escarpments, both near the western edge of the Cumberland Plateau and near the border of the Western Coal Field.
Hymenophyllaceae (Filmy fern family)

(Above)

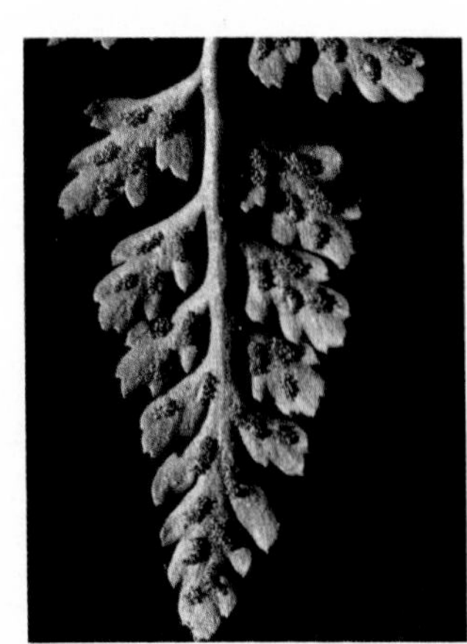

3.3 *Asplenium montanum*
MOUNTAIN SPLEENWORT

Fronds are evergreen though delicate, 2–5 inches long, and twice compound. Sporangium clusters on the lower surface are elongate. This little fern typically grows in moist shaded crevices in overhanging sandstone. It is fairly frequent in eastern Kentucky and also occurs in the area of sandstone cliffs bordering the Western Coal Field.
Polypodiaceae (Fern family)

(*Below opposite*)

3.4 *Asplenium ruta-muraria*
WALL-RUE

This tiny fern has fronds 2–4 inches long, thickish, evergreen, and twice divided, bearing the elongate clusters of sporangia characteristic of the genus *Asplenium*. It grows in crevices of limestone cliffs and is fairly frequent in the Bluegrass, Knobs, and Mississippian Plateau.
Polypodiaceae (Fern family)

3.5 *Asplenium pinnatifidum*

LOBED SPLEENWORT

This miniature evergreen fern, with fronds 3–6 inches long, has a tail-like tip and lobes cut nearly to the midrib. As in all spleenworts, the sporangium clusters are elongate. It grows in rock crevices, especially in noncalcareous rock, and is fairly frequent.
Polypodiaceae (Fern family)

3.6 *Asplenium trichomanes*

MAIDENHAIR SPLEENWORT

This miniature species, 2–6 inches high, is evergreen although tiny and delicate, and has a lustrous dark brown stalk and axis. Note the shape of the leaflets and do not confuse this species with immature specimens of the common ebony spleenwort (no. 3.7). This little fern lives in moist, shaded rock crevices; it is infrequent but widely distributed in the state.
Polypodiaceae (Fern family)

Two other species of small spleenworts, both of which have once-compound leaves, are as follows:

The black-stemmed spleenwort (*A. resiliens*) resembles the ebony spleenwort (no. 3.7) in having an "ear" at the base of each leaflet but differs in being smaller (4–8 inches high), having a darker brown or black stalk and axis, and having leaflets usually without teeth. It grows in shaded limestone crevices.

The cliff spleenwort (*A. bradleyi*), 2–6 inches high, has lobed leaflets, the segments of which are toothed. It grows in crevices of noncalcareous rock such as sandstone.

In the spleenworts there is some hybridization, which may occasionally make identification a problem.

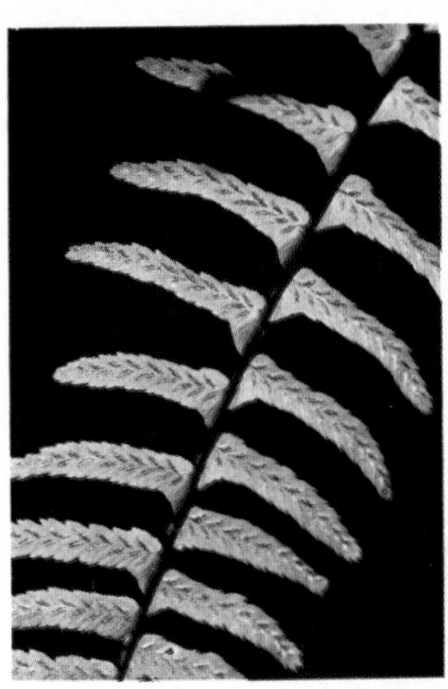

3.7 *Asplenium platyneuron*

EBONY SPLEENWORT

The stalk and axis are a lustrous dark brown (more like mahogany than ebony) and leaflets are evergreen. Fertile fronds are erect, 10–18 inches tall, and clusters of sporangia are elongate; sterile fronds are shorter and nearly prostrate. Individual plants vary in the depth of marginal teeth. This slender fern is common and widespread in open woods and thickets, especially in rocky ground, throughout the state.

Polypodiaceae (Fern family)

3.8 *Camptosorus rhizophyllus* WALKING FERN

The walking fern "walks" as the long, tail-like tip of a leaf roots when it touches the ground, forming a new plant, so that a parent plant is often surrounded by its "family" of plantlets. The evergreen leaf is 4–12 inches long, bearing elongate sporangium-clusters on the lower surface. This fern grows in moss and humus on shaded ledges, cliffs, and boulders, especially limestone, and is fairly frequent throughout the state.
Polypodiaceae (Fern family)

3.9 *Cheilanthes lanosa* HAIRY LIPFERN

Fronds, 6–12 inches high and covered with soft rusty hairs, are twice-compound. Subleaflets have obtuse lobes, with margins reflexed over the sporangium-clusters. This fern grows on dry shaly slopes and ledges. It is fairly frequent in southern and western Kentucky, infrequent in eastern Kentucky.
Polypodiaceae (Fern family)

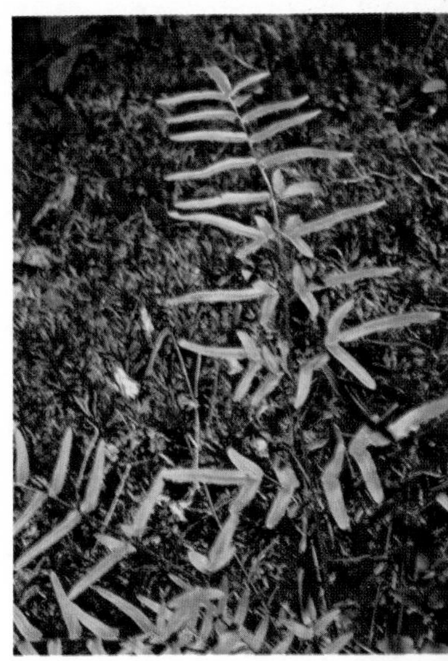

3.10 *Pellaea atropurpurea* PURPLE CLIFFBRAKE

The purple cliffbrake, 4–16 inches tall, has dark, wiry, brittle, hairy "stems"; leaflets are dull gray-green, with sporangia marginal on the lower surface. Since its habitat is limestone ledges and cliffs it is frequent in the Bluegrass region and the Mississippian Plateau, infrequent in other sections.
Polypodiaceae (Fern family)

3.11 *Woodsia obtusa* BLUNT-LOBED WOODSIA

Fronds are 8–16 inches high and glandular-hairy (the glands are visible with a hand lens); the stalk and axis are yellowish, hairy, and scaly, and leaflets are sessile on the axis. Lower leaflets are blunt-tipped, and subleaflets are blunt-lobed, with round clusters of sporangia on the lower surface. *Woodsia* grows in well-drained rocky woods and on forested cliffs, especially in limestone areas, and is frequent throughout the state. This fern slightly resembles *Cystopteris fragilis*, no. 3.12, and has the same habitat.
Polypodiaceae (Fern family)

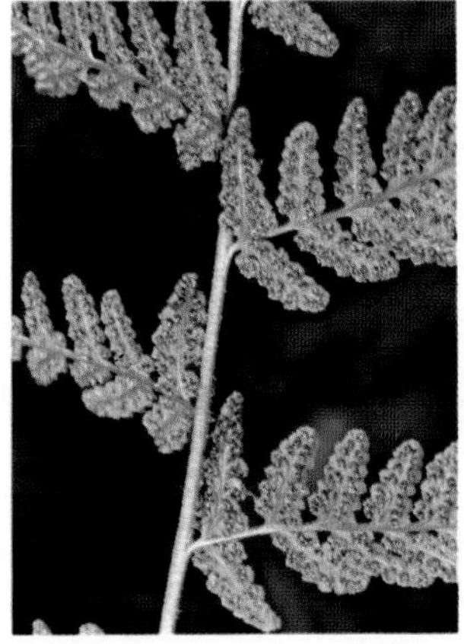

3.12 *Cystopteris fragilis* FRAGILE FERN

The fragile fern is so named because the stalk is brittle and breaks easily at the base. Fronds are 6–14 inches long and not hairy; the stalk, dark at the base, is smooth throughout; main leaflets have short stalks; sporangium clusters are round. It is found on rocky wooded slopes and wooded cliffs where there are pockets of moisture, most often in calcareous soil. It is frequent and widely distributed in the state.

The fragile fern may be confused with *Woodsia* (no. 3.11) and the bulblet fern (no. 3.13); note the differences.
Polypodiaceae (Fern family)

3.13 *Cystopteris bulbifera* BULBLET FERN

Fronds of the bulblet fern are soft, thin, light green, slender, 10–24 inches long, and usually pendent or reclining. Mature leaves bear on their lower surfaces a few green bulblets which easily fall off and give rise to new plants; small scattered clusters of sporangia are also present. When bulblets are found on the leaves, there can be no mistaking the identity of the species, but a specimen without bulblets growing in a less than optimum environ-

ment may resemble the fragile fern (no. 3.12); however, a hand lens will show the fronds of the bulblet fern to be minutely glandular. Typically the bulblet fern is found hanging from moist shaded limestone ledges. It is most frequent in the Bluegrass region and the Mississippian Plateau; it also grows in the eastern Knobs near the Cumberland Plateau.
Polypodiaceae (Fern family)

3.14 *Adiantum pedatum*

MAIDENHAIR FERN

The maidenhair is one of our loveliest and most graceful ferns. The slender, dark, shiny, erect stalk, 10–20 inches high, forks into 2 branches bearing a blade which fans out in a horizontal plane. The subleaflets are thin and bear spore-cases beneath the upper margin. The maidenhair would be more common if its habitat were not becoming so scarce: rich, moist, well-drained woods with deep humus. It is distributed throughout the state.
Polypodiaceae (Fern family)

3.15 *Phegopteris hexagonoptera*

BEECH FERN

The beech fern, 10–18 inches high, is easily recognized by the triangular outline of the blade, often broader than long, and the wings on the midrib between the pairs of leaflets. The groups of spore-cases on the lower surface are very small and round. It is found in woods and is fairly frequent in noncalcareous areas.
Polypodiaceae (Fern family)

3.16 *Thelypteris noveboracensis*

NEW YORK FERN

This is one of the most readily distinguished of our ferns because the lowest leaflets are much more reduced in size than in any other species. Fronds are thin, light green, and 12–24 inches tall, and the leaflets have uncut margins. The sporangium clusters are small, roundish (kidney-shaped when young), and located near the margins of the lower surface. The New York fern is common in moist woods in areas of acid soil.
Polypodiaceae (Fern family)

The marsh fern, *T. palustris,* also has leaflets with uncut margins but they are not as thin and pale, and the lowest leaflets are not greatly reduced, as in the New York fern. Margins of the spore-bearing leaflets are slightly rolled under. This species, growing in marshes and swamps, is infrequent but widely scattered in Kentucky.

3.17 *Athyrium thelypterioides*

SILVERY GLADEFERN

This is a graceful fern, 2–3½ feet tall, light green, soft, and delicate. Middle leaflets are the longest, and thus the frond tapers at both ends. Leaflets are deeply cut into blunt lobes having finely toothed margins; clusters of sporangia on the lower surface are elongate and appear lustrous and silvery. The silvery gladefern lives in moist rich woods and on shady banks of small streams. It is frequent in eastern Kentucky, infrequent in western Kentucky, and rare in the central part of the state.
Polypodiaceae (Fern family)

(*Below left*)

3.18 *Athyrium pycnocarpon*

GLADEFERN

Fronds of the gladefern, 1½–3 feet high, may superficially resemble sterile fronds of the Christmas fern (no. 2.4), but the gladefern is thin and deciduous whereas the Christmas fern is firm and evergreen. The spore-bearing structures also differ greatly, as the plates indicate. This species is found in moist areas in rich woods and is widely distributed over the state.
Polypodiaceae (Fern family)

3.19 *Athyrium asplenioides*

LADY-FERN

This is a graceful lacy fern, 18–32 inches tall, bipinnate, with subleaflets narrow and toothed. The lady-fern is variable in outline and in the depth of cutting of the leaflets, and several varieties have been named. The smooth stalk has only a few scales at the base; the clusters of sporangia are somewhat crescent-shaped. It is frequent in moist woods and on wooded stream banks, usually in noncalcareous soil, and is widely distributed in the state.

Other lacy ferns with which the lady-fern might be confused are the hay-scented fern (no. 3.20) and the spinulose shield-fern (no. 3.21); their distinguishing characteristics should be noted carefully.

Polypodiaceae (Fern family)

3.20 *Dennstaedtia punctilobula*

HAY-SCENTED FERN

A sweet odor when the fern is crushed gives this species its common name. Its fronds are 16–30 inches tall, thin, light green, hairy, and finely divided into deeply toothed or lobed subleaflets. Clusters of sporangia are minute and cup-shaped, borne on the marginal teeth of the subleaflets. The hay-scented fern grows in acid soil, especially in dry open woods and woodland borders but also in swampy areas and on moist banks. It is most common in the Knobs but is also found in eastern and southern Kentucky.
Polypodiaceae (Fern family)

(Below left)

3.21 *Dryopteris spinulosa*

SPINULOSE SHIELD-FERN, SPINULOSE WOODFERN

This handsome fern with lacy-cut leaves grows 14–28 inches tall and is nearly evergreen (sterile fronds are usually evergreen, fertile fronds often are). Stalks are scaly; subleaflets, which are minutely spiny-toothed, bear circular clusters of spore-cases. This species is variable in total outline, cutting of leaflets, characteristics of scales, and distribution of sporangium-clusters; several varieties have been named. It is found in moist woods and on wooded rocky banks where there is leafmold, usually in somewhat acid soil. It is frequent in the eastern, southern, and west-central parts of the state.

Characteristics of the spinulose shield-fern should be compared with those of the lady-fern (no. 3.19).
Polypodiaceae (Fern family)

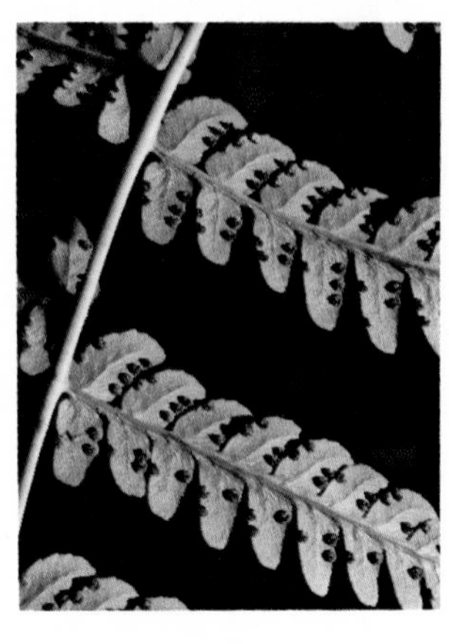

3.22 *Dryopteris marginalis*

MARGINAL SHIELD-FERN, MARGINAL WOODFERN

A dark green, thick-textured evergreen fern, 15–30 inches tall, and beautiful in all seasons, the marginal shield-fern is especially appreciated on winter walks through the woods. Stalks are scaly, subleaflets are blunt, and the roundish clusters of sporangia are marginal. It is found in all sections of the state where there are rich wooded slopes.
Polypodiaceae (Fern family)

The giant woodfern, also called Goldie's fern (*D. goldiana*), grows 2–4 feet high with fronds that may be as much as 12 inches across. Sporangium clusters are small and near the middle of a subleaflet. This species requires rich humus-laden woods.

3.23 *Pteridium latiusculum*

BRACKEN

The bracken is a robust fern 1½–3 feet high. The stalk has 3 main branches which give the whole blade a triangular outline. The leaflets are coarse-textured and bear spore-cases in a continuous line along the reflexed margin. It is common in dry open woods, thickets, and cut-over areas, usually in acid soil, in the hilly areas of the state.
Polypodiaceae (Fern family)

4.1 *Equisetum arvense*

FIELD HORSETAIL

The structure which suggests a horse's tail is the sterile shoot, 6–20 inches high, in which there is a whorl of branches at each joint in the stem. The unbranched fertile stem, 4–10 inches high and bearing a cone at the apex, appears in April and soon withers. In all species of *Equisetum* the stems are jointed and leaves are reduced to toothed sheaths at the joints. The horsetail may be found on stream banks, in thickets, in roadside ditches, and on railroad embankments. It is widely distributed over the state, is common in some places, and is almost weedy in its habit of spreading after it becomes established.
Equisetaceae (Horsetail family)

4.2 *Equisetum hyemale* var. *affine*

SCOURING RUSH

In pioneer days this plant was useful as an abrasive in scouring iron pots because of the large amount of silica in the outer region of the stem. Accumulation of silica is a characteristic of all *Equisetum* but this species contains more than others. Note the sound when one stem is rubbed against another. The stem, bearing a cone at the apex, is 2–4 feet tall, unbranched, evergreen, and fluted. The scouring rush is found along watercourses, especially on alluvial flats, in sun or shade in all sections of the state.
Equisetaceae (Horsetail family)

4.3 *Lycopodium lucidulum*

SHINING CLUBMOSS

Widely spreading leaves and the absence of a definite cone characterize the shining clubmoss. It has a horizontal stem from which rise upright stems 4–8 inches high; its leaves are evergreen, ¼–½ inch long. The fertile leaves, which bear sporangia in their axils, are near the apex and are similar to the foliage leaves but shorter. This species is found in eastern and southern Kentucky; its habitat is shady, damp, acid, humus-rich soil, such as that under dripping sandstone cliffs and on stream-banks in forested areas.
Lycopodiaceae (Clubmoss family)

4.4 *Lycopodium porophilum*

ROCK CLUBMOSS

In this species the stems curve up from a short horizontal stem and reach approximately the same height, 3–6 inches, forming a close tuft. The evergreen leaves are only slightly spreading; the fertile leaves, bearing sporangia in their axils, are similar to the foliage leaves. This clubmoss grows on moist shaded ledges and, though widely scattered in the state, is infrequent.
Lycopodiaceae (Clubmoss family)

4.5 *Lycopodium flabelliforme*

GROUND-CEDAR

Branches rising from a creeping horizontal stem fork into fanlike groups of spreading, flattened branchlets. Leaves are scale-like, in 4 rows down the stem. Fertile branches, standing above the foliage, bear slender cylindrical cones; the overall height is 6–10 inches. The gathering of this pretty evergreen species for use as Christmas greens has reduced its frequence. It grows in eastern Kentucky where it is usually associated with pine and mountain laurel in upland woods in acid soil.
Lycopodiaceae (Clubmoss family)

Another similar *Lycopodium* is *L. tristachyum*, in which the fanlike branches are whitish green and more erect, not arching as in *L. flabelliforme*. The 2 species have the same habitat and the same common names.

4.6 *Lycopodium obscurum*

GROUNDPINE

The groundpine has erect stems branching like a miniature tree about 8 inches tall. Leaves are small, awl-shaped, acute, spreading, and evergreen; in late summer there are several cylindric cones per "tree." It occurs, infrequently, in eastern and southeastern Kentucky, where it is found in wet acid soil in rocky wooded areas.
Lycopodiaceae (Clubmoss family)

Series Two: **Monocotyledons (1)**

Monocotyledons typically have parallel-veined leaves and perianth-parts in threes or sixes; plants combining these characteristics comprise this series. (It should be noted that in a few bilaterally symmetrical flowers, such as some orchids, the perianth may not be recognized at first as six-parted, but the leaves are plainly parallel-veined.)

A few exceptional monocotyledons with net-veined leaves or with no leaves, and a few grasses and sedges are included in Series Three, p. 73.

ARRANGEMENT OF PLATES

Group 1. Flowers radially symmetrical

Flowers orange or yellow 1.1–1.9

Flowers white 1.10–1.19

(A few blue-flowered plants may rarely have white flowers; these are grouped with the blues.)

Flowers greenish, brownish, pinkish, or yellowish 1.20–1.25

Flowers blue, rose, purple, or lavender 1.26–1.32

Group 2. Flowers bilaterally symmetrical

2.1–2.15

The Genus *Lilium*, the True Lilies

The lilies are probably the most stately of all our wildflowers. They grow in open woods, edges of woods, and meadows, but unfortunately are infrequent. The true lilies can readily be distinguished from lily-like plants (such as the daylily and the blackberry-lily) by their whorled leaves.

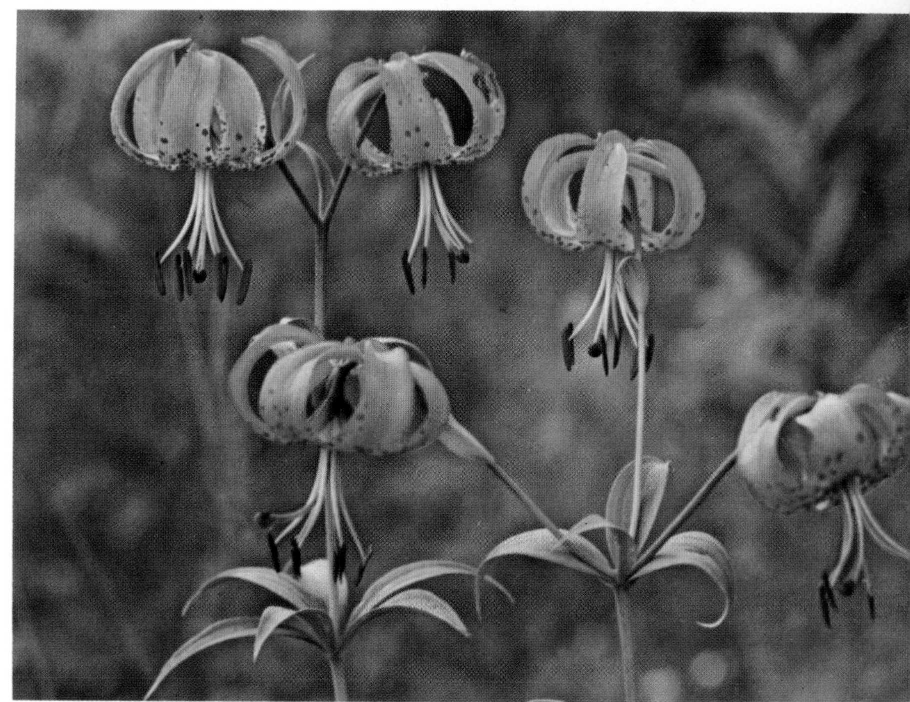

1.1 *Lilium superbum*

TURK'S-CAP LILY

The tallest of our lilies, the Turk's-cap is 3–7 feet high. The nodding flowers, 2½–3½ inches long, have their perianth segments strongly recurved almost from the base. In Kentucky it is found only in the south and southeast and is rare.

Liliaceae (Lily family) July–August

1.2 *Lilium canadense*

CANADA LILY

The Canada lily stands 2–5 feet tall. The flowers, 2–3 inches long, are nodding and the perianth segments flare gracefully, being recurved near the tip. Although it occurs in most sections of the state, it is infrequent.
Liliaceae (Lily family)
Late June–July

Another species of lily in Kentucky is *L. michiganense,* the Michigan lily, which is 2–5 feet tall, also with nodding flowers. Perianth segments are recurved from near the middle, more than in the Canada lily and less than in the Turk's-cap. It is found only in wet ground, whereas the other species may be in either wet or somewhat dry ground.

1.3 *Lilium philadelphicum*

WOOD LILY, PHILADELPHIA LILY

This is the only lily with erect flowers and perianth segments much narrowed at the base. It grows 1–3 feet tall and the flower is 2½–3 inches long. It is infrequently found in eastern and southern Kentucky.
Liliaceae (Lily family)
Late June–July

1.4 *Hemerocallis fulva*

ORANGE DAYLILY

Individual flowers of the daylily are open for one day only. The stem is 2½–3½ feet tall, all leaves are basal, and the flowers, 4–4½ inches long, are erect and unspotted. (Contrast this species with the true lilies, nos. 1.1–1.3.) The daylily is an escape from cultivation often found on roadsides, where its attractiveness justifies its being spared from herbicides.

Liliaceae (Lily family) June–July

1.5 *Belamcanda chinensis*

BLACKBERRY-LILY

Leaves are sword-shaped and are folded lengthwise, making a flattened, one-plane design. The stem is 1½–3½ feet tall and the flower is 1¼–1¾ inches across (smaller than the flower of a true lily). The "blackberry" feature is the cluster of shiny black seeds which are exposed when the fruit breaks open. A native of Asia, it has become naturalized especially in calcareous soil in dry open woods, woodland borders, thickets, and occasionally on roadsides. It is fairly frequent in the Bluegrass and Mississippian Plateau and is infrequent elsewhere.

Iridaceae (Iris family)

July

1.6 *Uvularia grandiflora*

LARGE-FLOWERED BELLWORT

The arching stem, the pendulous, slender yellow flower 1–2 inches long, and the immature leaves which have not fully unfurled at flowering time, all give the large-flowered bellwort a wilted appearance even though the plant is perfectly healthy. This species is perfoliate as well as the one so named (no. 1.7) but, unlike *U. perfoliata,* the leaves of *U. grandiflora* have short hairs on the lower surface. This bellwort is frequent in rich moist woods throughout the state, especially in calcareous areas; it is also frequent in dry woods in the Bluegrass region.

Liliaceae (Lily family) April

1.7 *Uvularia perfoliata*

BELLWORT

As in the preceding species, the leaves appear to be pierced by the stem (perfoliate), but *U. perfoliata* is a larger plant with smaller flowers, ¾–1⅜ inches long. It is frequent in either dry or moist woods throughout the state except in the Bluegrass region.

Liliaceae (Lily family)
Late April–early May

1.8 *Hypoxis hirsuta*

YELLOW STARGRASS

This hairy little plant has stems 4–7 inches tall with flowers ½–¾ inch across, surpassed in height by narrow grasslike leaves. It is fairly frequent in dry woods throughout the state except in the Bluegrass region, where it is rare.
Amaryllidaceae (Amaryllis family)
May

1.9 *Erythronium americanum*

YELLOW TROUT-LILY

This is an example of a species to which many common names have been applied. Either "trout-lily" or "fawn-lily" is apt since its pair of leaves are spotted like a trout or a fawn and since it belongs to the lily family. One name, "adder's-tongue," refers to the appearance of the immature fruit. The name "dog-tooth violet" has no justification, for this plant is far removed from a violet. This species, with a perianth 1–1¾ inches long, is frequent in rich woods throughout the state.
Liliaceae (Lily family) Early April

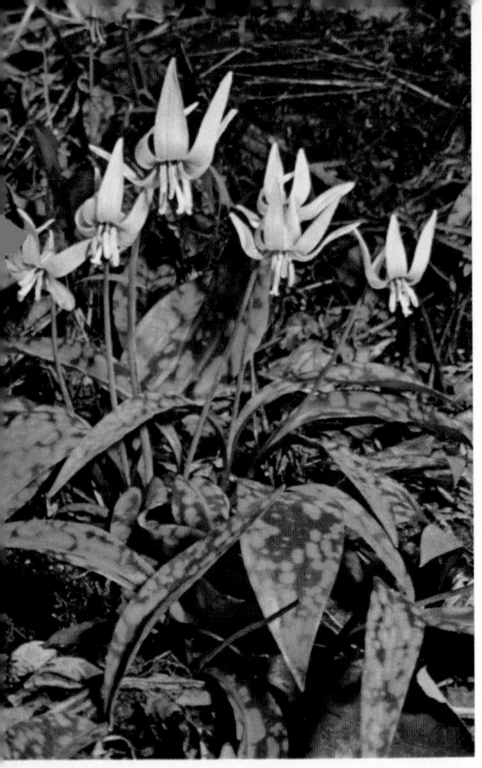

1.10 *Erythronium albidum*

WHITE TROUT-LILY

The white trout-lily, in which the perianth, 1–1½ inches long, is sometimes tinted with lavender, is one of our earliest spring flowers. It grows on wooded limestone slopes, especially in the Bluegrass region and the Mississippian Plateau, and sometimes blankets a cliffside. It is apparently absent from the eastern mountain section.
Liliaceae (Lily family) March

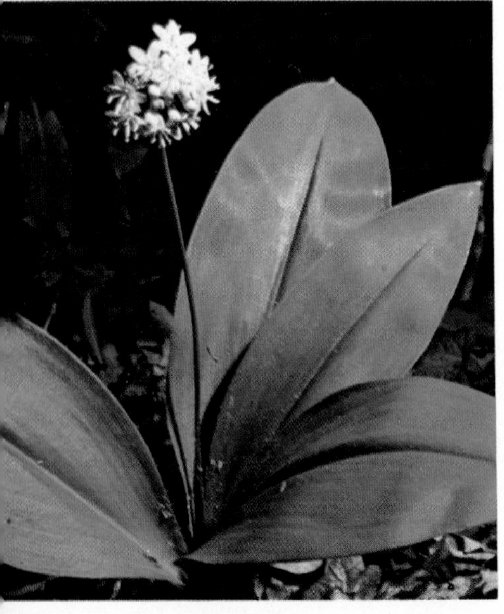

1.11 *Clintonia umbellulata*

WHITE CLINTONIA, SPECKLED WOOD-LILY

Two to four large elliptic leaves sheathe the base of the stem, which is 8–20 inches high. Fragrant white flowers, ¼–⅜ inch long and flecked with pale purple, grow in a terminal umbel; they are followed by blue-black berries. This species is found in the rich moist forests of eastern Kentucky, especially in cool shady ravines of sandstone areas, but is not frequent.
Liliaceae (Lily family) May

1.12 *Smilacina racemosa*

FALSE SOLOMON'S-SEAL, SOLOMON'S-PLUME

The false Solomon's-seal resembles the Solomon's-seal (no. 1.25) in having oval leaves on arching, unbranched stems 1½–3 feet long; it differs in having small white flowers in a dense terminal panicle 2–6 inches long, followed by mottled red berries. It is frequent in rich woods throughout the state.
Liliaceae (Lily family) May

1.13 *Maianthemum canadense*

CANADA MAYFLOWER

This dainty little plant has flowering stems usually about 4 inches high rising from a slender creeping stem which also supports single leaves. It is characteristic of woods of the far north but also grows in the cool high elevations of the southern Appalachians. Its rare occurrence in the Cumberland Plateau at a much lower elevation is a surprising survival of a northern relict from the glacial epoch, and it must be zealously protected.
Liliaceae (Lily family) May

1.14 *Nothoscordum bivalve*

FALSE GARLIC

The common name is not flattering to this pretty—and odorless—little plant. The leaves are linear and basal, the stem is 6–10 inches high, and the flowers are about ½ inch long. It is restricted to dry sunny areas on limestone outcrops, where it often grows with red cedar, and is frequent in central and western Kentucky.

Liliaceae (Lily family)
Late April–early May

1.15 *Ornithogalum umbellatum*

STAR-OF-BETHLEHEM

Perianth segments, ½–¾ inch long, are white with a green stripe on the back, and the leaves have a white stripe down the center. As an escape from old gardens into which it was introduced from Europe, it is found on roadsides, in lawns, and in open woodlands near houses.

Liliaceae (Lily family) May

1.16 *Chamaelirium luteum*

FAIRY-WAND, DEVIL'S-BIT

The gracefully curved spike of small white flowers on a slender wandlike stem 1–3 feet tall accounts for the name "fairy-wand," but the other common name is not so easily explained. Flowers bearing stamens and those bearing pistils are produced on separate plants; the staminate ones (illustrated) are more conspicuous since the flowers are whiter and denser than the greenish white pistillate flowers. The species is found in upland woods in eastern Kentucky and other hilly areas of the state where the soil is acid, but is not frequent.

Liliaceae (Lily family) June

1.17 *Aletris farinosa*

STARGRASS, COLIC-ROOT

The mealy surface of the tubular perianth, ⅜–½ inch long, is responsible for the species name. Leaves are dull pale green, firm, and all basal. The plant grows in acid soil, usually sandy, in open woods and meadows in eastern and southern Kentucky, but is infrequent.

Liliaceae (Lily family) June–July

1.18 *Hymenocallis occidentalis*

SPIDER-LILY

The flowering stem of this handsome plant is 1½–2 feet high, bearing large showy flowers in an umbel; leaves, 1–2 feet long, are all basal. The perianth has spreading linear segments 2–4 inches long and a funnel-shaped crown 1–1½ inches long connecting the filaments of the stamens. It is found in moist ground in southern and western Kentucky but is infrequent.
Amaryllidaceae (Amaryllis family) August

1.19 *Disporum maculatum*

SPOTTED MANDARIN, FAIRY-BELLS

This beautiful plant has white flowers, 1½ inches across, spotted with purple; perianth segments are long-pointed, widely spreading, and strongly narrowed at the base; stamens are long. It is becoming more and more rare as its habitat, the rich climax forests of eastern Kentucky, is destroyed.
Liliaceae (Lily family) May

1.20 *Disporum lanuginosum*

YELLOW MANDARIN

The yellow mandarin, about 2 feet high, has stems forking and then approaching a somewhat horizontal plane. Yellow-green flowers with narrow perianth segments hang singly or in clusters of 2 or 3 at the end of the stem. Essentially an Appalachian species, it is frequent in rich woods in eastern, southeastern, and south-central Kentucky.

Liliaceae (Lily family)

May

1.21 *Agave virginica*

FALSE ALOE

The flowering stem, bearing scattered greenish yellow tubular flowers ¾–1 inch long, stands 3–6 feet tall above a basal rosette of thick, fleshy leaves, unlike anything else in our native flora. It grows in dry sunny areas, usually calcareous, where the soil is thin and in such situations is fairly frequent from the Bluegrass region and Knobs southward and westward. Although this is the only *Agave* in eastern United States, the genus is well represented in the southwestern states.

Amaryllidaceae (Amaryllis family) July

1.22 *Allium cernuum*

NODDING WILD ONION

This nonweedy species of wild onion is distinguished by a crook at the base of the umbel of pink flowers, each about ¼ inch long. Growing in open rocky woods and borders, it is widely scattered and fairly frequent, sometimes locally plentiful in calcareous areas.

Liliaceae (Lily family) July

1.23 *Allium canadense*

WILD GARLIC

In both this native wild garlic and the introduced weed, A. *vineale*, called field garlic or crow garlic (popularly but incorrectly known as "wild onion"), the flowers are pinkish, less than ¼ inch long, and many in an umbel are replaced by bulblets. The 2 species can best be distinguished by their leaves, which are cylindrical in the foreign weed and flat in the native species. It is the foreign field garlic (A. *vineale*) which is a very troublesome weed in pastures, lawns, and gardens, although the native garlic, common throughout the state, sometimes occurs in pastures as well as on roadsides and in open woods.

Liliaceae (Lily family) May–June

1.24 *Medeola virginiana*

INDIAN CUCUMBER-ROOT

The Indian cucumber-root, 12–18 inches high, has a two-tiered design, with a lower whorl of 5–9 leaves at midstem and an upper smaller whorl of 3 leaves subtending the few small greenish yellow flowers, which are followed by purple berries in late summer. Young plants have only one whorl, which is terminal. The Indian cucumber-root is frequent in rich woods in noncalcareous areas of the eastern two-thirds of the state.

Liliaceae (Lily family) May

1.25 *Polygonatum biflorum*

SOLOMON'S-SEAL

Kentucky has three species of Solomon's-seal, all with arching unbranched stems and small, greenish bell-shaped flowers hanging from the axils of the leaves. All are found in woods throughout the state.

P. biflorum and *P. pubescens* are similar in general appearance, 1–3 feet long with 1–3 flowers per cluster, but *P. pubescens* can be distinguished by short hairs on the veins beneath. Both flower in May; *P. biflorum* is more frequent.

P. canaliculatum is the largest and the only coarse one of the three species, having stems 2–6 feet long. It has slightly puckered leaves clasping at the base and 2–8 flowers in each cluster. It flowers in early June and is more frequent in the Bluegrass than elsewhere.

Liliaceae (Lily family)

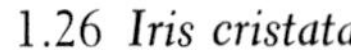

1.26 *Iris cristata*

CRESTED DWARF IRIS

Both species of dwarf iris (*I. cristata* and *I. verna*, no. 1.27) have large showy flowers on small plants; flowering stems are only 4–6 inches high, overtopped by the sterile shoots.

In *I. cristata* the leaves of the sterile shoots (¼–¾ inch wide) are curved and make a gracefully arching fan. Each of the sepals (the 3 down-curved segments of the perianth) has a small fluted crest on a yellow band bordered with white. Widespread in the state, this species is frequent on moist wooded hillsides, especially ravine slopes and ledges, in most regions except the Bluegrass.

Iridaceae (Iris family) May

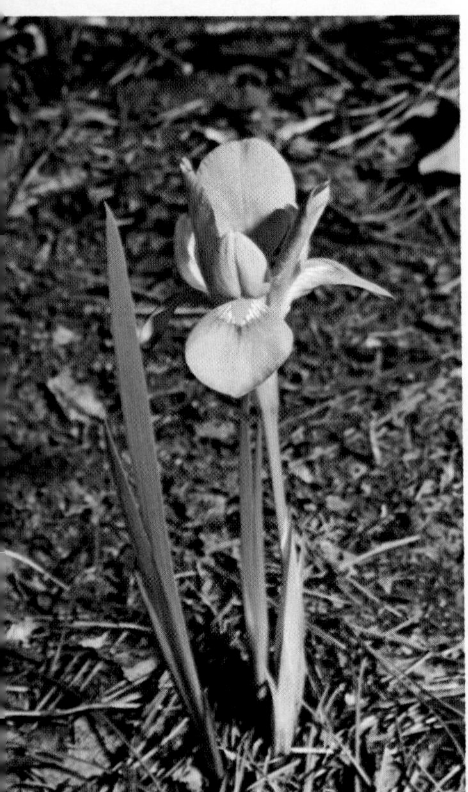

1.27 *Iris verna*

DWARF IRIS

In this species of dwarf iris the leaves are narrow and vertical, only ⅛–⅜ inch wide, and up to 12 inches high. Each of the three sepals has a hairy orange band but is not crested. This species is frequent in open oak and pine woods on dry sandy uplands in eastern Kentucky.

Iridaceae (Iris family) May

1.28 *Iris virginica* var. *shrevei*

SOUTHERN BLUE FLAG

This beautiful plant, with sword-like leaves and blue flowers 2½–3 inches across, stands 2½–3 feet tall. Growing in open swampy woods and marshes, it is widely scattered but infrequent.
Iridaceae (Iris family) June

1.29 *Sisyrinchium angustifolium*

BLUE-EYED GRASS

The so-called blue-eyed grass is a small member of the iris family, not a grass. Its stem is winged, ⅛–¼ inch wide (the same width as the linear leaves), flexed, and 6–18 inches tall. It is frequent in meadows, thickets, and woodland borders throughout the state.
Iridaceae (Iris family)
May–June

Another *Sisyrinchium* in Kentucky is *S. albidum*, called white blue-eyed grass, in which the flowers are white or pale blue and the stems are erect and less than ⅛ inch in width.

1.30 *Camassia scilloides*

WILD HYACINTH

The raceme of pale blue (rarely white) flowers about ½ inch long stands 1–1½ feet high on a leafless stem above basal linear leaves and is followed by triangular capsules. It is found in calcareous areas, especially on ravine slopes, in central and western Kentucky, and is frequent in the Bluegrass region.
Liliaceae (Lily family) May

1.31 *Tradescantia virginiana*

EARLY SPIDERWORT

The early spiderwort, 6–12 inches tall, has leaves ⅜–¾ inch wide and flowers 1–1½ inches across. The richly colored petals vary from purple to rose. It grows in dry open woods and edges of woods, and is more frequent from central Kentucky westward than in eastern Kentucky.
Commelinaceae (Spiderwort family) May

1.32 *Tradescantia subaspera*

ZIGZAG SPIDERWORT

This plant with slightly zigzag stems 1½–2½ feet tall is somewhat coarser than the early species (no. 1.31). It bears bluish purple flowers ¾–1¼ inches across and lance-shaped leaves ½–2 inches wide. It grows in woods and thickets and is more frequent in the western two-thirds of the state than in the eastern third.
Commelinaceae (Spiderwort family) June

Another species of spiderwort less frequent in Kentucky is *T. ohiensis*. Some hybrid spiderworts have been cultivated.

2.1 *Commelina communis*

DAYFLOWER

This introduced weed is a weak-stemmed annual which bears its flowers in a folded bract. Each of the two larger blue petals averages ½ inch in length, with the third white petal much smaller. It is common in dooryards, roadside ditches, and other places near man's habitations, especially in moist ground.
Commelinaceae (Spiderwort family) July–September

A smaller and less common native species of dayflower is *C. diffusa*, found along streams.

2.2 *Liparis lilifolia*

LILY-LEAVED TWAYBLADE

The lily-leaved twayblade (an orchid) has a pair of glossy leaves 2–5 inches long sheathing the base of the stem, which grows 4–10 inches high. The raceme has a delicate appearance since each flower has a long slender stalk, threadlike sepals, and a translucent, purplish brown lip. This species grows on wooded banks of small streams and moist forest slopes; it is infrequent but occurs in all sections of the state.

Orchidaceae (Orchid family)

June

The green adder's-mouth, *Malaxis unifolia,* has a single, oval, sheathing leaf near the middle of the stem, which is 4–10 inches high. The tiny greenish flowers with threadlike lateral petals are in a loose raceme. It is fairly frequent in oak woods in eastern Kentucky and flowers in July.

2.3 *Goodyera pubescens*

RATTLESNAKE-PLANTAIN

The most striking feature of this species of orchid is the basal rosette of evergreen leaves bearing a beautiful and intricate tracery of white veins on a dark green background. The leaves are somewhat succulent, 1–2½ inches long; the raceme of small, dull white flowers (each not over ¼ inch long) stands 6–20 inches tall. It is fairly frequent in rich woods in the mountains and other hilly sections of the state.

Orchidaceae (Orchid family)

August

2.4 *Spiranthes vernalis*

LADIES'-TRESSES

Flowers spiral around the axis of a spike in the ladies'-tresses. Six species are found in Kentucky, all with white flowers save the rare *S. lucida,* which has a yellow lip.

In no. 2.4 a single row of flowers makes the spiral. (Compare with no. 2.5.) The stem is 8–24 inches tall and the flowers are ¼–½ inch long. It grows in dry or moist open woods, borders, thickets, and meadows; though widely scattered in Kentucky, it is infrequent.

Orchidaceae (Orchid family)

July–August

Two smaller species, *S. gracilis* and *S. tuberosa,* flowering in August and September, also have a single spiral.

2.5 *Spiranthes cernua*

LADIES'-TRESSES

In this species 2 or more rows of flowers are spirally twisted around the axis, thereby making a denser spike than no. 2.4. Flowers are ¼–½ inch long, and the stem is 8–24 inches high. It grows in open woods and meadows in low ground and is fairly frequent in eastern Kentucky.

Orchidaceae (Orchid family)

September

A smaller upland species with a double spiral is *S. ovalis.*

2.6 *Cypripedium calceolus* var. *pubescens*

YELLOW LADY'S-SLIPPER, MOCCASIN-FLOWER

The rare and strange-looking lady's-slippers, both the yellow and the pink, are a wildflower fancier's delight. In both species the perianth consists of 2 united sepals, 1 separate sepal, 2 lateral petals, and 1 petal (called the lip) modified into a pouch or inflated sac. The resemblance of this pouch to a moccasin is more pronounced in the yellow species than in the pink.

In the yellow lady's-slipper, which has spirally twisted lateral petals, there are 1 or 2 flowers and 4 or 5 leaves on the stem, which stands 1–2 feet high; the "shoe size" is 1–2 inches. This species grows in deep leafmold on rich, moist, wooded slopes. Though rare, it is widely scattered in the state.

Orchidaceae (Orchid family) May

2.7 *Cypripedium acaule*

PINK LADY'S-SLIPPER, STEMLESS LADY'S-SLIPPER

The pink lady's-slipper has a pair of basal leaves 5–8 inches long; the flower stalk, bearing a solitary flower, is leafless. The pouch, which is infolded down the center, is 1½–2 inches long. This lady's-slipper requires the acid humus of pine needles in pine and oak-pine woods in either wet or dry situations. It is infrequent in eastern Kentucky but may be plentiful in a very few localities. See the account of the genus under no. 2.6.

Orchidaceae (Orchid family) May

Note concerning leaves similar to those of Cypripedium

Seeing in the woods in April a pair of large, oval, parallel-veined leaves before flower stalks are produced, one might wonder if it is a lady's-slipper, a showy orchis (no. 2.8), or a juvenile plant of *Clintonia* (no. 1.11). Leaf surfaces of the stemless lady's-slipper are finely hairy whereas leaves of the showy orchis are without hairs, and in *Clintonia* hairs are restricted to the leaf margins. A single leaf of the same size and shape might be a juvenile plant of any of these species, but if it appears somewhat dry and withered, it is likely to belong to the putty-root (*Aplectrum hyemale,* Series Three, no. 3.3), which has lived through the winter.

2.8 *Orchis spectabilis*

SHOWY ORCHIS

The showy orchis has a pair of thick glossy leaves at the base of the stem, which is 6–12 inches high. Each individual flower, subtended by a large green bract, is approximately 1 inch long and has a white lip, which is prolonged at the base into a spur, and a pinkish purple hood formed by the lateral petals and the sepals. This lovely orchid grows in rich moist woods where there is deep leafmold, and, though infrequent, is widely distributed in the state.

Its beauty may tempt the admirer to appropriate it. As with all orchids, however, the habitat requirements are very precise and success in transplanting is unlikely. All orchids should be left, protected, and admired in place.

Orchidaceae (Orchid family) April–May

2.9 *Isotria verticillata*

WHORLED POGONIA

The whorled pogonia, 4–12 inches high, has a single erect flower above a single whorl of 5 (or 6) leaves. While the flower is open the leaves enlarge from about 1 inch long to 2 inches and later to about 3 inches. The flower has brownish purple linear sepals, 1½–2½ inches long, twice the length of the yellow-green petals. This species grows in acid leafmold in oak-pine and hemlock woods in eastern and southern Kentucky, where it is often associated with mountain laurel, but is infrequent.

Sterile plants of the more common *Medeola*, Indian cucumber-root (no. 1.24), should not be mistaken for *Isotria*. The stem of the whorled pogonia is succulent, hollow, and without hairs, as contrasted with a wiry, slightly hairy stem in *Medeola*.

Orchidaceae (Orchid family)

Early May

2.10 *Cleistes divaricata*

SPREADING POGONIA

Three linear greenish or brownish sepals, 2–3 inches long, and a funnel-shaped corolla, 1–1½ inches long, pale pink or lavender with darker lines on the lip, characterize the spreading pogonia. There are also a green bract, a single clasping leaf midway on the 12–18 inch stem, and usually one basal leaf. It grows in open woods on dry, sandy uplands in eastern Kentucky but is infrequent.

Orchidaceae (Orchid family)

July

2.11 *Calopogon pulchellus*

GRASS-PINK, SWAMP-PINK

Common names can be misleading; this is actually an orchid and not a member of the pink family. Its purplish pink flowers are 1–1¾ inches across, with sepals larger than the lateral petals; the lip, which is bearded, is uppermost instead of lowermost, as it is in most orchids. The stem, bearing several flowers, is 12–18 inches high and has a single, tall, linear basal leaf. It is found, infrequently, in wet meadows and sunny wet depressions in acid soil in eastern and southern Kentucky.

Orchidaceae (Orchid family) June

The Genus *Habenaria*, the Fringed Orchids

In the so-called fringed orchids the lip of the flower, which may or may not be fringed, is prolonged at the base into a spur. The flowers, usually showy, are in dense racemes or spikes.

2.12 *Habenaria peramoena*

PURPLE FRINGELESS ORCHID, FAN-LIP ORCHID

The specific name translated from Greek means "very beautiful" and is apt indeed. The lip is 3-parted, ½ inch long, and ¾ inch across; the middle lobe is fan-shaped and fringeless. The plant, with lower leaves broadly lance-shaped and upper leaves narrower, is 12–30 inches high. It grows in wet acid soil in sun or partial shade and is widely distributed in the state although infrequent.
Orchidaceae (Orchid family)
July

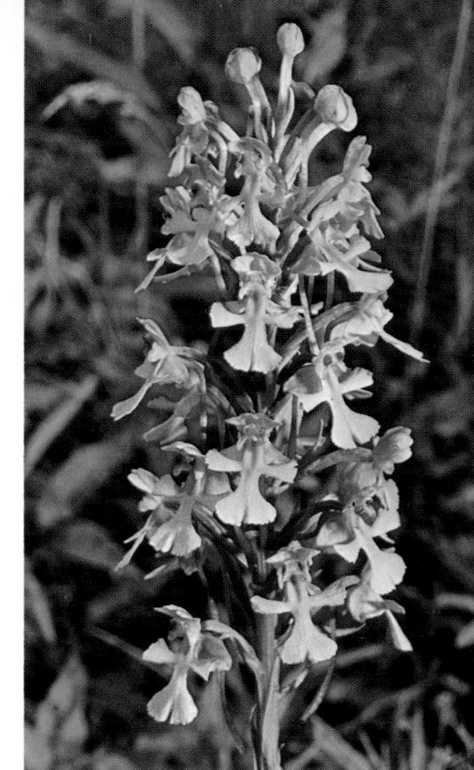

2.13 *Habenaria psycodes*

PURPLE FRINGED ORCHID

The illustration shows an individual flower from the raceme. The fringed 3-parted lip is ⅜–½ inch long, and the spur is ⅔–1 inch. The plant, with narrow pointed leaves, is 12–20 inches high. A northern relict species rare in Kentucky, it grows in wet acid soil in the high Cumberland Mountains, and in the Cumberland Plateau it is known to occur in only one area.
Orchidaceae (Orchid family)
July

2.14 *Habenaria flava*

PALE GREEN ORCHIS

The stem, 6–20 inches high, bears 2–4 large lanceolate leaves. In one variety (pictured) the bracts are longer than the pale green flowers, which are about ¼ inch across, and in another they equal the flowers in length. This species grows in wet grassy areas and clearings in swamp forests in southeastern Kentucky but is rare.
Orchidaceae (Orchid family) June

Another pale greenish *Habenaria* is *H. clavellata*, 4–15 inches high, which has only one well-developed leaf on the stem and which has bracts shorter than the flowers. *H. lacera*, the ragged orchis, has a fringed pale greenish lip. *H. blephariglottis* has white flowers. All of these species are rare in Kentucky.

2.15 *Habenaria ciliaris*

YELLOW FRINGED ORCHID

In this handsome plant the lip of the flower is narrow, ⅜–½ inch long, and fringed. The leaves are lance-shaped, the upper ones smaller than the lower, and the stem is 12–24 inches high. It grows in wet acid soil in sun or partial shade in eastern and southern Kentucky and is infrequent.
Orchidaceae (Orchid family) July

Series Three: **Monocotyledons (2)**

Exceptional monocotyledons which have net-veined leaves or no leaves, and those with parallel-veined leaves which do not have perianth parts in threes or sixes.

ARRANGEMENT OF PLATES

Group 1. *Plants with net-veined leaves and perianth parts in threes or sixes or absent*

- Flowers lacking a perianth 1.1–1.2
- Flowers with 3 sepals and 3 petals; leaves in a single whorl of 3 1.3–1.10
- Flowers having a 3- or 6-parted perianth; leaves not in a single whorl of 3 1.11–1.15

Group 2. *Selected grasses, sedges, and rushes, all with linear leaves*

- Marsh plants 2.1–2.9
- Grasses of mesic situations 2.10–2.12

Group 3. *Plants lacking green leaves, at least at flowering time*

- Green leaves present at a season different from flowering time 3.1–3.3
- Saprophytic or parasitic plants, never green 3.4–3.5

1.1 *Arisaema atrorubens*

JACK-IN-THE-PULPIT, INDIAN TURNIP

"Jack" in his canopied "pulpit" is a fleshy, club-shaped inflorescence which bears minute flowers near the base. The "pulpit," which is a sheathing bract, is 2–4 inches long and can be purple, green, or striped. By August the bract has withered and "Jack" has become a mass of scarlet berries. Leaves are trifoliate, 1 or 2 per plant. This interesting plant is frequent in rich woods throughout the state.

Araceae (Arum family) May

The species illustrated, having the lateral leaflets oblique and slightly whitened beneath, is more frequent than A. *triphyllum,* in which the lateral leaflets are nearly symmetrical and green beneath.

1.2 *Arisaema dracontium*

GREEN DRAGON

The 5–15 leaflets are arranged on one side of an axis which forms an arc. The long "tongue" of the dragon extends from the fleshy inflorescence and protrudes 1–7 inches beyond the sheathing bract, which is 1–2 inches long. The green dragon is fairly frequent in wet shady areas such as floodplains, swamps, stream margins, and seepage areas throughout the state.

Araceae (Arum family) May–June

1.3 *Trillium sessile*

SESSILE TRILLIUM

This species is well named, for the flower has no stalk and the leaves have no petioles. The plant is 4–10 inches high. The leaves are mottled; the petals are slender, 1–1½ inches long, and usually maroon but sometimes greenish yellow. In general this trillium is found in wooded bottomlands, but in the Bluegrass region it also grows on wooded cliffs and ledges and in upland woods and thickets. It is frequent in the central and northern parts of the state and rare in the eastern and western sections.
Liliaceae (Lily family) April

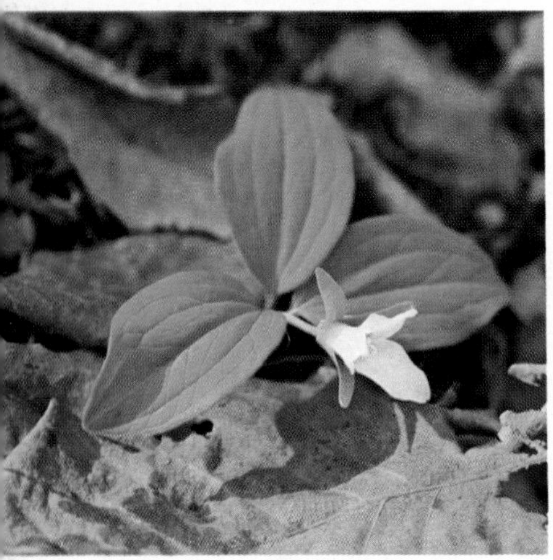

1.4 *Trillium nivale*

DWARF WHITE TRILLIUM, SNOW TRILLIUM

One of the very earliest spring flowers, this diminutive trillium, only 2–5 inches tall, has petioled leaves and a stalked flower with petals ½–1¼ inches long. It grows on wooded limestone ledges in the Inner Bluegrass; the species is rare, even endangered, and should not be disturbed.
Liliaceae (Lily family) March

1.5 *Trillium recurvatum*

RECURVED TRILLIUM

In this species the leaves are petioled but the flower is sessile; the maroon petals, 1–1¾ inches long, are strongly narrowed at the base, and the sepals are bent downward. The stem is 6–16 inches high. It grows in rich woods, and in Kentucky is apparently restricted to the western third of the state.

Liliaceae (Lily family) April–May

1.6 *Trillium luteum*

YELLOW TRILLIUM

Both leaves and flowers are sessile, and the leaves are mottled. The flowers, which have a lemon-oil scent, have petals 1½–2¼ inches long, and the plant grows 8–18 inches tall. In Kentucky this species is restricted to upland woods in calcareous soil in the southern part of the state. It should not be confused with the greenish-yellow form of *T. sessile* (no. 1.3), which is smaller and more frequent.

Liliaceae (Lily family) April–May

1.7 *Trillium undulatum*

PAINTED TRILLIUM

A white corolla with a rose-colored triangle at the center and bronzy-green leaves on a plant 8–18 inches tall characterize the painted trillium at a distance. Each petal is wavy-edged, white with a magenta or rose spot at the base. In Kentucky this species is found only in the southeastern mountain counties where it grows in acid soil and is associated with hemlock, rhododendron, and mountain laurel.

Liliaceae (Lily family) May

1.8 *Trillium grandiflorum*

LARGE-FLOWERED TRILLIUM

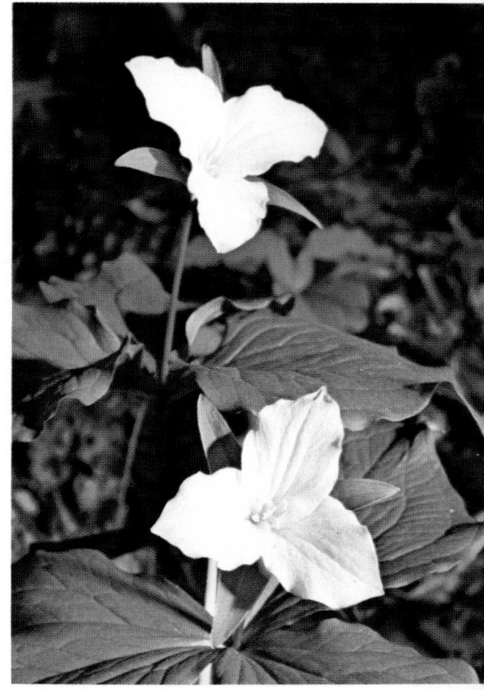

This is the most showy of all trilliums in the state although the plant is no taller than some others (8–18 inches high). Petals, broadest near the tip, 1½–2½ inches long, and decidedly longer than the sepals, are white, turning pink with age. The ovary also is white. A cove, mountainside, or ravine slope covered with these handsome flowers is a spectacle not to be forgotten. The species is frequent in rich woods in eastern and southern Kentucky.

Sports or "freaks" occur in all species of *Trillium* but are most frequent in *T. grandiflorum*.

Liliaceae (Lily family)

April–May

1.9 *Trillium erectum*

ERECT TRILLIUM

This is a large species, 10–20 inches tall with petals ¾–2 inches long. Petals are usually lanceolate or ovate-lanceolate but may sometimes be broadly ovate, as in the photograph; they are usually dark reddish or brownish purple but may be white or any intermediate shade. The white form can be distinguished from the white form of *T. flexipes* (no. 1.10) and from *T. grandiflorum* (no. 1.8) by the dark ovary in *T. erectum*. The flowers are usually somewhat erect but may be declined, and are often ill-scented. This species is frequent in rich moist woods, especially on ravine slopes in eastern and southeastern Kentucky.

Liliaceae (Lily family)

April

1.10 *Trillium flexipes*

BENT TRILLIUM

The flower in this species is usually nodding beneath the leaves. The petals, ¾–1¾ inches long, are most often white but may be maroon or an intermediate color; however, the ovary is always white or pale. (The color of the ovary is constant in any one species of *Trillium* and is thus useful in distinguishing between species in which petal color varies.) The bent trillium grows in rich woods in the Bluegrass region and thence westward and southwestward.

Liliaceae (Lily family) April

1.11 *Smilax herbacea*

CARRION-FLOWER

This annual vine, held up by tendrils, has greenish flowers in spherical umbels. Each flower has a 6-parted perianth, but pistillate and staminate flowers are on different plants. Having the odor of carrion, they are pollinated by carrion flies, as shown in the photograph. The plant, widely distributed and fairly frequent, grows in thickets in rich ground.

Liliaceae (Lily family) June

Another species of carrion-flower (*S. ecirrhata*) grows erect, without tendrils; otherwise it is similar.

1.12 *Dioscorea quaternata*

WILD YAM

The leaves and fruit of this herbaceous twiner attract more attention than the minute greenish flowers. Bearing staminate and pistillate flowers on separate plants, the stems are 3–6 feet long and the leaf blades 2½–4 inches long. The 3-winged capsules persist all winter and rattle in the wind. The wild yam, so-called because of a large starchy rootstock, grows in woodlands throughout the state but is most frequent in the calcareous areas of central Kentucky.

Dioscoreaceae (Yam family) May

The species pictured has its lowest leaves in a whorl of 4 to 7; another similar species, *D. villosa*, has all leaves alternate or the lowest opposite or in a whorl of 3.

1.13 *Alisma subcordatum*

WATER-PLANTAIN

The leaves have elliptical blades 3–6 inches in length and long petioles, the length of which varies with the depth of the water. Flowers, with 3 green sepals and 3 white petals, rarely over ⅛ inch across, are numerous on whorled branches of a large panicle 1–3 feet tall. The water-plantain is common in shallow water, especially at the edge of ponds but also in slow streams and ditches, and is distributed throughout the state.

Alismataceae (Water-plantain family) June–July

1.14 *Sagittaria latifolia*

ARROWHEAD, DUCK-POTATO

Leaf-blades, 6–12 inches long and variable in width, are long-petioled and arrow-shaped with long basal lobes. Flowers, 1–1¼ inches across with 3 green sepals and 3 white petals, are borne in whorls in a raceme. Tubers on long runners provide food for waterfowl and hence account for the name "duck-potato." This plant is frequent in shallow water at the edge of ponds, in sluggish streams, and in ditches, and is widespread in the state.

Alismataceae (Water-plantain family) July–August

A similar species, S. *australis*, differing mainly in the fruit but also having lance-shaped instead of ovate bracts, is also frequent.

1.15 *Sagittaria graminea*

GRASS-LEAF ARROWHEAD

Not all "arrowheads" have arrow-shaped leaves; this species has blades linear-lanceolate or oblong-lanceolate and nearly parallel venation. Flowers are similar to those of *S. latifolia* (no. 1.14). It also grows in shallow water but is less frequent than no. 1.14.

Alismataceae (Water-plantain family)
June-August

2.1 *Typha latifolia*

CAT-TAIL

The "tail" is composed of thousands of minute flowers which lack both calyx and corolla. The thick brown portion consists of pistillate flowers and the slender upper portion of staminate flowers, which fall off after shedding pollen. In late winter it becomes more "furry" as seeds, each with a tuft of hair at the base, are loosened and scattered by the wind. This species, which grows 3–6 feet tall, is common throughout the state in marshes, pond borders, and shallow sluggish streams. A cat-tail colony provides homes for marsh-dwelling birds; the rootstock furnishes food for muskrats and wild geese; and man can use the spikes in autumn bouquets.

Typhaceae (Cat-tail family) Summer

A smaller, less common species is *T. angustifolia,* which differs principally in having a gap between the pistillate and the staminate portions of the spike.

2.2 *Acorus americanus*

SWEET FLAG, AMERICAN CALAMUS

The leaves are lustrous, 2–3 feet high. The stem producing the inflorescence is of the same width as the leaves, and the inflorescence is topped by a bract of the same width which rises to the height of the leaves. The thick horizontal rhizome is highly aromatic. The sweet flag grows at the edge of quiet shallow water; though scattered over the state, it is not frequent.

Araceae (Arum family) May

2.3 *Cyperus strigosus* UMBRELLA SEDGE

This is the most common of several species of umbrella sedges occurring in the state. The actual flowers are in the axils of the straw-colored scales which make up the spikelets; these in turn make up the spikes, which are arranged in an umbrella-like design. This sedge is found in moist ground throughout the state and is especially common in ditches.

Cyperaceae (Sedge family) September

2.4 *Scirpus validus* var. *creber*

GREAT BULRUSH

Stems are round, thick but soft and easily compressed, and are usually 4–6 feet tall. The inflorescence of many spikelets appears lateral because of the erect position of the subtending bract. The great bulrush is widely scattered and fairly frequent in the shallow water of marshes.

Cyperaceae (Sedge family)

June–August

2.5 *Scirpus pedicellatus*

WOOL-GRASS

The so-called wool-grass is one of the bulrushes, a sedge and not a grass. Growing 3–6 feet tall, it has a full graceful inflorescence with nodding branches 4–10 inches long. The long, soft, curly bristles surrounding the one-seeded fruits give the spikelets a woolly appearance. This species and the similar *S. cyperinus* are common in swamps and marshes and are widely distributed.

Cyperaceae (Sedge family)

August–September

2.6 *Scirpus atrovirens*

SMALL BULRUSH

This is the most common bulrush in Kentucky. It is 2–5 feet tall; the spikelets are dark greenish brown, less than 1/3 inch long, and crowded on the branches of the inflorescence. It is found in swamps, marshes, ditches, and wet meadows throughout the state.

Cyperaceae (Sedge family) July–August

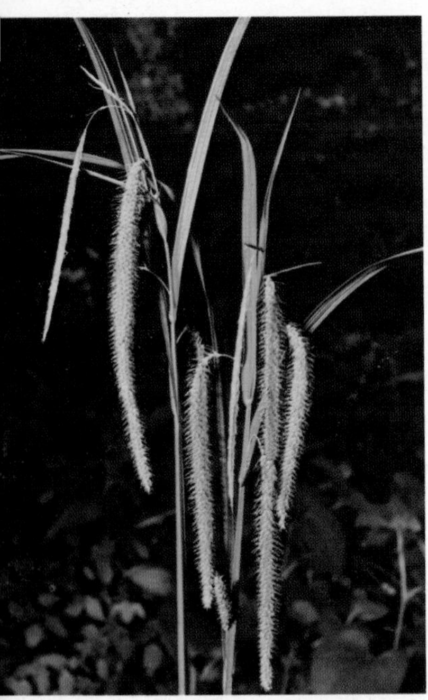

2.7 *Carex crinita*

DROOPING SEDGE

From almost a hundred species of *Carex* in the state we select this one because of the unusual grace and attractiveness of its slender, pendulous spikes on a stem 3–5 feet tall. These are pistillate spikes bearing flowers in the axils of bristle-tipped scales; the spikes bearing staminate flowers are more slender and terminal. This beautiful sedge is frequent in swamps and wet woods.

Cyperaceae (Sedge family)

June–July

2.8 *Carex lupulina*

HOP SEDGE

As in all species of *Carex*, the individual flowers are minute but an entire spike of them is conspicuous. In *Carex* a pistillate flower consists of one pistil enclosed in a sac; in the section of the genus to which this species belongs, the sac is inflated, ribbed, and beaked; and in this species it is nearly ½ inch long. The staminate spikes are much more slender than the big, bur-like pistillate ones. This sedge is frequent in swamps and wet ground in meadows, woods, and thickets throughout the state.

Cyperaceae (Sedge family)

June–August

2.9 *Juncus effusus*

COMMON RUSH

At least 18 species of rushes, of the genus *Juncus,* occur in Kentucky. Their flowers are characterized by a 6-parted perianth surrounding at maturity a capsule containing many minute seeds. The common rush lacks leaves; its stem is green, pliant, and 2–4 feet high. The flowers are about ⅛ inch long in a much branched inflorescence which appears to be lateral because of an erect bract. It grows in dense clumps and is common in marshes and wet meadows in various sections of the state. It has been used extensively for chair bottoms and formerly also for matting.

Juncaceae (Rush family) July–August

2.10 *Uniola latifolia*

SPANGLE GRASS

The slender branches of the panicle droop gracefully with the weight of the large flat spikelets. This handsome grass can be attractive in a flower arrangement but when grown as an ornamental, it spreads and needs to be held within bounds. It grows 2–4 feet tall with spikelets ¾–1¼ inches long, large enough to demonstrate the structure and arrangement of grass flowers. In this species there are 8–16 flowers per spikelet, each between a pair of scales: the outer, conspicuous scales making the overlapping pattern of the spikelet and the small inner ones invisible unless dissected. The spangle grass is frequent in moist ground throughout the state.

Gramineae (Grass family)

August–September

2.11 *Hystrix patula*

BOTTLE-BRUSH GRASS

This is a distinctive and easily recognized grass having spikelets extending horizontally when mature and bearing stiff 1-inch bristles. The spikelets occur in close pairs which are distantly spaced in the spike. The bottle-brush is common in woodlands throughout the state.

Gramineae (Grass family) July

2.12 *Poa pratensis*

KENTUCKY BLUEGRASS

This species of bluegrass is one of the chief turf, pasture, and lawn grasses in the northeastern quarter of the United States and the north-central states, south to the southern boundary of Kentucky and Virginia, to a lesser extent in Tennessee, and in the humid northwest. Over most of the United States it is usually called "Kentucky bluegrass" though it is occasionally called "June grass" in the north.

As to whether the species was native to a section of Kentucky (and possibly a small area of southern Ohio) and was growing wild here before the white man brought it is a question that may never be answered with certainty. That it is a native of England, where it is called "meadow grass," that it was introduced early into the American colonies, where the colonists called it "English grass," that it was not native to the coastal states, that in its present cultivated form it is of European origin—these are indisputable facts.

Most botanists have believed that it was all introduced and that it became known as "Kentucky bluegrass" well over a century ago because it flourished more in this rich limestone region than in many other areas, and because much seed was commercially produced here. However, there is some evidence that it was here before the first settlers arrived. Some early land surveys prior to 1780, before these tracts were settled, mention quantities of "English grass." A tradition is that it was accidentally introduced by the early explorers of the 1750s and 1760s and had become established by the time the state was settled in the 1770s. This is unlikely, for the primeval vegetation would have so covered the land that a new grass which is not aggressive in its habits could not have replaced a substantial part of the native vegetation so quickly. It is known that Indians had practiced some burning of the land before the settlement of Kentucky, and it is remotely possible that they could have sown in these plots some "English grass" obtained from eastern colonists. On the other hand, a variety of *Poa pratensis* may have been indigenous.

The genus *Poa* consists of over 50 species of bluegrasses in all the United States; 7 species other than *P. pratensis* are definitely native to Kentucky but are predominantly woodland species and are not forage grasses.

Gramineae (Grass family) May

3.1 *Allium tricoccum*

WILD LEEK, RAMP

In late winter and early spring the wild leek produces rich, verdant patches of lily-of-the-valley-like leaves which provide a bright contrast with the brown forest floor. By late spring they are yellowing, and by the time flowers appear in July no trace of leaf remains. In late summer large, shiny, jet-black seeds are conspicuous after the capsule splits. Leaves are 4–10 inches long, with a rank odor; sepals and petals are white and about ¼ inch long. The wild leek grows in rich woods, especially on ravine slopes, and, though scattered in most regions of the state, is not frequent.

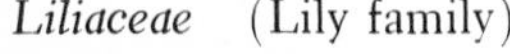

Liliaceae (Lily family) July

3.2 *Tipularia discolor*

CRANEFLY ORCHID (*Below left*)

In August the cranefly orchid has long-spurred, pale purplish green flowers in a slender raceme that stands leafless and 8–16 inches high. In autumn it produces a single elliptical, petioled leaf, veiny and almost pleated, purple beneath, and 2–5 inches long, which persists through winter until it dies in late spring. This orchid is frequent in oak woods in the hilly sections of the state.

Orchidaceae (Orchid family) August

3.3 *Aplectrum hyemale*

PUTTY-ROOT

The solitary leaf in winter is more conspicuous than the flowers in summer. The blade, which is 4–7 inches long and dark, dull green with light "pleated" veins, appears in autumn and withers before flowering occurs in late May or June. The flower stem, 8–20 inches tall and sheathed at the base, bears a raceme of greenish flowers in which the lip is white with purple markings. Sepals and petals are approximately ½ inch long. In hilly sections of the state the putty-root orchid is fairly frequent in moist spots in rich woods.

Orchidaceae (Orchid family) May–June

3.4 *Hexalectris spicata*

CRESTED CORAL-ROOT

The crested coral-root is a colorful and handsome saprophytic orchid. The stem, 6–24 inches tall, is golden-brown or red-brown with purplish scales and bears a raceme of flowers, each ¾ inch or more long and combining red, purple, yellow, and brown. The lip is crested, that is, with ridges down the middle. This interesting orchid grows especially in calcareous rocky woods in the Knobs and the Mississippian Plateau region but is not common.
Orchidaceae (Orchid family) August

3.5 *Corallorhiza wisteriana*

CORAL-ROOT

The coral-roots are small saprophytic orchids (4–12 inches high) in which stem, scale-like reduced leaves, and flowers are brownish or purplish. The flowers have a short spur, and the lip is white with purple spots. Kentucky has two species, both found in woodlands and probably fairly frequent though often overlooked: C. *wisteriana*, chiefly in central and western Kentucky and flowering in May, and C. *odontorhiza*, widely distributed and flowering in August and September.
Orchidaceae (Orchid family)

Series Four: **Dicotyledons (1)**

Dicotyledons having radially symmetrical flowers with perianth parts in fours or fives and net-veined leaves.

Radial symmetry

(Can be cut into 2 equal halves in many ways provided the plane of cutting passes through the center)

ARRANGEMENT OF PLATES

Group 1. Individual flowers ½ inch or more in diameter or length

Flowers yellow or orange
- With separate petals 1.1–1.17, 1.24, 1.25
- With united corolla 1.18–1.23

Flowers white
- With separate petals 1.26–1.43
- With united corolla 1.44–1.52

Flowers red 1.53–1.56

Flowers pink, blue, or purple
- With separate petals 1.57–1.66
- With united corolla 1.67–1.90

Flowers of miscellaneous pale colors
- With separate petals 1.91–1.98
- With united corolla 1.99–1.108

Group 2. Individual flowers less than ½ inch in any dimension

Flowers in racemes, spikes, or headlike spikes (in sequence: yellow, white, and pink or blue) 2.1–2.20

Flowers in umbels (yellow, white) 2.21–2.35

Flowers in panicles (listed first) and various other types of inflorescences or clusters 2.36–2.60

Solitary flower 2.61

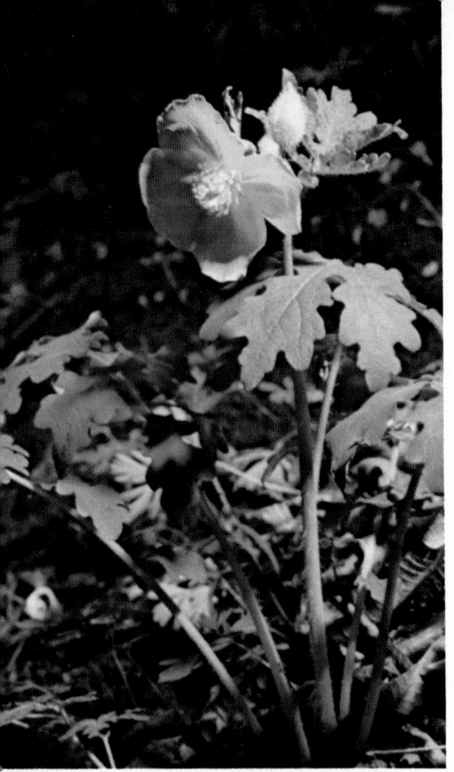

1.1 *Stylophorum diphyllum*

CELANDINE POPPY, WOOD POPPY

The celandine poppy has yellow juice as well as yellow flowers. There are 4 petals, each ¾–1 inch long; buds are covered with 2 hairy sepals, and the fruit is bristly hairy. The leaves, predominantly basal, are pinnately lobed. This species, which grows 10–18 inches high, is widely distributed in the state and is frequent in rich mesophytic woods, especially on slopes where leafmold is deep.

Papaveraceae (Poppy family)

April

A similar plant, the celandine (*Chelidonium majus*), differs in having narrower petals which are only ½ inch long. It was introduced from Europe and has escaped to roadsides in rich ground.

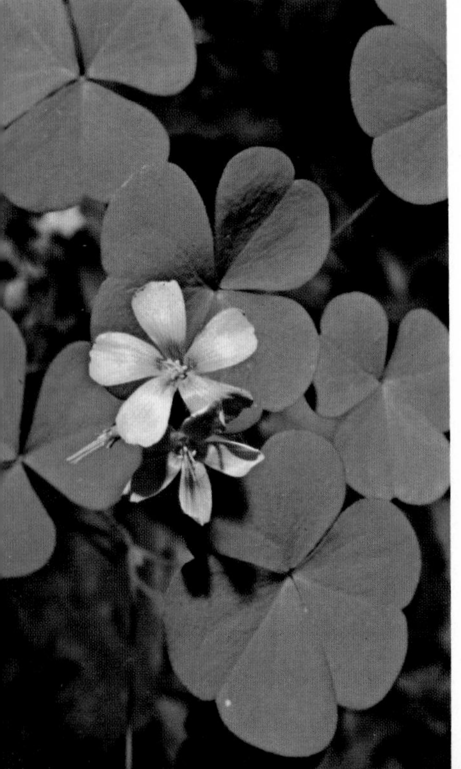

1.2 *Oxalis grandis*

LARGE WOOD-SORREL

The large yellow wood-sorrel has flowers ½–¾ inch long, leaflets 1¼–1½ inches broad and often edged with purple, and stems 12–24 inches high. It grows in rich moist woods and is frequent throughout the state.

Oxalidaceae (Wood-sorrel family)

June

This native woodland plant has several much smaller weedy relatives, also called yellow wood-sorrels, which grow in lawns, gardens, and waste places, and on roadsides (*O. europaea*, *O. corniculata*, and *O. stricta*).

1.3 *Ranunculus hispidus* HAIRY BUTTERCUP

The so-called hairy buttercup, with petioles and stems usually hairy at least at the base, has palmately cut leaves and grows 6–18 inches high. Flowers are ½–¾ inch across and lustrous. It is frequent in moist ground in woods throughout the state.
Ranunculaceae (Buttercup family) April

Among other buttercups in Kentucky is the swamp buttercup (*R. septentrionalis*), which has weak stems 1–2 feet long at flowering time, later 3 feet long and reclining.

Some European species, such as the tall buttercup (*R. acris*), the bulbous buttercup (*R. bulbosus*), and the creeping buttercup (*R. repens*), have become established in a few areas.

1.4 *Ranunculus fascicularis* EARLY BUTTERCUP

Leaves are silky, the earliest ones 3-lobed, the later, principal ones pinnately cut into 5 main segments with slender blunt lobes. Flowers, ½–¾ inch across, have narrowly oblong, waxy petals. The plant is 6–12 inches tall and grows in dry open, chiefly calcareous, woods in central and western Kentucky.
Ranunculaceae (Buttercup family) April

1.5 *Duchesnea indica*

INDIAN STRAWBERRY, MOCK STRAWBERRY

The bright red strawberry-like fruit of this Asiatic weed is tempting but spongy and insipid. Also in contrast to the edible strawberry, the petals are yellow instead of white, the flowers, ½ inch across, are solitary on flower stems that rise from the nodes of the runners, and both flowers and fruit have a "collar" of green bracts beneath. It is a common weed, especially in lawns.

Rosaceae (Rose family) April–September (chiefly April)

1.6 *Waldsteinia fragarioides*

BARREN STRAWBERRY

This plant is strawberry-like in its flower structure and its trifoliate leaves but differs from the true strawberry in having yellow petals, no runners, and dry fruits. Its fruit has the "straws," but the receptacle does not become fleshy as in the strawberry. The flowers are usually ½ inch across, and the plant is 4–8 inches high. It grows in rich woods in eastern, central, and southern Kentucky but is infrequent.

Rosaceae (Rose family)

Late April–early May

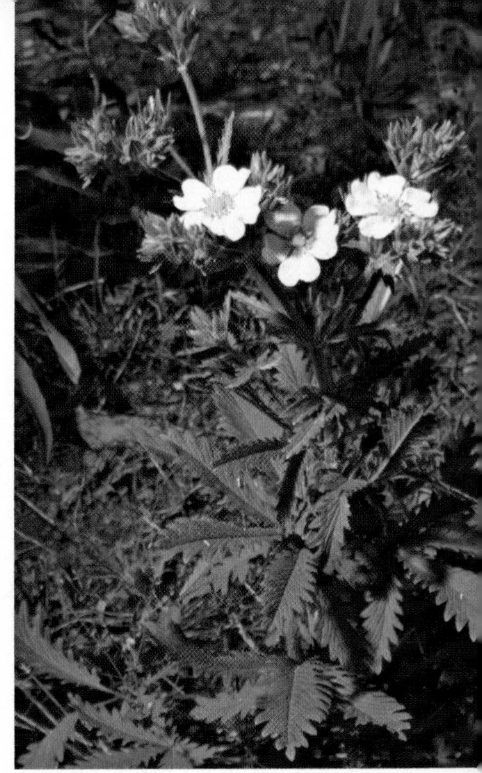

1.7 *Potentilla recta*

ROUGH-FRUITED CINQUEFOIL, SULPHUR CINQUEFOIL

The cinquefoils are also called five-fingers.

This species of *Potentilla* has erect, much-branched stems 1–2 feet high, and 5–7 narrow leaflets per leaf. The sulphur-yellow flowers are ½–1 inch across. A European weed, it has become common in fields and fencerows and on roadsides in many parts of the state.

Rosaceae (Rose family)

Late May–June

1.8 *Potentilla canadensis*

DWARF CINQUEFOIL, EARLY CINQUEFOIL

The flower in this species is about ½ inch across; at flowering time the stem is only 2–6 inches long and the leaves are still expanding. It is frequent in open woods and borders of woods, chiefly in noncalcareous soil, in eastern Kentucky and in the Knobs.

Rosaceae (Rose family) March–April

A similar species, distributed throughout the state and common in some areas, is *P. simplex*, called old-field cinquefoil or common cinquefoil. It grows in old fields as well as thickets and open woods. When it flowers in late April and May, the stem is 6–18 inches long and the leaves are fully expanded.

1.9 *Hypericum spathulatum*

SHRUBBY ST. JOHN'S-WORT

A big fluff of stamens in a bright yellow corolla ¾–1 inch across make this shrub showy when in full flower. It is 3–6 feet high and has lance-oblong, lustrous leaves. It grows in dry or moist soil in open places and is frequent in various sections of the state.

Hypericaceae (St. John's-wort family) July

Another shrubby St. John's-wort, *H. frondosum,* which has larger flowers, 1–1¾ inches across, is restricted in Kentucky to limestone bluffs and slopes in the south-central counties.

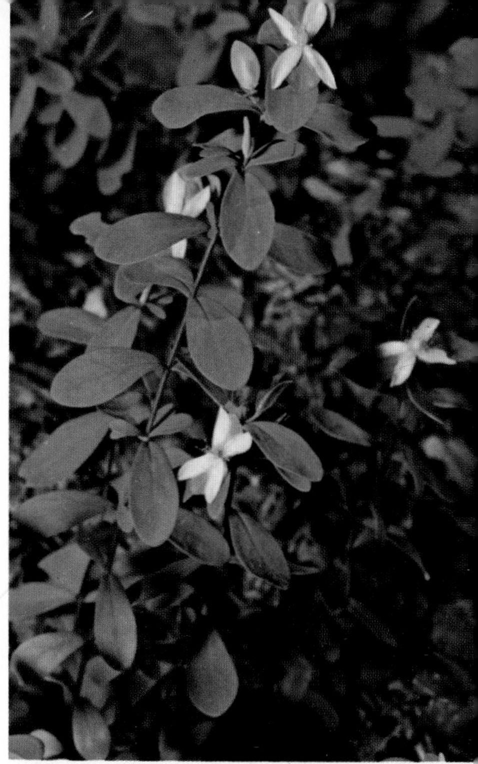

1.10 *Ascyrum hypericoides*

ST. ANDREW'S CROSS

The St. Andrew's cross with its slender, somewhat woody stems is technically a semi-shrub although it grows only 4–8 inches high. The plant has many branches bearing light green, narrowly oblong leaves ½–1 inch long, and solitary flowers, each ½–¾ inch broad. The flowers have 4 pale yellow petals forming an oblique cross, 2 large sepals, and 2 minute ones. The plant is frequent in dry, open oak woods and clearings in noncalcareous areas and is found in most regions of the state except the Bluegrass.

Hypericaceae July–August
(St. John's-wort family)

1.11 *Hypericum perforatum*

COMMON ST. JOHN'S-WORT

All species of St. John's-wort have opposite leaves without marginal teeth and with either translucent or black dots; in most species stamens are numerous.

The common St. John's-wort is 1–2½ feet high and has many leafy branches and numerous flowers. Leaves are narrowly oblong; flowers are ⅝–¾ inch across and the petals have black dots on the margins. Of the 13 species of *Hypericum* in Kentucky, this is the only alien. Distributed over the state, it is a common weed of fields, waste places, and roadsides.

Hypericaceae July–August
(St. John's-wort family)

1.12 *Hypericum dolabriforme*

ST. JOHN'S-WORT

The showy flowers about 1 inch across with oblique petals make this a beautiful species. The stems are slender, slightly woody at the base, and 8–15 inches high, and the leaves are linear-lanceolate. It grows on dry open red cedar slopes and in other dry openings and borders in calcareous soil of the Mississippian Plateau and the Inner and Outer Bluegrass regions. Though infrequent in the Bluegrass, it is common in south-central Kentucky.

Hypericaceae July
(St. John's-wort family)

1.13 *Hypericum sphaerocarpum*

ST. JOHN'S-WORT

In this species, the flowers are ½–⅝ inch across and the leaves are linear-oblong or narrowly elliptic. The stems are 4-angled, slightly woody at the base, and 12–20 inches high. It is frequent in rocky ground in the Bluegrass region and also grows in southern and western Kentucky.

Hypericaceae July
(St. John's-wort family)

Of the other species of *Hypericum* in Kentucky, 6 have flowers less than ½ inch across and 2 are rare.

1.14 *Oenothera biennis*

EVENING PRIMROSE

All species of *Oenothera* have 4 broad petals, 8 stamens, a cross-shaped stigma, and, below the petals, a slender calyx-tube enclosing the ovary at the base.

In the evening primrose each fragrant flower (about 1 inch across) opens near sunset and wilts in hot sunshine. The stem, often reddish tinged, is coarse and 2–5 feet tall, and the leaf margins have a slightly wavy outline. It is a common biennial in old fields and along roadsides throughout the state.

Onagraceae July–September
(Evening primrose family)

1.15 *Oenothera tetragona*

SUNDROPS

The sundrops flower in the day, in contrast to the evening primrose (no. 1.14). Not at all weedy, this species has a slender stem 1–2 feet high, leaves without teeth, and flowers about 1 inch across. It grows in open woods, woodland borders, and grassy fields; though scattered in all regions of the state, it is only fairly frequent.

Onagraceae July–August
(Evening primrose family)

1.16 *Ludwigia alternifolia*

SEEDBOX, RATTLEBOX

The flowers, ½–⅝ inch across, are borne in the leaf axils. The 4 petals fall off easily but the conspicuous calyx-lobes, as long as the petals, remain atop the squarish capsules, which are responsible for the common names. The plant, 2–3 feet high, grows in borders of ponds and sluggish streams, ditches, and other wet ground, and is frequent in all sections of the state except the Inner Bluegrass.

Onagraceae July
(Evening primrose family)

1.17 *Jussiaea repens*

PRIMROSE-WILLOW, WATER PRIMROSE

This aquatic plant has creeping or floating stems, often rooting at the nodes and ascending at the tips. Its flowers, ¾–1 inch across and long-stalked, bear 5 glistening petals; the leaves are lance-shaped or slightly broader, tapering into a petiole. Growing in quiet shallow water, the primrose-willow is distributed over the state but is only fairly frequent.

Onagraceae June–September
(Evening primrose family)

Another species of water primrose, *J. decurrens*, has erect, 4-angled stems 1–3 feet high and flowers with 4 petals.

1.18 *Lysimachia nummularia*

MONEYWORT

Trailing stems and opposite round leaves, together with bright yellow flowers, make this species easily recognized. The flowers, about 1 inch across, are borne in the axils of the leaves. The moneywort was introduced from Europe, has become naturalized, and in Kentucky is fairly frequent in wet ground, especially along damp roadsides and creek banks.

Primulaceae (Primrose family) July

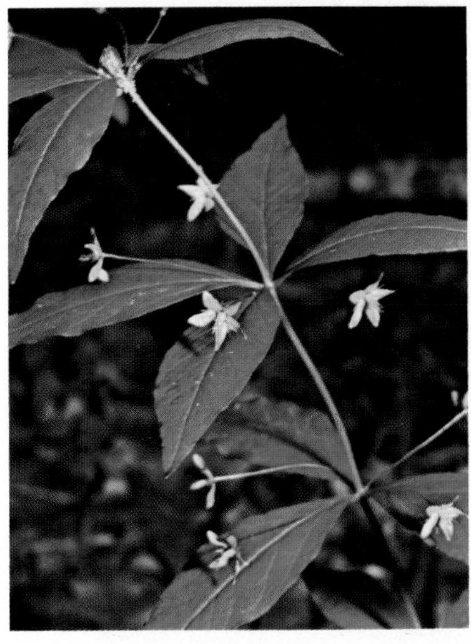

1.19 *Lysimachia quadrifolia*

WHORLED LOOSESTRIFE

Leaves are in whorls of 4 or 5, and the stems, 1½–2½ feet tall, are usually unbranched. Flowers are ½–⅝ inch across and are borne one to each leaf axil. The whorled loosestrife grows in open oak woods and is frequent in most sections of the state except the Inner Bluegrass.

Primulaceae June–July
(Primrose family)

1.20 *Lysimachia ciliata*

FRINGED LOOSESTRIFE

In the fringed loosestrife leaves are narrowly ovate and opposite, with minute fringe on the petioles. Flowers, ¾–1 inch across and slightly nodding, are borne singly in several of the upper axils; petals have an abrupt point and tiny teeth. This species grows 1–3 feet high and is found on stream banks and in other moist ground. Though only fairly frequent, it is distributed throughout the state.

Primulaceae (Primrose family)

July

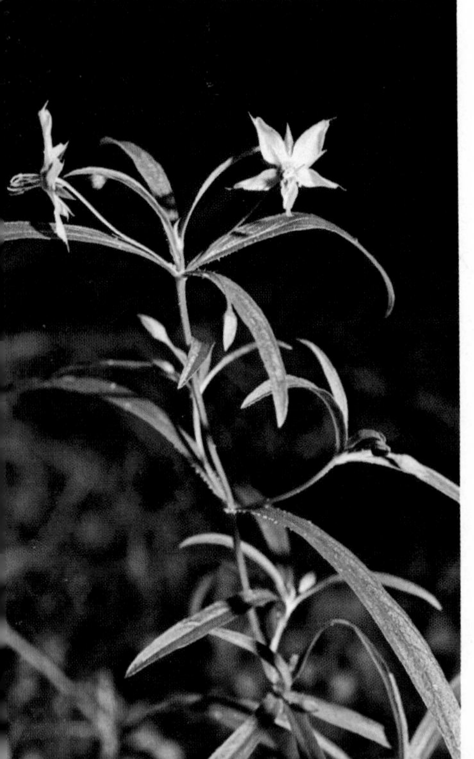

1.21 *Lysimachia lanceolata*

LANCE-LEAVED LOOSESTRIFE

Leaves are lance-shaped, tapering at the base without a distinct petiole. Flowers, with an abrupt point on each petal, are ½–¾ inch across and are borne in the upper axils. The stem stands 1–2 feet tall and produces runners at the base. The lance-leaved loosestrife is fairly frequent in open woods and thickets in all sections of Kentucky.

Primulaceae (Primrose family)

July

1.22 *Asclepias tuberosa*

BUTTERFLY WEED, ORANGE MILKWEED

The butterfly weed is a relative of the milkweeds but lacks white latex. The flowers, like those of the milkweeds, have reflexed corolla lobes and, attached to the corolla, a circle of 5 erect hoods. The color varies from orange-red to yellow-orange (rarely yellow). The total length of a single flower is about ½ inch. The hairy stem bearing narrow leaves grows 12–30 inches high. It is frequent on dry sunny slopes and in prairie patches from the eastern Knobs across the state to the Mississippi River but is infrequent in the Cumberland Plateau, Cumberland Mountains, and Inner Bluegrass.

Asclepiadaceae (Milkweed family) July

1.23 *Lithospermum canescens*

HOARY PUCCOON

The flowers are tubular with 5 spreading lobes and are ½ inch across. The plant, with lance-oblong leaves, is densely covered with fine, soft hairs and is usually 6–12 inches high. It is fairly frequent in dry ground in limestone areas, such as sunny slopes, clearings, woodland borders, and prairie patches, especially in the Mississippian Plateau and calcareous areas of the eastern knobs.

Boraginaceae (Borage family) May

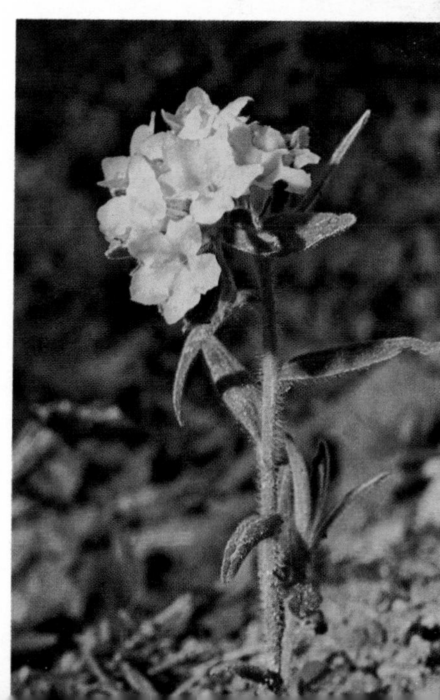

1.24 *Nuphar advena*

YELLOW POND-LILY, SPATTERDOCK

In the yellow pond-lily the flowers are cup-shaped, 1¼–2 inches across, with outer sepals green and inner ones yellow. Petals are minute and stamens short; the most conspicuous feature within the cup is the disk-like stigma. Leaf blades, erect or floating, are 4–12 inches long. Growing in pond margins and other shallow, sluggish water in various sections of the state, this is the most common member of the water-lily family in Kentucky.

Nymphaeaceae (Water-lily family) June-September

1.25 *Nelumbo lutea*

AMERICAN LOTUS, YELLOW NELUMBO

This is our largest and most striking aquatic plant. The leaf blades, resembling giant saucers 12–20 inches across, are held 1–2 feet above the water, and the pale yellow flowers are 4–8 inches across. Infrequent in Kentucky, this species grows in ponds in a few scattered localities from the northern to the southwestern parts of the state.

Nymphaeaceae (Water-lily family) July–August

1.26 *Nymphaea odorata*

FRAGRANT WATER-LILY

This water-lily has large, fragrant, many-petaled flowers 3–6 inches across, which open in the morning. Its leaf blades are roundish, 3–8 inches across, and floating. Infrequent in Kentucky, it is found in ponds in a few widely scattered localities.

Nymphaeaceae (Water-lily family) July–August

1.27 *Silene stellata*

STARRY CAMPION

White flowers with fringed petals and leaves in whorls of 4 make the starry campion unmistakable. In a loose and open inflorescence, the flowers are about ¾ inch across, and the calyx is bell-shaped. The stem grows 2–3 feet tall. This species is frequent in open woods in all parts of the state.

Caryophyllaceae (Pink family) July

1.28 *Stellaria pubera*

STAR CHICKWEED, GREAT CHICKWEED

Five white, deeply cleft petals give a starlike appearance to the flowers which are usually about ½ inch across. The stems, with opposite, elliptical sessile leaves, are ascending and 6–12 inches long. The star chickweed is frequent in woods, especially on slopes, in all sections of the state except the far west.
Caryophyllaceae (Pink family) April

This lovely woodland plant has a weedy relative, the common chickweed (*S. media*), which is a profuse-growing, weak-stemmed annual found especially in lawns and gardens in early spring. It has ovate, petioled leaves usually less than ¾ inch long, and the flowers, with sepals longer than the petals, are only about ¼ inch across.

1.29 *Hepatica acutiloba*

HEPATICA

The name resulted from a fancied resemblance of the lobed leaf to a liver. In the flowers of hepatica, about ¾ inch broad, no petals are present; the sepals are petal-like, white, pink, or blue, and variable in number, and the 3 bracts are sepal-like. The flower stem is softly hairy, 4–8 inches high; the old 3-lobed leaves, having persisted through the winter, may be a bit bronzed and weatherbeaten, and the young leaves, covered with soft hair, have not completely unfurled at flowering time. This species with pointed leaves is widespread in Kentucky and is frequent wherever rich, mesophytic wooded slopes are found. It is also shown as no. 1.91.
Ranunculaceae (Buttercup family)
Late March–early April

A species with blunt-lobed leaves is *H. americana*, which is also found in rich woods but usually in areas of sandy acid soil. It is less widely distributed in the state than *H. acutiloba*.

1.30 *Anemonella thalictroides*

RUE ANEMONE

This is a delicate little plant 6–8 inches tall. Petals are absent; the sepals, which are petal-like, are usually white, though occasionally pink, and number from 5 to 10. The flowers are ⅝–1¼ inches across, the earliest ones largest and the last ones smallest. The leaves are compound, all basal except the bract-like leaves subtending the flower-cluster at the top of the stem. The resemblance of the leaflets, 3-lobed at the apex, to those of the meadow rue (the genus *Thalictrum*) accounts for both the common name and the species name. The rue anemone is very frequent in woods throughout the state.

Ranunculaceae (Buttercup family) April

1.31 *Isopyrum biternatum*

FALSE RUE ANEMONE

In this species 5 bright-white sepals are petal-like (petals are absent). The leaves are compound; the principal ones are basal but also there is a leaf midway on the stem in addition to the bract-like leaves beneath the flowers. *Isopyrum* resembles *Anemonella* (no. 1.30) but is more leafy; also the flowers are smaller, ½–¾ inch across, and the stem is taller, 8–16 inches high. In Kentucky it is apparently confined to calcareous soil and is frequent in rich moist woods in the Bluegrass region and the Mississippian Plateau.

Ranunculaceae (Buttercup family) April

1.32 *Anemone quinquefolia*

WOOD ANEMONE

In the wood anemone the flower is solitary, subtended by a whorl of 3 bract-like leaves each composed of 3 (-5) leaflets. The principal leaf is solitary, basal, and long-petioled, bearing 5 leaflets; leaflet margins are toothed. The flower is ¾–1¼ inches across, with 4–9 petal-like sepals and no petals. This little woodland plant grows 4–8 inches high. In Kentucky it is restricted to the Cumberland Plateau and Cumberland Mountains.

Ranunculaceae (Buttercup family)

Late April

1.33 *Anemone virginiana*

TALL ANEMONE, THIMBLEWEED

The tall anemone grows 20–30 inches high. Flowers, 1–1¼ inches across with greenish white sepals and no petals, are solitary on 1–3 long stalks standing above a circle of 3 compound bract-like leaves. Both these leaves and the long-petioled basal leaves have sharply toothed leaflets. It is the fruit which suggests the name "thimbleweed." This plant grows in open woods, thickets, and woodland borders in all sections of the state; it is very frequent in limestone soils, infrequent in others.

Ranunculaceae (Buttercup family)

July

1.34 *Clematis virginiana*

VIRGIN'S-BOWER

A slightly woody vine with slender stems, the virgin's bower is conspicuous when laden with fragrant flowers borne in axillary panicles. Each flower is ¾–1 inch across with 4 petal-like sepals and no petals, and in fruit becomes a group of radiating silvery-gray plumes. The leaves are trifoliate and opposite, and the vine climbs over shrubs by the bending of its petioles over twigs. It is frequent in moist thickets throughout the state. *Ranunculaceae* (Buttercup family) August–September

1.35 *Podophyllum peltatum*

MAY-APPLE, MANDRAKE

Large umbrella-like leaves, with the petiole attached near the center of the blade, make the may-apple conspicuous. Plants bearing a single "umbrella" have no flower; plants 12–18 inches tall and bearing two leaves have a solitary flower in the fork between the petioles. The flower, 1–2 inches broad, has thick petals, the number varying between 6 and 9. The fruit is edible but the leaves and rootstock are poisonous if eaten. The may-apple, often growing in colonies, is common in open woods, borders, and clearings throughout Kentucky. *Berberidaceae* (Barberry family) Late April–early May

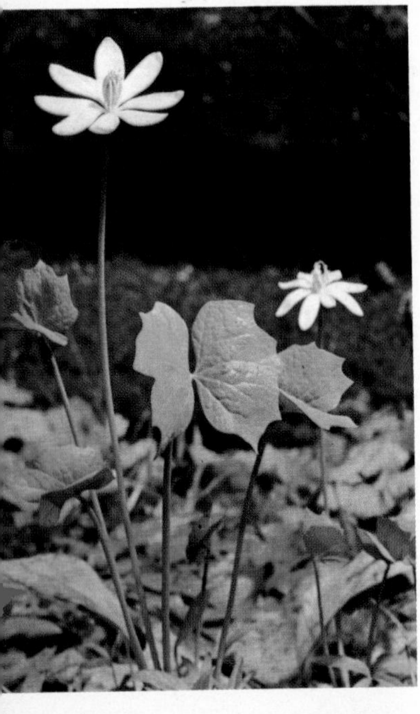

1.36 *Jeffersonia diphylla*

TWINLEAF

The genus was named for Thomas Jefferson; the species name and the common name refer to its leaves, which are divided into 2 segments. Solitary on leafless stalks, the flowers, with 8 petals, are about 1 inch broad. Following the flowers, the seed capsules are unusual in their manner of opening by a lid that remains hinged at the back. The twinleaf grows on rich wooded slopes in limestone areas; hence it is frequent in the Bluegrass region and the Mississippian Plateau and rare in eastern Kentucky.

Berberidaceae (Barberry family)
Late March–early April

1.37 *Sanguinaria canadensis*

BLOODROOT

The bloodroot is one of America's favorite wildflowers both because of its beauty and because its early appearance in the bare forest imparts hope and cheer to all who find it. The flower, with a young leaf embracing its stalk, has 8 (occasionally 12) brilliant white petals and is 1–2 inches across. After flowering time the palmately lobed leaves greatly enlarge. The rootstock, containing bright red latex, "bleeds" when cut, accounting for the name. This lovely plant is frequent in woods, especially on slopes throughout the state.

Papaveraceae (Poppy family)
Late March–early April

1.38 *Dentaria laciniata*

CUT-LEAF TOOTHWORT

In all species of *Dentaria* the flowers have 4 petals and are in racemes, and the pods are slender.

In the cut-leaf toothwort the leaves are in a whorl of 3 on the stem, each with 3–5 narrow, deeply toothed segments. The flowers, which are usually white but occasionally pinkish, are about ½ inch long, and the plant is 8–12 inches high. It is common in woods throughout Kentucky.

Cruciferae (Mustard family)

Late March–April

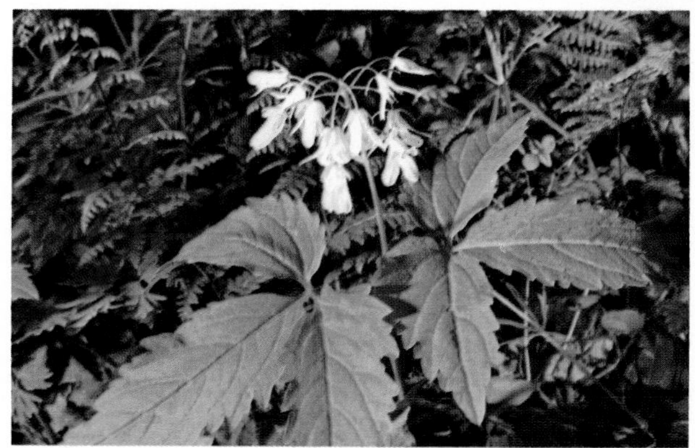

1.39 *Dentaria diphylla*

CRINKLEROOT, TWO-LEAVED TOOTHWORT

This species has a pair of leaves, each with 3 broad leaflets, on the 10- to 12-inch stem and a similar but long-petioled basal leaf. The flowers are about ½ inch long, white but often pinkish when fading. It is fairly frequent in moist ravines in mesophytic woods in the eastern two-thirds of the state.

Cruciferae (Mustard family) Late April

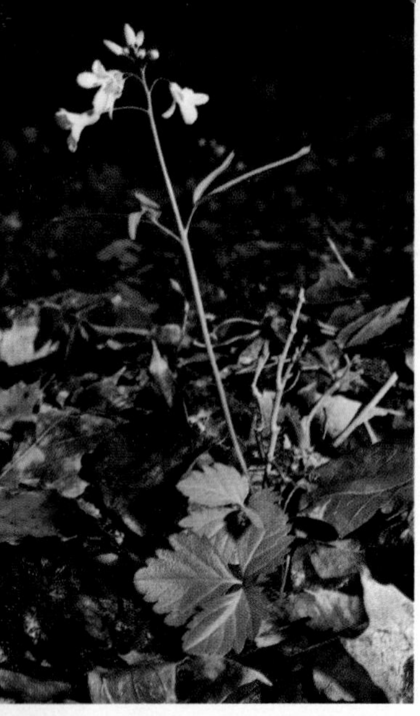

1.40 *Dentaria heterophylla*

SLENDER TOOTHWORT

The slender toothwort has a pair of stem-leaves, each with 3 narrow segments, unlike the broad, long-petioled basal leaf. The flowers, ⅜–½ inch long, are white or pinkish. This species is frequent in oak woods, chiefly in noncalcareous soil, in eastern Kentucky, the Knobs, and the noncalcareous portions of the Mississippian Plateau.

Cruciferae (Mustard family) April

1.41 *Fragaria virginiana*

WILD STRAWBERRY

Wild strawberries often form colonies by the production of runners. The leaves, which are basal, have 3 coarsely toothed leaflets on slender, hairy petioles. Flowers are borne several in a cluster on an erect stem 2–6 inches high. Each flower, ½–¾ inch across, has many separate pistils inserted on a dome-shaped receptacle, and it is the receptacle which enlarges and becomes fleshy rather than the ovary wall as in most fruits. The "straws" are the actual botanical fruits, the type known as achenes, which are single-seeded and dry. The wild strawberries, though small, are sweeter, more juicy, and superior in flavor to the large cultivated ones, and hence anyone with the patience to pick them is well rewarded. The plant is common in old fields, clearings, and borders of thickets, and on railroad embankments and other sunny banks throughout the state. This plant must not be confused with the inedible mock strawberry, no. 1.5.

Rosaceae (Rose family) April

1.42 *Gillenia stipulata*

AMERICAN IPECAC, INDIAN PHYSIC

The American ipecac has stems 12–36 inches high and flowers with narrow white petals ½ inch long. Its leaves have 3 sharply toothed leaflets, but ovate toothed stipules make the leaf appear to have 5 leaflets. Though occurring in most sections of the state, with the apparent exception of the Inner Bluegrass and southeastern Kentucky, it is most frequent in the Knobs.
Rosaceae (Rose family) June

A similar species differing in having minute stipules, *G. trifoliata*, is found in southeastern Kentucky.

1.43 *Geum canadense*

WHITE AVENS

In the white avens, which is 18–30 inches high, the flowers are about ½ inch broad and the fruits are bristly. The principal leaves have 3 leaflets, but the upper ones are simple. It is common in thickets in all sections of Kentucky.
Rosaceae (Rose family) June–July

1.44 *Chimaphila maculata*

SPOTTED WINTERGREEN, STRIPED PIPSISSIWA

Leathery evergreen leaves having the vein pattern marked with white make this little plant attractive at all seasons, but it is especially interesting in flower. The flowers, nodding and ½–¾ inch across, have waxy petals which are reflexed when mature, and a broad, conspicuous pistil. The stem is 6–9 inches tall. The spotted wintergreen grows in pine, oak, or beech woods in noncalcareous soil; it is fairly frequent in the eastern two-thirds of the state with the exception of the Bluegrass region.

Pyrolaceae (Wintergreen family)

July

1.45 *Dodecatheon meadia*

SHOOTING STAR

The rocket-like flowers of this strikingly beautiful plant appear designed for space flight. The stamens are held together, forming a narrow cone, and the corolla lobes, ½–¾ inch long, are reflexed. The leaves, smooth, oblong, and 3–6 inches in length, form a basal rosette above which the flower stem stands 10–18 inches high. Its typical habitat is moist or dripping areas on wooded cliffs, either limestone or sandstone, although it may occasionally grow in other situations. It is frequent from central Kentucky westward but rare in eastern Kentucky.

Primulaceae (Primrose family)

Late April–early May

1.46 *Obolaria virginica*

PENNYWORT

The pennywort is a small plant, only 3–6 inches high, with thick, rounded, purplish green leaves. The flowers, which are borne in the axils of the leaves, are ⅜–½ inch long, funnel-shaped, 4-lobed, and dull white or slightly tinted. Growing in oak and mesophytic woods, it is widely scattered in the state but is frequent only in eastern Kentucky, the Knobs, and west-central Kentucky.

Gentianaceae (Gentian family) April

1.47 *Asclepias variegata*

WHITE MILKWEED

As in all milkweeds, the corolla is bent back and the erect portion of the flower is the additional crown composed of 5 hoods, each attached to the back of a stamen. Each flower is about ½ inch long, including both the corolla lobes and the hoods. The flowers are in umbels; the leaves are broadly oblong and opposite. The white milkweed grows in open oak and oak-pine woods and borders. Although it is infrequent, it is distributed over most sections of the state, with the apparent exception of the Bluegrass region.

Asclepiadaceae (Milkweed family) June

Kentucky has 2 other species which are predominantly white or slightly tinted: A. *exaltata*, the poke milkweed, which has loosely flowered drooping umbels, and A. *perennis*, which has lanceolate leaves, a slender stem, and small flowers.

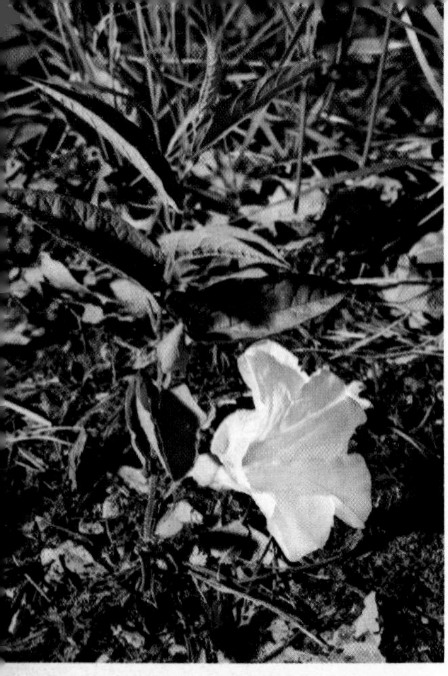

1.48 *Convolvulus spithamaeus*

UPRIGHT BINDWEED

All the bindweeds and the related morning glories have funnel-shaped or bell-shaped corollas.

The upright bindweed, which is not weedy in its habits, grows 6–18 inches high. The flower is 1¾–2½ inches long, borne low on the stem. This species grows in dry open woods and edges of woods and, though infrequent, is widely distributed in the state.

Convolvulaceae (Morning-glory family)

May–June

The small bindweed, *C. arvensis,* is a trailing or twining weed with arrow-shaped leaves 1–2 inches long and white flowers ¾ inch long. This native of Europe is common in waste places and fields.

1.49 *Ipomoea pandurata*

WILD POTATO VINE

The trailing or climbing stems of this vine may be 15 feet long. The flowers are 2–3 inches long, and the leaves are heart-shaped at the base. This is a very common and troublesome weed in waste places, along roadsides, and in thickets throughout the state.

Convolvulaceae (Morning-glory family)

July–August

Another vine with large, white, funnel-shaped flowers is the hedge bindweed, *Convolvulus sepium,* with which the wild potato vine may be confused. The leaves of the hedge bindweed are arrow-shaped at the base; its flower, which lacks the purple center of the wild potato vine, has 2 linear-oblong stigmas instead of the single roundish stigma of *Ipomoea.* It is common in clearings, thickets, and fields and along roadsides in all parts of Kentucky.

1.50 *Hydrophyllum macrophyllum*

LARGE-LEAF WATERLEAF

In all species of waterleaf the flowers have 5 shallow lobes and the stamens and style extend beyond the corolla.

In this species the plant is rough-hairy, 12–24 inches high; the leaves are pinnately divided, often having a 2-tone pattern of light and dark green; the dull white flowers are about ½ inch long. It grows in rich moist woods and may be found in most sections of Kentucky but is most frequent in the central part of the state.

Hydrophyllaceae (Waterleaf family)
Late May–early June

1.51 *Hydrophyllum canadense*

BROAD-LEAF WATERLEAF

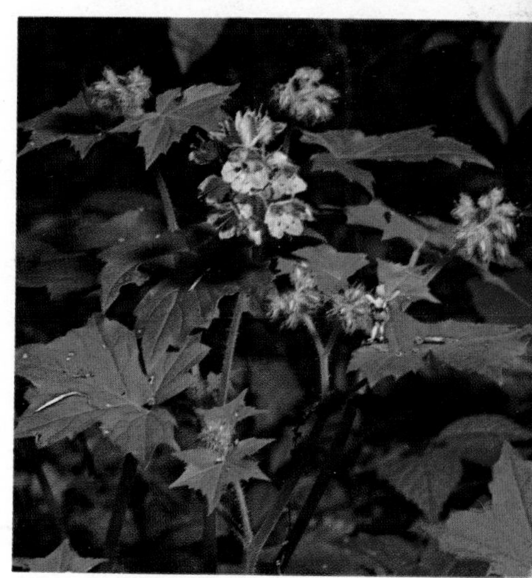

This species, which is essentially glabrous, has palmately lobed leaves 3–8 inches broad. The corolla, usually white though rarely tinted, is ⅜–½ inch long. This waterleaf grows in moist ravines in mesophytic woods and in moist ground at the base of mesophytic wooded slopes. Restricted to such habitats, it is only fairly frequent but is widely distributed over the state.

Hydrophyllaceae June
(Waterleaf family)

1.52 *Mitchella repens*
PARTRIDGE-BERRY

A diminutive trailing evergreen herb, the partridge-berry is one of our most interesting woodland plants. A pair of flowers, joined like Siamese twins, produce a single berry which bears the marks where two corollas were attached. A few of the red berries persist through winter until the next flowering season. The fragrant flowers, which are fuzzy inside, average 1/2 inch in length; the roundish leaves are 1/3–2/3 inch long. The partridge-berry carpets hummocks and small banks in woods in acid soil; it is frequent in eastern and southern Kentucky and rare in a few other localities.

Rubiaceae (Madder family) June–July

1.53 *Aquilegia canadensis*
COLUMBINE

The columbine is one of our most graceful wildflowers. The colorful flowers, red outside, yellow inside, and 1½–2 inches long, hang upside down from slender stems. They have 5 petal-like sepals and 5 petals which are extended backward into long spurs containing nectar at the far end. The leaves are compound, 2–3 times divided into blunt-lobed leaflets. The plants range in height from 1 to 3 feet, depending on the habitat; the smaller plants grow in crevices in cliffs and large boulders (chiefly limestone but occasionally sandstone), and the large ones grow in moist rocky valleys. Fortunately this charming plant is frequent and widespread in Kentucky.
Ranunculaceae (Buttercup family) May

1.54 *Spigelia marilandica*

INDIAN PINK, PINKROOT

Scarlet without and yellow within, the flowers are tubular-funnelform with 5 flaring lobes and are 1–2 inches long. The leaves are ovate, opposite, and sessile; the stem grows 1–2 feet high. This striking plant is found in moist woods and thickets in southern Kentucky but is infrequent.
Loganiaceae (Logania family) May–June

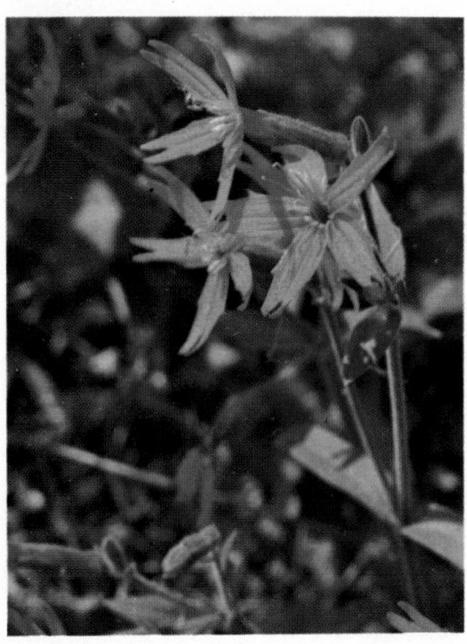

1.55 *Silene virginica*

FIRE PINK, RED CATCHFLY

The bright flowers of the fire pink, 1–1½ inches across with 5 notched petals, are borne on weak stems 1–2 feet long. The sticky stems and calyx tube are responsible for the name "catchfly," applied to several members of this genus. The leaves are opposite and lanceolate. This species is frequent in open woods and on rocky slopes in all sections of Kentucky.
Caryophyllaceae (Pink family) Late April–June

1.56 *Silene rotundifolia*

ROUND-LEAVED FIRE PINK, ROUND-LEAVED CATCHFLY

This species differs from the more common fire pink (no. 1.55) in having nearly round or elliptic rather than narrow leaves. It grows on shaded cliffs, chiefly sandstone but occasionally limestone. In its restricted habitat it is fairly frequent, especially in eastern, south-central, and southern Kentucky.
Caryophyllaceae (Pink family)
June–July

1.57 *Silene caroliniana* var. *wherryi*

WILD PINK

Creating a mass of bright pink on cliff or hillside, this is one of our very showy wildflowers. A superficial glance at the flower may suggest a phlox, but if the calyx tube is slit, the petals can be seen to be completely separate in contrast to the united corolla tube in *Phlox*. The flowers, with wedge-shaped petals, are ¾–1 inch across; the stem is 4–10 inches long. Though often profuse where it grows, it is apparently restricted to limestone cliffs of the Inner Bluegrass and shaly slopes of the eastern and southern Knobs.
Caryophyllaceae (Pink family) Early May

1.58 *Dianthus armeria*

DEPTFORD PINK

The Deptford pink, an annual or biennial, has slender, stiff, erect stems, 10–24 inches high, and opposite linear leaves. The rose flowers, with toothed petals, are about ½ inch across. This native of Europe is frequent in thickets and old fields and along roadsides and fencerows throughout the state.
Caryophyllaceae (Pink family) June

1.59 *Agrostemma githago*

CORN COCKLE

This native of Europe is especially associated with wheat fields. (In England "corn" refers to small grain.) The stem grows 1½–3 feet high, bearing opposite linear leaves. The corolla, which is exceeded by the calyx lobes, is 1–1¾ inches across. Though widely distributed in fields and waste places, it is less common than formerly due to an effort to eradicate it from grain fields because of its poisonous seeds.
Caryophyllaceae (Pink family)
June–July

1.60 *Hesperis matronalis*

DAME'S ROCKET, SWEET ROCKET

The fragrant flowers of the dame's rocket, which may be purple, lilac, pink, or white, have 4 separate petals and are about ¾ inch broad. Seedpods are long and slender, leaves are alternate, and the stem grows 1–3 feet high. As an escape from old gardens, it is sometimes found along roadsides and in thickets near old homesites.
Cruciferae (Mustard family) May

1.61 *Clematis viorna*

LEATHER FLOWER

These interesting flowers, resembling urns hanging upside down, have a thick, leathery calyx nearly an inch long (no petals are present), and are followed by plume-like fruits. The leaves are opposite and compound with 3–7 leaflets. This vine, which is herbaceous or slightly woody, grows in rich thickets and woodland borders and is fairly frequent throughout Kentucky.

Ranunculaceae (Buttercup family)

June–July

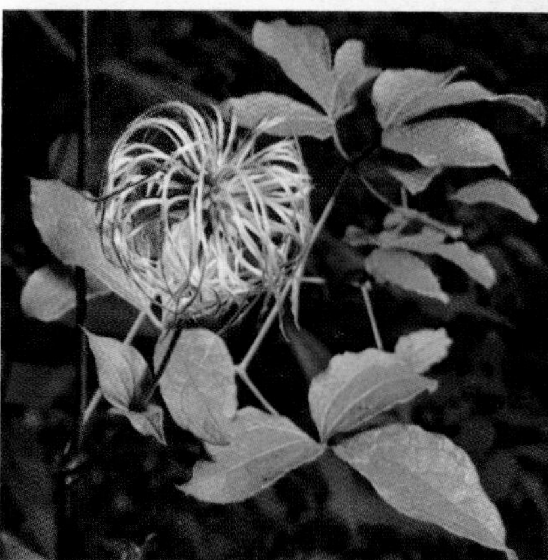

Several other species of leather flower occur only in the southern and western parts of the state. *C. glaucophylla* and *C. versicolor* both have leaves glaucous beneath; *C. pitcheri* has all veins raised beneath.

1.62 *Rosa carolina*

CAROLINA ROSE, PASTURE ROSE

The Carolina rose has a slender stem 1–3 feet tall, straight slender prickles, 5–7 leaflets, and flowers mostly solitary. It grows in dry open woods, woodland borders, and old fields, and is frequent throughout the state.

Rosaceae (Rose family) June

Our other wild roses are the swamp rose, *R. palustris*, a large erect shrub 3–7 feet tall, and *R. setigera*, the prairie rose, which has long-arching or climbing stems up to 14 feet long.

1.63 *Geranium maculatum*

WILD GERANIUM

Because of its long slender fruits this plant is also called crane's-bill. Its rose-purple flowers, which are an inch or more across, have separate petals and 10 stamens. The leaves are palmately cleft into 5–7 segments, and the stem grows 1½–2 feet high. This lovely wildflower is common in woods throughout Kentucky.

Geraniaceae (Geranium family)
Late April–May

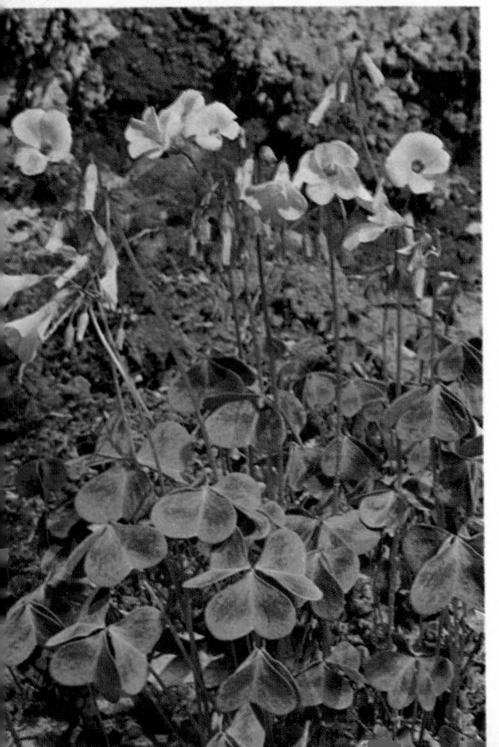

1.64 *Oxalis violacea*

VIOLET WOOD-SORREL

The 3-parted leaves, all basal, are usually red-purple beneath. The flowers, with petals about ½ inch long, are pale pinkish violet. This little plant, 4–8 inches high, is very frequent in dry open woods over the entire state.

Oxalidaceae Late April–May
(Wood-sorrel family)

1.65 *Hibiscus militaris*

ROSE MALLOW

The rose mallows are tall, stout, and herbaceous, with large showy flowers having the stamens united into a column surrounding the style. In this species the flower is pale pink with a dark purple center and is 2½–3 inches long. The leaves are somewhat triangular and some have 2 divergent basal lobes. Growing 3–5 feet tall, it is found along sluggish streams and in marshy ground. Though widely scattered, it is most frequent in the western half of the state.
Malvaceae (Mallow family) August

A larger species of rose mallow is *H. moscheutos*, with whitish or creamy flowers with dark purple centers. It differs also in having ovate or lanceolate leaves which are velvety-hairy beneath. It too is more frequent in western than eastern Kentucky.

1.66 *Rhexia virginica*

VIRGINIA MEADOWBEAUTY

Eight long, curved, golden anthers and 4 purplish rose petals distinguish the meadowbeauty. The flowers are about 1 inch broad and the plant is 8–18 inches tall. The stem is square and slightly winged on the angles; the finely toothed leaves have 3–5 prominent veins. This plant grows in wet meadows and along swampy margins of creeks in most sections of the state except the Bluegrass region; it is most frequent in the Knobs.
Melastomataceae (Melastome family) July

The Maryland meadowbeauty, *R. mariana*, has pale pink flowers and narrower, nearly lance-shaped leaves. It is infrequent but is found in the same habitats and geographical areas as the Virginia meadowbeauty.

1.67 *Sabatia angularis*

ROSE GENTIAN, ROSE-PINK

With a pyramidal inflorescence of bright rose-pink flowers, each with a yellow-green center, this is one of our prettiest midsummer wildflowers. The flowers are fragrant and about 1 inch across. Both the leaves and the flowering branches are opposite; the stem is strongly 4-angled, usually 1½–2 feet high. This lovely annual or biennial plant grows in moist ground in meadows, clearings, and woodland borders, and is frequent in all sections of the state save the Bluegrass.
Gentianaceae (Gentian family) July

1.68 *Gentiana saponaria*

SOAPWORT GENTIAN

The blue gentians are all strikingly beautiful flowers of late autumn.

In the soapwort gentian the corolla lobes are held together at the tips by a pleated membrane but are not completely closed because the pleats are slightly shorter than the lobes. (This can be observed by spreading out the corolla.) The flowers are 1½–1¾ inches long; the deep blue becomes more purple with age. This species, which is usually 1–2 feet high, grows in swampy thickets and wet woodland borders. Though it is infrequent in the state, it is widely scattered and locally plentiful.
Gentianaceae (Gentian family) October

In the closed or bottle gentian, G. *andrewsii,* which is rare in Kentucky, the pleated membrane surpasses the corolla lobes and completely closes the flower.

In the downy gentian, G. *puberula,* which is infrequent, the corolla lobes are pointed, spreading, and much longer than the connecting membranes.

Two other blue gentians are rare in Kentucky: G. *decora,* the showy gentian, having flowers open but not spreading, and G. *quinquefolia,* the stiff gentian, having flowers only ¾ inch long in dense clusters.

1.69 *Asclepias purpurascens*

PURPLE MILKWEED

As in all milkweeds, the most conspicuous part of the flower is not the corolla, which is bent back, but an additional erect crown composed of 5 concave hoods attached to the stamens, which are joined together and to the stigma to form a column.

In this species the corolla lobes are usually a magenta-purple, about ⅜ inch long, and the hoods, which are paler, are about ¼ inch long; the plant grows 2–3 feet tall. It is found in woodland borders and thickets and is fairly frequent in most of the state.

Asclepiadaceae (Milkweed family) June–July

The common milkweed, A. *syriaca,* which has dull grayish lavender or dull dusty rose flowers, is an abundant weed in old fields and along roadsides throughout the state.

A. *amplexicaulis,* the blunt-leaved milkweed, which has greenish purple flowers and wavy leaves with clasping bases, grows in open grassy areas in southern and western Kentucky.

1.70 *Asclepias incarnata*

SWAMP MILKWEED

The swamp milkweed, growing 2–4 feet tall, has lance-shaped leaves and bright, clear pink flowers. Frequent in most sections of the state, it is a beautiful plant on margins of creeks and ponds, near springs, and in swamps.

Asclepiadaceae (Milkweed family)

July

1.71 *Gonolobus shortii*

ANGLE-POD

The leaves are large, roundish or broadly ovate, and heart-shaped at the base. The flowers, in axillary clusters, are brownish purple with linear spreading lobes, each ½ inch or more long. A crown is present in the flower but is much shorter than that in the milkweeds. This twining herbaceous vine is frequent in thickets in central and western Kentucky.

Asclepiadaceae (Milkweed family) June

Another species of angle-pod, G. *obliquus*, with smaller greenish purple flowers (corolla lobes each ¼–½ inch long) is more widespread in the state.

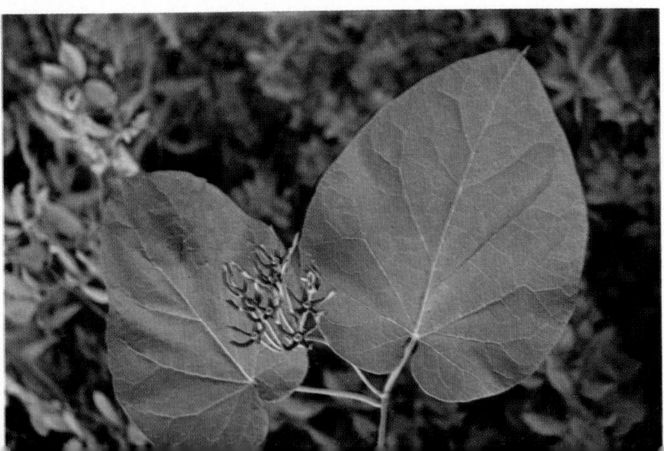

1.72 *Vinca minor*

MYRTLE, PERIWINKLE

The myrtle is an evergreen trailing vine which forms an attractive ground cover. The leaves are dark green, opposite, and shining; the axillary blue flowers, which have a slender corolla tube, measure about 1 inch across the spreading lobes. This native of Europe, which has been extensively planted, persists in old homesites and cemeteries and has sometimes escaped to roadsides.

Apocynaceae (Dogbane family)
April

1.73 *Ipomoea purpurea*

COMMON MORNING-GLORY

This familiar annual weedy vine, though a pest in cultivated ground, has beautiful flowers opening in the morning. Varying in color from blue, through purple, to pink, the corolla is about 2 inches long. The leaves are ovate and heart-shaped. It is abundant and widespread in fields, on roadsides, and in waste places.

Convolvulaceae August–October
(Morning-glory family)

1.74 *Ipomoea hederacea*

IVY-LEAVED MORNING-GLORY

The ivy-leaved morning-glory, with 3-lobed leaves, is also a weedy annual vine with beautiful blue or purple flowers, which are 1½–2 inches long. It is common in cultivated ground, along roadsides, and in waste places.

Convolvulaceae August–October
(Morning-glory family)

1.75 *Verbena canadensis* ROSE VERBENA

The flowers, about ½ inch wide, usually rose but occasionally purple or lilac, have 5 notched corolla lobes which spread abruptly from the corolla tube. The cluster is dense in flower but the axis elongates in fruit. The stem, reclining at the base, is 12–20 inches long, and the opposite leaves are pinnately lobed and toothed. The rose verbena grows in rocky ground, is infrequent but widely scattered, and is frequently cultivated.
Verbenaceae (Verbena family) May–June

The Genus *Phlox*

All species of phlox have opposite leaves without marginal teeth, and flowers with a slender corolla tube and abruptly spreading lobes. Some species are occasionally confused with pinks. Note that pinks (such as no. 1.57) have petals separate within the calyx tube, in *Phlox* they are united. Also in all pinks, but never in phlox, the stems are swollen at the nodes.

1.76 *Phlox subulata* MOSS PHLOX

This phlox, sometimes erroneously called moss-pink, has prostrate stems with numerous flowering branches and narrowly linear, sharply pointed leaves ¼–¾ inch long. The flowers, ½–¾ inch across and usually pink, have notched corolla lobes. Abundantly cultivated for its mass of color, it infrequently grows wild on dry hilltops in eastern and central Kentucky.
Polemoniaceae (Phlox family) Late April–early May

Another phlox with linear leaves is the sand phlox, *P. bifida,* which has leaves ¾–1½ inches long and pale violet corolla lobes cleft for nearly half their length. In Kentucky it is known to occur only on limestone cliffs of the Inner Bluegrass.

1.77 *Phlox pilosa*

DOWNY PHLOX, PRAIRIE PHLOX

This phlox has lance-shaped leaves narrowed to a sharp, stiff, needle-like tip. The corolla is usually pale rose-purple, ⅝–¾ inch across, and the stem is 12–20 inches high. Growing in open woods and grassy areas, usually dry, this species is widely scattered in the state but is only fairly frequent.

Polemoniaceae (Phlox family) April–May

Two other spring-flowering pink or rose-purple species of *Phlox*, 6–12 inches high, occur in the state. *P. amoena*, the hairy phlox, with dense, compact clusters of flowers each ¾ inch across, is found in southern Kentucky. *P. stolonifera*, the creeping phlox, which has loose clusters of few flowers, each about 1 inch across, is found in eastern Kentucky. Both are infrequent.

1.78 *Phlox carolina* var. *triflora*

THICK-LEAF PHLOX

This handsome phlox with flowers ⅝–⅞ inch across grows 1–2 feet tall. The stem is slender and smooth and the leaves are firm, varying from linear to broadly lance-shaped. It is frequent in eastern Kentucky, especially in open oak woods on shaly slopes in the Knobs, and infrequent in southern and southwestern Kentucky.

Polemoniaceae (Phlox family) May

A similar species is the smooth phlox, *P. glaberrima,* which grows 2–4 feet tall. In Kentucky it is found principally in open wet woods and grassy areas in the western half of the state, although there are isolated occurrences in eastern Kentucky.

1.79 *Phlox divaricata*

BLUE PHLOX

The blue phlox contributes much to a woodland's loveliness in spring. The flowers, each ¾–1 inch across, usually blue but occasionally rose-purple, have corolla lobes usually notched but sometimes without a notch. The stems are hairy and 12–20 inches high; the leaves are lance-ovate to oblong. In rich woods throughout the state this is a common species, but such habitats are unfortunately becoming fewer.

The name "wild sweet William" is sometimes applied to it but this is misleading since "sweet William" usually refers to a member of the pink family.

Polemoniaceae (Phlox family) April–May

1.80 *Phlox maculata*

MEADOW PHLOX

The meadow phlox has a stiffly erect stem 20–30 inches high, usually spotted with purple. The inflorescence is compound, broadly cylindric in outline, and the flowers are reddish-purple, ½–¾ inch broad. The leaves are lance-shaped. Widely scattered in the state, it is fairly frequent in low ground in open woods and meadows.

Polemoniaceae (Phlox family) July

Another large purple phlox flowering in late summer, found in all sections of Kentucky and more frequent than the preceding species, is *P. paniculata,* called fall phlox, veiny-leaved phlox, or panicled phlox. This is the same species as the familiar garden phlox. It differs from the meadow phlox in having narrowly elliptic leaves that are thinner and more veiny, in having a broader inflorescence, in growing 3–4 feet tall, and in not having a spotted stem.

A species similar to *P. paniculata,* though less frequent, is the broad-leaved phlox, *P. amplifolia,* which has wider and more hairy leaves. Both of these grow chiefly in alluvium.

1.81 *Polemonium reptans*

JACOB'S-LADDER,
GREEK VALERIAN

A "ladder" of leaflets and blue or blue-violet bell-shaped flowers with white stamens distinguish the Jacob's-ladder. The flowers are ½–⅝ inch long, and the plant is 10–15 inches high. It grows in rich moist woods and is frequent throughout the state.

Polemoniaceae (Phlox family) April

1.82 *Phacelia bipinnatifida*

PURPLE PHACELIA

In midspring the biennial purple phacelia adds beautiful masses of color to the woods and ledges where it grows. The flowers are bell-shaped, ½ inch across, usually purple though sometimes blue-violet, with a white center and long stamens. The stems are 1–2 feet high; the leaves are twice pinnately divided and the ultimate segments are coarsely toothed. Widespread in the state, it is frequent in rich woods, especially in deep leafmold on rocky slopes and ledges; it is most frequent in the Inner Bluegrass region.

Hydrophyllaceae (Waterleaf family)
April–early May

1.83 *Hydrophyllum appendiculatum*

APPENDAGED WATERLEAF, LAVENDER WATERLEAF

As in all species of waterleaf, the flowers are bell-shaped, about ½ inch across, and the stamens are longer than the corolla. In this species the corolla is lavender and there are small reflexed appendages alternating with the sepals. The leaves are shallowly lobed and approximately as broad as long. Between 1 and 2 feet in height, this biennial grows in rich moist woods and thickets; it is very frequent in both the Inner and Outer Bluegrass, less frequent in southern and western Kentucky, and infrequent in eastern Kentucky.
Hydrophyllaceae (Waterleaf family)
May

1.84 *Mertensia virginica*

VIRGINIA BLUEBELLS, VIRGINIA COWSLIP

Hanging like bells but shaped more like trumpets, the fully opened flowers, ¾–1 inch long, are blue while the buds are pink. The somewhat succulent stem, with smooth, pale green, alternate, oblong leaves, grows 1–2½ feet tall. One of our most attractive spring flowers, this lovely plant grows especially in shady alluvial ground but also on moist rocky hillsides. It is widespread in Kentucky, frequent, and in some places plentiful.
Boraginaceae (Borage family) April

1.85 *Ruellia strepens*

RUELLIA

There are 3 species of *Ruellia* in Kentucky: *R. strepens, R. caroliniensis,* and *R. humilis*. All have large, axillary violet flowers 1–3 inches long, each with a slender corolla tube, 5 flaring corolla lobes, and 4 stamens; all have opposite leaves without marginal teeth. The stem is 1–3 feet tall and the leaves are petioled in the first 2 species, which grow in thickets, open woods, and woodland borders; the stem is shorter, 8–20 inches, and the leaves are sessile in *R. humilis,* which grows in dry, calcareous, rocky ground. One or more species will be found frequently in all parts of the state except the Cumberland Plateau and Cumberland Mountains, where they are infrequent.

Acanthaceae (Acanthus family) June-July

1.86 *Houstonia caerulea*

BLUETS, QUAKER-LADIES

A tiny plant, a delicate flower, but conspicuous en masse, the bluet grows 2–6 inches high on a threadlike stem and has a light blue corolla, about ½ inch across, with a yellow eye. The corolla tube is slender and the 4 lobes spread abruptly. The lovely little bluets grow especially in spots of low fertility, both in dry open woods and in wet meadows. Absent from the Bluegrass, they are frequent in the remaining eastern two-thirds of the state and less frequent in the west. Annual.

Rubiaceae (Madder family) April–May

The thyme-leaved bluets, *H. serpyllifolia,* have similar flowers but prostrate stems and round or oval leaves. This species grows in southeastern Kentucky but is infrequent. A smaller species which grows in western Kentucky is shown as no. 2.64.

1.87 *Datura stramonium* var. *tatula*

JIMSONWEED

"Jimson" is a corruption of Jamestown, referring to the early Virginia colony; this annual weed is sometimes called thorn-apple, a name applied to any member of the genus, several of which are grown ornamentally.

Most persons know only the vigorous, rank-smelling dark green herbage of the Jimsonweed without realizing the beauty of its flowers, which are white in one variety and lavender with a purple throat in the variety illustrated. The funnel-shaped corolla, 3–4 inches long, pleated, and gracefully swirled, opens at sunset. Emitting an exotic perfume in the evening, it is pollinated by nocturnal moths and withers in the morning. The plant contains a narcotic poison and is widespread in cultivated and waste ground.

Solanaceae (Nightshade family)

July-September

1.88 *Nicandra physalodes*

APPLE-OF-PERU

The erect bell-shaped flowers, 1–1½ inches across and borne in the leaf axils, are light blue with a white throat; the 5-angled calyx becomes inflated and resembles a Japanese lantern when in fruit. The toothed and lobed leaves are 3–6 inches long, and the plant stands 2–4 feet high. Introduced as an ornamental plant but no longer cultivated, the apple-of-Peru has escaped as a weed. It is found especially near cultivated fields in alluvial soil but is not common.

Solanaceae (Nightshade family)

July–August

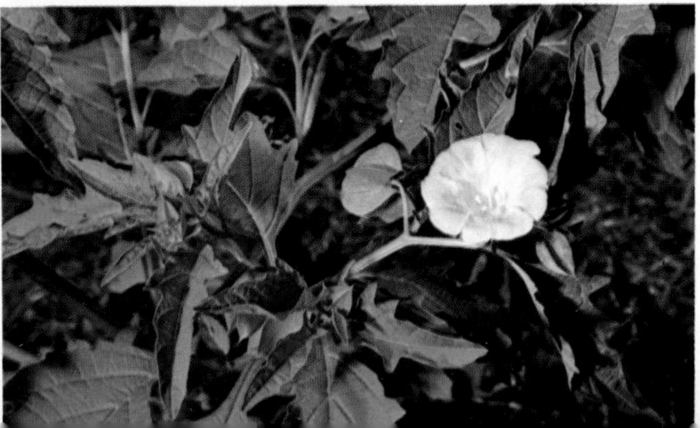

1.89 *Specularia perfoliata*

VENUS' LOOKING-GLASS

Deep purple flowers sessile in the axils of roundish, clasping leaves make this species easily recognized. The flowers are about ½ inch across; the plant, usually with an unbranched stem, is 6–24 inches high. It is a frequent annual throughout the state in old fields and other dry open places.

Campanulaceae (Bluebell family)

May–June

1.90 *Campanula americana*

TALL BELLFLOWER

Blue flowers with pale centers bloom in a tall, erect leafy spike for several weeks in midsummer. The 5-lobed corolla is flat, not bell-shaped as in other species of *Campanula,* and is about 1 inch broad; the style is long and curved. The plant is annual, 2–6 feet tall, with broadly lanceolate, long-pointed leaves. It is frequent in rich moist ground in woodlands, borders, and thickets throughout the state.

Campanulaceae (Bluebell family)

Late June–early August

1.91 *Hepatica acutiloba*

HEPATICA

Nothing can compare with the early-spring thrill of finding hepaticas and other little beauties in flower on a woodland bank after a bleak winter. Hepatica flowers shatter soon, but there is the assurance that in another spring they will again bring loveliness if man does not destroy the woods of which they are a part.

Hepatica flowers may be white, pink, or blue. They are described under no. 1.29.

Ranunculaceae (Buttercup family) Late March–early April

1.92 *Oxalis montana*

TRUE WOOD-SORREL

The flower stems, 2½–5 inches high, bear solitary flowers, and the shamrock-like leaves are all basal. The flowers are ½–¾ inch across, white veined with pink. A northern species extending south in the mountains, it is rare in Kentucky but may be found growing in rhododendron thickets and on moss-covered sandstone in deep shade in several localities in the Cumberland Plateau and Cumberland Mountains.

Oxalidaceae (Wood-sorrel family) June

1.93 *Saponaria officinalis*

BOUNCING BET, SOAPWORT

The roots of this European immigrant will produce a soapy lather in water. As in all members of the pink family, the leaves are opposite and the stem is swollen at the nodes; in this species the leaves are elliptical and smooth. Masses of the pinkish or whitish 5-petaled flowers, on stems 1–2 feet high, often cover roadsides and railroad embankments. The species is abundant and widespread.

Caryophyllaceae (Pink family)

June–September

1.94 *Claytonia virginica*

SPRING-BEAUTY

Spring-beauty flowers, ½–¾ inch wide and borne in racemes, have 2 sepals, 5 petals marked with pink, and 5 pink stamens. The plant, with its pair of succulent leaves, is 3–6 inches high. In woods, spring-beauties usually grow scattered but in lawns and parks in partial shade they often make a real display. It should be noted that in such places they are not weeds, for they do not seriously interfere with the grass; they have a deep corm and an unbranched stem, and by late spring have disappeared. The species pictured has lance-shaped leaves and is common and widespread in the state. A species with elliptic or oblong leaves, *C. caroliniana*, is much less frequent in Kentucky than *C. virginica*.

Portulacaceae (Purslane family) March–April

1.95 *Cardamine douglassii*

PURPLE CRESS

The purple cress is one of our earliest wildflowers. The flowers are in racemes on stems 5–12 inches high; the 4 petals, about ½ inch long, are pinkish lavender, pale violet, or rarely whitish; the pods are slender. The basal leaves are long-petioled with roundish blades but the stem leaves are sessile and ovate. This species is especially frequent in rich woods in central and northern Kentucky but also occurs in other areas.

Cruciferae (Mustard family)

March–April

Other similar species of *Cardamine*, but with smaller flowers, are described at no. 2.5.

1.96 *Iodanthus pinnatifidus*

PURPLE ROCKET

This plant grows 1½–3 feet high, bearing pale violet or whitish flowers in a small panicle and lance-elliptic, sharply toothed leaves. The petals are abruptly narrowed at the base and are about ½ inch long; the seedpods are slender. The purple rocket grows in moist alluvial woods and thickets and near springs. It is frequent from northern and central Kentucky westward.

Cruciferae (Mustard family) May

1.97 *Passiflora incarnata*

PASSION-FLOWER

This beautiful flower has a lavender fringed crown above white sepals and petals, and has 5 stamens and 3 styles standing in the center. The flower is 1½–2 inches across and is followed by an edible yellow, lemon-sized fruit. The leaves are deeply 3-lobed. This tendril-bearing vine grows in fencerows, old fields, and other dry sunny areas; it is frequent and widespread in the state, especially in central, southern, and western Kentucky.
Passifloraceae (Passion-flower family) June–July

1.98 *Passiflora lutea*

YELLOW PASSION-FLOWER

This diminutive greenish yellow flower, ¾–1 inch across, has the same structure as its larger relative, no. 1.97. The slender vine has numerous coiled tendrils, and leaves with 3 shallow, rounded lobes. It is frequent in woods and thickets in moist ground throughout the state.
Passifloraceae (Passion-flower family)
June–August

1.99 *Epigaea repens*

TRAILING ARBUTUS

Technically a small prostrate shrub, the trailing arbutus is only 2–3 inches high. Oblong, leathery, evergreen leaves are borne on stems 8–15 inches long, and clusters of pink or white flowers, each about ¾ inch long, may be nearly concealed. The corolla is tubular, flaring into 5 lobes, and has a delicate spicy fragrance. Its popularity, resulting from its beauty and fragrance, has been its undoing. It can be destroyed easily by breaking, and attempts to transplant it are almost always unsuccessful, at least after a year or two. It should be protected in its own habitat, which is sandy acid soil in open pine or oak woods on hillsides and ridges, in eastern and southeastern Kentucky.

Ericaceae (Heath family) March–April

1.100 *Gentiana villosa*

STRIPED GENTIAN

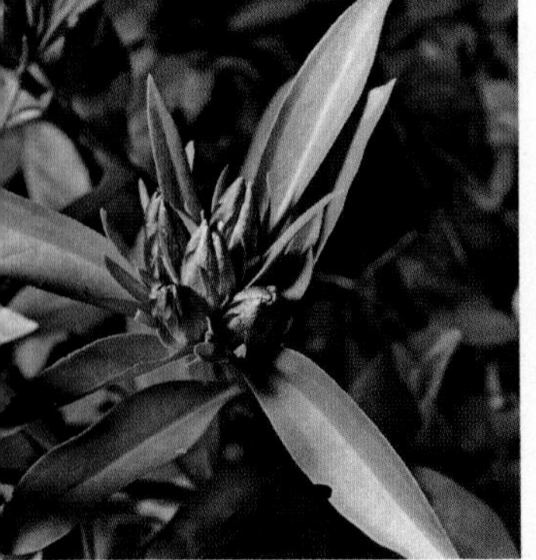

Also called Sampson's snakeroot, this gentian differs from most of its relatives in not being blue. The corolla, 1¼–1¾ inches long, is greenish white, striped with pale purple within; the corolla lobes are joined by a pleated membrane but are not completely closed. The flowers are crowded, the leaves are broad, smooth, and opposite, and the stem is 8–15 inches high. It grows in oak and oak-pine woods on hills in the Knobs, Mississippian Plateau, Cumberland Plateau, and Cumberland Mountains, but is infrequent.

Gentianaceae (Gentian family) October

1.101 *Swertia caroliniensis*

AMERICAN COLUMBO

This monumental plant, which may stand 7 feet tall when flowering, is usually a triennial: that is, the first year it produces a rosette of leaves, the second year the rosette becomes larger, and the third year, as a climax and finale, a single tall stem grows from the center. At this time the leaves in the basal whorl are 12–15 inches long, and those in the upper whorls are progressively smaller. The branches of the large panicle-like inflorescence are also whorled. The individual greenish flowers, about 1 inch broad, are spotted with purple and bear a gland on each corolla lobe. Growing in woods, usually in limestone soil, the columbo is fairly frequent and is widely distributed over the state.

Gentianaceae (Gentian family) June

1.102 *Amsonia tabernaemontana*

AMSONIA, BLUE DOGBANE

The pale blue flowers, about ½ inch across, have 5 slender lobes abruptly spreading from a corolla tube. The leaves are lanceolate, and the stem is 2–3 feet high. The blue dogbane, also called bluestar, is common in moist soil in western Kentucky.

Apocynaceae (Dogbane family) May

1.103 *Asclepias quadrifolia*

FOUR-LEAVED MILKWEED

This is a more delicate plant than other milkweeds. It has a slender stem, 1–1½ feet high, bearing a single whorl of 4 leaves at midstem, with other leaves in pairs, and 1–3 terminal umbels of whitish or pinkish flowers. The flowers have the characteristic milkweed form, with an erect crown of hood-like structures and reflexed corolla lobes. This species is frequent in woods throughout the state.

Asclepiadaceae (Milkweed family) Late May–early June

1.104 *Asclepias viridiflora*

GREEN MILKWEED

The umbels are densely flowered and lateral on a stem 1–2½ feet tall. Each green flower is about ½ inch long, including reflexed corolla lobes and erect hoods. Leaf shape varies from lance-linear to oblong or elliptic. The green milkweed grows in cedar barrens, on dry banks, and in other dry upland situations; it is fairly frequent from the eastern Knobs westward.

Asclepiadaceae (Milkweed family) July

1.105 *Phacelia purshii*

PHACELIA, MIAMI MIST

The lovely pale blue flowers, about ½ inch across, have fringed margins. The leaves are pinnately lobed and the stem is 10–15 inches high. This annual is common and locally abundant in the Bluegrass region, rare in eastern Kentucky, and frequent or locally common in the rest of the state. Typically it grows in alluvial woods but in the Bluegrass it is also found along roadsides.

Hydrophyllaceae (Waterleaf family) April–May

1.106 *Cynoglossum virginianum*

WILD COMFREY

Observation of the leaves shows the aptness of the genus name, which means "hound's tongue." The basal leaves have an elliptic-oblong blade 4–8 inches long, tapering into a petiole; stem leaves are smaller and clasping. Both stem and leaves are hairy. Several racemes of pale blue flowers, each flower about ½ inch across, terminate the stem, which is 1½–2 feet high. This plant is frequent in woods throughout the state.

Boraginaceae (Borage family) May

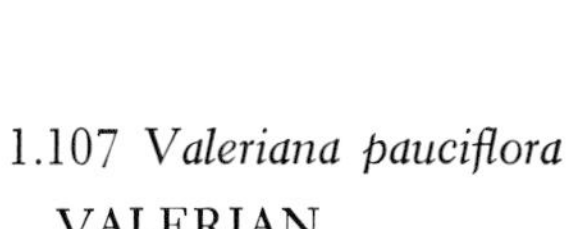

1.107 *Valeriana pauciflora*

VALERIAN

The valerian is a delicate, slender plant, 15–30 inches high, with a terminal cluster of pale pink flowers. The corolla, ⅝–¾ inch long, has a slender tube and 5 small lobes. The leaves are opposite and pinnately divided, with the terminal lobe much longer than the lateral lobes. It grows in rich moist woods, especially on lower slopes and in alluvium; though not frequent except in the Bluegrass, it is widespread through the state.

Valerianaceae (Valerian family)

May

2.1 *Agrimonia parviflora*

AGRIMONY

There are 5 species of *Agrimonia* in Kentucky. All have small yellow flowers in spikes, each flower with 5 separate petals; all have pinnate leaves composed of sharply toothed leaflets, usually with small leaflets interspersed with the larger ones; all have top-shaped fruit bearing hooked bristles. The species pictured has 11 or more lance-shaped leaflets, in contrast to all other species with 3–9 wider leaflets, and is 2–5 feet tall, whereas others are 1½–3 feet. Also *A. parviflora* grows in wet ground in woods, but the other species grow in moderately dry woods. Agrimonies are distributed over the state, and as a group are fairly frequent.

Rosaceae (Rose family) July–August

2.2 *Barbarea vulgaris*

WINTER CRESS

This species is conspicuous in the abundance of its golden flowers, sometimes covering whole fields and roadsides in moist ground. The lowest leaves have a petiole and a large, roundish terminal segment with smaller elliptic lateral lobes; upper leaves are small, sessile, and not deeply lobed. The flowers, having 4 petals, are ⅜ inch wide; the fruit is long and narrow. This biennial is common or abundant throughout the state.

Cruciferae (Mustard family)

April–May

Kentucky has another species of *Barbarea* (with smaller flowers and leaves), plus 8 other genera of weedy yellow-flowered mustards, some flowering in spring and some in summer. Most are such weedy alien species that they are not included here.

2.3 *Alliaria officinalis*

GARLIC-MUSTARD

Alliaria is a member of the mustard family with the odor of garlic. It grows 1½–3 feet high and has sharply toothed, triangular, petioled leaves. The 4 white petals, abruptly narrowed at the base, are about ¼ inch long. This introduced biennial weed is frequent along roadsides, at the edge of woods, and in waste places.
Cruciferae (Mustard family) May

2.4 *Nasturtium officinale*

WATERCRESS

Watercress grows partly submersed in the shallow water of brooks and springs or on mud which is often covered with water. The leaves are pinnate with 3–9 obtuse segments, the terminal one roundish and much larger than the lateral ones. The flowers, with 4 white petals, are about ¼ inch wide. This edible plant, often used in salads, is a native of Europe which is thoroughly naturalized throughout the state.
Cruciferae (Mustard family)
May–July

2.5 *Cardamine bulbosa*

SPRING CRESS

The spring cress is 10–20 inches tall. All leaves are simple; the basal ones are roundish and long-petioled; the stem leaves are ovate-oblong and sessile or short-petioled. The 4 white petals are ⅜–½ inch long. It grows near springs, in seepage areas, and in other wet ground. It is fairly frequent in such habitats anywhere in the state.

Cruciferae (Mustard family) April–May

The mountain watercress, *C. rotundifolia*, has weak stems reclining in the shallow water of mountain brooks. Its principal leaves have a roundish terminal segment and 2 minute lobes on the petiole; other leaves are roundish and petioled. Flowers, in racemes, have 4 white petals ¼–⅜ inch long. This species grows in eastern and southeastern Kentucky and flowers in May.

2.6 *Arabis laevigata*

SMOOTH ROCK-CRESS

The raceme of greenish white flowers is less conspicuous than the long sickle-shaped pods which follow. The leaves are gray-green, glaucous, and clasping at the base. It is usually 1–2 feet tall and is frequent in rocky woods throughout Kentucky.

Cruciferae (Mustard family) April–May

Another similar but less frequent species is the sicklepod, *A. canadensis*, which has even more strongly downcurved pods. Its leaves are not glaucous and not clasping at the base.

2.7 *Phytolacca americana*

POKEWEED, POKEBERRY

The pokeweed is a stout, widely branched plant 4–9 feet tall, with red stems and oblong leaves 4–12 inches long. The flowers, about ¼ inch wide, have petal-like sepals, no petals, 10 stamens, and 10 pistils joined in a disk-like ring, and are followed by dark purple berries on red stalks. The roots are poisonous but the young shoots and leaves are edible; the seeds also contain some poison. The pokeweed grows at the edge of cultivated ground and in fencerows, recent clearings, and waste places.

Phytolaccaceae (Pokeweed family) July–September

2.8 *Circaea quadrisulcata*

ENCHANTER'S NIGHTSHADE

Each of the small flowers (about ¼ inch across) has 2 sepals, 2 notched white petals, and 2 stamens. The ovary, which is below the attachment of other parts, develops into a fruit covered with hooked bristles. The leaves are ovate, opposite, and petioled, and the slender plant is usually 1–2 feet tall. The enchanter's nightshade is frequent in moist woods throughout the state.

Onagraceae (Evening primrose family) June–July

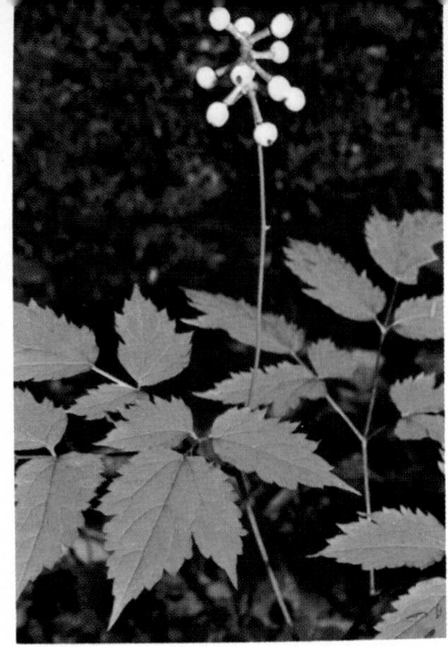

2.9 *Actaea pachypoda*

WHITE BANEBERRY

The numerous white stamens are longer than the minute petals. More conspicuous than the short raceme of flowers is the fruit, which is poisonous. The white berries, each with a thick stalk and a black spot, suggest the name "doll's-eyes" for the plant. The stem is 1–2 feet tall, the leaves are twice or thrice compound, and the leaflets are sharply toothed. The baneberry grows in mesophytic woods in all parts of the state but is not frequent.

Ranunculaceae (Buttercup family) Flowers: May

Fruit: August

2.10 *Cimicifuga racemosa*

BLACK SNAKEROOT,
BLACK COHOSH

The tall, slender, white racemes suggest cathedral candles in the forest. Petals are absent and sepals fall early, leaving only a tuft of white stamens and a pistil in each flower. The stately plant is 4–7 feet tall, the compound leaves are twice divided into 3s, and the leaflets are coarsely toothed. It is fairly frequent in woods, thickets, and woodland borders in most sections of the state but is apparently absent from the Inner Bluegrass.

Ranunculaceae (Buttercup family)

June–July

2.11 *Tiarella cordifolia*

FOAMFLOWER

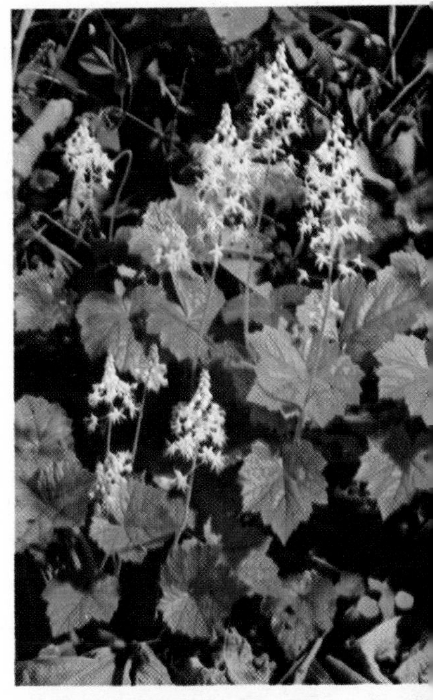

Delicate white flowers, about 1/3 inch across, with 5 petals and 10 long stamens, are borne in a raceme on a stem 6–12 inches high. The leaves, all basal, are lobed, with a toothed margin. The foamflower is frequent on rich wooded slopes in eastern and southern Kentucky.
Saxifragaceae (Saxifrage family)
April–May

2.12 *Mitella diphylla*

MITERWORT, BISHOP'S-CAP

A slender unbranched stem, 10–18 inches high, bears scattered small white flowers. Magnification of a flower with a hand lens reveals the extraordinary beauty of a snowflake. There are basal petioled leaves and a single opposite pair of sessile leaves on the stem. The bishop's-cap is fairly frequent in mesophytic woods throughout the state.
Saxifragaceae (Saxifrage family)
April–May

2.13 *Galax aphylla*

GALAX

The very lustrous leaves are the most notable feature of the galax. They are heart-shaped, petioled, persistent and coppery through the winter. The leafless stem bearing a spike of white flowers stands 10–20 inches high. This species grows in sandy acid soil in oak-pine woods; in Kentucky it occurs only in the eastern part of the state, especially the southeastern, where it is infrequent.
Diapensiaceae (Diapensia family)

June

2.14 *Pachysandra procumbens*

MOUNTAIN SPURGE, ALLEGHENY SPURGE

The evergreen leaves are crowded near the summit of the stem, which is 6–10 inches long, reclining, and turning up at the tip. Spikes 2–3 inches long are borne along the base of the stem. Most flowers in a spike are staminate, having thick white filaments and 4 greenish or purplish sepals but no petals; pistillate flowers, with 5 sepals, are near the base of the spike. The mountain spurge is infrequent but locally plentiful in mesophytic woods in calcareous soil from the Inner Bluegrass southward.
Buxaceae (Box family)

April

2.15 *Desmanthus illinoensis*

PRAIRIE MIMOSA

This is a bushy plant, 3–4 feet tall, having twice pinnate leaves with many tiny leaflets. The whitish flowers are borne in dense stalked "heads" in the upper axils. Petals are minute, and each flower has 5 long stamens. The pods are curved, often twisted together in the globe-like clusters. The prairie mimosa grows in dry, sunny, rocky ground and on river banks. It is found in northern, central, and western Kentucky but is infrequent.

Leguminosae (Legume family) June–July

2.16 *Schrankia microphylla*

SENSITIVE BRIER

This trailing vine, armed with hooked prickles, has twice pinnate leaves which close their tiny leaflets when touched. The pink or rose-purple flowers, each with a united corolla and 10 stamens, are borne in spherical clusters ½–⅝ inch in diameter. The pods are linear, and spiny. This species grows in sandy soil in southern Kentucky but is infrequent.

Leguminosae (Legume family) July-August

2.17 *Verbena simplex*

NARROW-LEAVED VERVAIN

The stem, 6–20 inches high, bears lanceolate leaves which taper at the base, and long, slender spikes of lavender flowers which have a corolla of 5 nearly equal lobes. It is frequent in sunny, rocky ground, especially in limestone, and is most frequent in central, southern, and western Kentucky.

Verbenaceae (Verbena family)

Late May–June

The blue vervain, V. *hastata*, which flowers later, has many pencil-like spikes on a stem 1½–5 feet tall. It grows in moist fields and meadows and is widely scattered in the state.

2.18 *Mentha spicata*

SPEARMINT

The true mints differ from most of their family in having radially symmetrical flowers with 4 nearly equal corolla lobes. Spearmint (illustrated) differs from peppermint, *M. piperita,* as follows, in addition to a difference in flavor: spearmint has leaves sessile or nearly so, and peppermint has definitely petioled leaves; the inflorescence in peppermint tends to be wider and the flowers more purplish than in spearmint. Both are natives of Europe which have become naturalized and are found near springs, on stream banks, and in other wet, sunny areas. In Kentucky spearmint is more frequent than peppermint.

Labiatae (Mint family)

July–August

2.19 *Myosotis scorpioides*

FORGET-ME-NOT

The pretty little flower, blue with a yellow eye, is ¼–⅜ inch across. The leaves are lance-oblong and the stem is 8–20 inches long. This species, naturalized from Europe, grows in wet ground in scattered localities but is not frequent.
Boraginaceae (Borage family) June

Our 2 native species of forget-me-not, *M. verna* and *M. macrosperma,* have white flowers.

Cynoglossum virginianum, the wild comfrey, which is a coarse plant in the same family, has pale blue flowers suggestive of the forget-me-not. It is illustrated as no. 1.106.

2.20 *Eryngium prostratum*

PROSTRATE ERYNGO

This little plant has stems 6–20 inches long, often rooting at the nodes. Blue flower-heads, ¼–⅜ inch long on slender stalks, are borne in the axils of petioled leaves. The prostrate eryngo grows in wet ground, and in Kentucky is restricted to the southwestern part of the state.
Umbelliferae (Parsley family) July–September

A larger species of eryngo, *E. yuccifolium,* with stiffly erect stems and strictly parallel-veined leaves is illustrated in Series Seven, no. 2.6.

2.21 *Bupleurum rotundifolium*

HARE'S EAR, THOROUGHWAX

This is an introduced annual weed which is noteworthy for the distinctive aspect of the plant rather than for showy flowers. The upper leaves appear to be pierced by the slender, wiry stem, and the minute, yellow, nearly sessile flowers in a compound umbel are encircled by broad, sharply pointed bracts. The plant is smooth, gray-green, and 12–20 inches high, and grows in fields, especially in central Kentucky.

Umbelliferae (Parsley family) June

2.22 *Pastinaca sativa*

WILD PARSNIP

This biennial European weed is the same species as the cultivated parsnip. The stem is stout, grooved, 2½–5 feet tall; the leaves are pinnately compound, having ovate, coarsely toothed leaflets and sheathing petioles. Yellow flowers are in large umbels 4–6 inches broad. The wild parsnip is abundant on the state's roadsides and in waste places.

Umbelliferae (Parsley family) June

2.23 *Taenidia integerrima*

YELLOW PIMPERNEL

Untoothed leaflets on leaves twice 3-parted distinguish the yellow pimpernel from other species with small yellow umbels. The plant, 1–2½ feet high, is fairly frequent on rocky wooded hillsides throughout the state.

Umbelliferae (Parsley family) May

2.24 *Thaspium barbinode*

MEADOW-PARSNIP

Creamy yellow flowers and tufts of hair at the nodes distinguish this species from others with which it might be confused. The stem is 2–3½ feet tall and branched; the principal leaves are twice compound, and the leaflets are toothed. This meadow-parsnip grows in woods, is widely distributed in Kentucky, and is fairly frequent.

Umbelliferae (Parsley family)

Late May–early June

2.25 *Zizia aptera*

GOLDEN ALEXANDERS

Compound umbels of bright yellow flowers, trifoliate stem leaves, simple heart-shaped basal leaves, and stems 1–2 feet tall are characteristics shared by *Zizia aptera* and *Thaspium trifoliatum* var. *flavum*. However, in *Zizia aptera* the central flower in each small secondary umbel is sessile, whereas in *Thaspium* it is stalked like the others; also in *Zizia* the fruit is ribbed but not winged, whereas in *Thaspium* the fruit has thin projecting membranes. Both species are fairly frequent in dry open woods and woodland borders in most of the state.

Umbelliferae (Parsley family) May

Another variety of *T. trifoliatum*, with purple flowers, is found in southeastern Kentucky but is not frequent.

Zizia aurea has twice compound leaves and leaflets finely toothed. It grows in wet thickets and meadows, is widely scattered in the state, but is infrequent.

2.26 *Angelica venenosa*

HAIRY ANGELICA

The upper part of the stem and the umbels are densely covered with short, whitish, velvety hairs. The lower leaves are twice or thrice pinnate, the leaflets are elliptic and thick, and the petioles are sheathing. The leaves are progressively reduced up the stem, which is usually 2–4 feet tall, and the uppermost may consist of only the sheath. The hairy angelica grows in open oak woods and borders, especially on dry slopes. Though widely scattered and occurring in most regions except the Inner Bluegrass, it is only fairly frequent.

Umbelliferae (Parsley family) August

2.27 *Osmorhiza longistylis*

SWEET CICELY, SWEET ANISE

The roots when broken are spicy-aromatic. The compound leaves are twice or thrice divided in thirds, and the ultimate leaflets are lance-shaped and bluntly toothed. The white flowers are minute and in small umbels; the fruit is slender, tapered at both ends, and prolonged at the base into a barbed tail. This species, which is without hairs except at the nodes, grows 1½–3 feet high; it is widely distributed in woods and fairly frequent.

Umbelliferae (Parsley family) May

The hairy sweet cicely, *O. claytoni,* differs in being softly hairy throughout and in not having a spicy aroma. It is probably more frequent than the preceding species.

2.28 *Daucus carota*

WILD CARROT, QUEEN ANNE'S LACE

Lacy, white, flat-topped umbels 2–4 inches across account for one common name of this biennial European weed; the other common name is a reminder that the cultivated carrot was developed from a race of this species. In fruit the outer rays arch inward causing the umbel to resemble a bird's nest. The leaves and bracts are finely divided into linear segments. The stem is rough-hairy, 2–5 feet tall. This abundant weed, troublesome in fields and pastures, also grows along roadsides and in waste places throughout the state.

Umbelliferae (Parsley family)
July–August

2.29 *Torilis japonica*

HEDGE PARSLEY

Radiating branches of the inflorescence, usually ¾–1 inch long, are few and the stalks of individual flowers are very short. The fruit is beset with hooked prickles. Leaflets of the twice pinnate leaves are sharply toothed. This alien annual weed, which grows 12–30 inches high, is abundant in fields and pastures and along roadsides especially in the Bluegrass region.

Umbelliferae (Parsley family) July

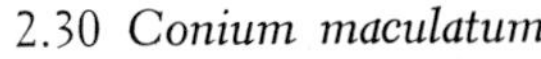

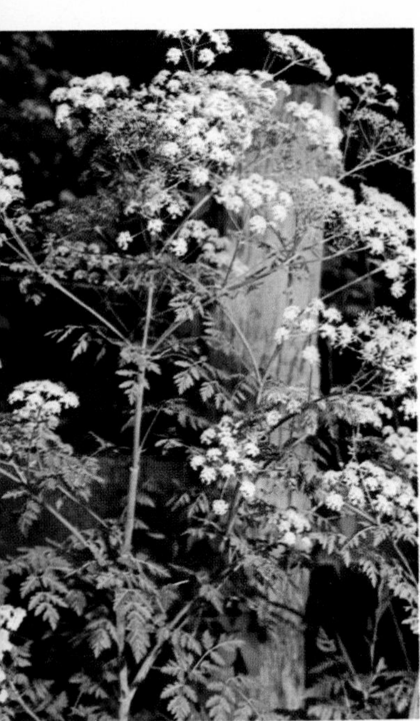

2.30 *Conium maculatum*

POISON HEMLOCK

This species supplied the deadly potion which the Greeks administered to Socrates and other state prisoners. Livestock can also be killed by eating the foliage.

It is a much-branched biennial, 5–8 feet tall, with a smooth, spotted, hollow stem, very finely divided leaves, and numerous umbels of white flowers. The crushed foliage has a rank odor. This foreign weed is more common in central and northern Kentucky than in other sections and is locally abundant in alluvial soil and along roadsides and railroads in the Bluegrass region.

Umbelliferae (Parsley family) June

2.31 *Cicuta maculata*

WATER HEMLOCK

The water hemlock is a native perennial which has a violently poisonous root; however, the foliage and fruit do not contain enough of the poison to harm livestock. The stem, which is streaked with purple, is 3–5 feet tall; the twice or thrice compound leaves have toothed, lance-shaped leaflets and sheathing petioles. Growing in wet meadows and along streams, it is frequent in most sections of Kentucky.

Umbelliferae (Parsley family) July

2.32 *Erigenia bulbosa*

HARBINGER-OF-SPRING

Only 3–6 inches high, this is a tiny representative of a family that has many coarse members. The minute white flowers with black anthers have suggested the name "salt-and-pepper"; the more frequently used name refers to its early flowering. The ultimate segments of the much-divided leaf are linear-oblong. It is frequent in rich woods throughout the state.
Umbelliferae (Parsley family)
March–early April

2.33 *Aralia racemosa*

SPIKENARD

The spikenard is a widely branched plant 3–6 feet tall with twice compound leaves. The flowers are in umbels which are arranged in a panicle and are followed by dark purple berries. It is fairly frequent in rich woods throughout the state.
Araliaceae (Ginseng family) July

2.34 *Panax quinquefolium*

GINSENG

The unbranched stem is 8–16 inches high, producing a single terminal umbel of minute greenish white flowers, which are less conspicuous than the red berries that follow. The stem bears a single whorl of 3 palmately compound leaves, each composed of 5 leaflets.

The dried roots, long in demand in Chinese folk medicine and bringing a high price, have been sought, dug, and sold for export. As a result, this native species, once common in most of the rich forests of the state, has been exterminated in many places and is now rare throughout Kentucky, as well as in other states. The species should be protected by law from further exploitation, and any plants to be sold should be propagated and grown commercially.

Araliaceae (Ginseng family)

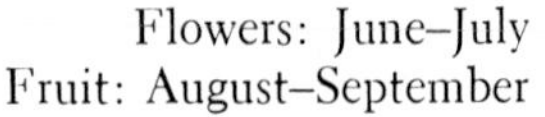

Flowers: June–July
Fruit: August–September

2.35 *Panax trifolium*

DWARF GINSENG

This diminutive ginseng is only 4–6 inches high; the leaflets are usually 3 (rarely 5); the flowers, in a single terminal umbel, are white; and the berries are yellow. Like its larger and more famous relative (no. 2.34), it has an unbranched stem and a whorl of 3 leaves. It is a northern species which is found in rich moist woods in only a few localities in eastern Kentucky.

Araliaceae (Ginseng family)

April–early May

2.36 *Spiraea tomentosa*

STEEPLE-BUSH, HARDHACK

The lovely, pink, spire-like inflorescence in this small shrub accounts for one common name, and the tough, wiry stem for the other. Stems are 2–4 feet high; leaves have tawny "felt" on the lower surface. It is fairly frequent in sunny, wet, poorly drained ground in various sections of the state except the Bluegrass region.

Rosaceae (Rose family) July

2.37 *Aruncus dioicus*

GOAT'S-BEARD

Small white flowers are nearly sessile in a large terminal panicle, and the entire plant is 3–5 feet tall. The leaves are twice or thrice pinnately divided; the leaflets, 2–4 inches long, are coarsely toothed, the lateral ones often oblique. Stamens and pistils are in separate flowers. The goat's-beard grows on mesophytic slopes and moist shady cliffs; it is widely distributed across the state, but is most frequent in eastern Kentucky.

Rosaceae (Rose family) June

Astilbe biternata, the false goat's-beard, of the saxifrage family, resembles *Aruncus* in general aspect. However, *Astilbe* has 10 stamens to the flower, *Aruncus* 15 or more; *Astilbe* usually produces 2 pods per flower, *Aruncus* 3; in *Astilbe* the fruits are erect and 4 mm. or 1/6 inch long, while in *Aruncus* they are reflexed and 2 mm. or 1/12 inch long. The false goat's-beard is found in eastern Kentucky, especially the southeastern section, but is not frequent.

2.38 *Saxifraga virginiensis*

EARLY SAXIFRAGE

Rosettes of leaves appear bright green all winter on a cliff or ledge where no fallen leaves accumulate, and the earliest spring warmth will initiate a panicle of white flowers, short and dense at first but lengthening and opening out as later flowers bloom. The leaves are narrowed to a petiole and toothed, and the flowers have 5 petals and 10 stamens. The early saxifrage is common on limestone cliffs in the Inner Bluegrass and occurs in less frequence on limestone and sandstone in other sections of the state.
Saxifragaceae (Saxifrage family)
March–April

The Genus *Heuchera*, the Alum-roots

Kentucky has 6 species of alum-root of the genus *Heuchera*. All have long-petioled, palmately lobed, toothed basal leaves and a panicle of small flowers on a leafless stalk. The calyx is united, but the petals are separate, minute, and spatulate.

2.39 *Heuchera americana*

ALUM-ROOT

The flowers may be slightly oblique in this species. The stamens and style are much longer than the perianth, and the outside of the flower when magnified is seen to have glands and minute hairs. The petioles either have a few hairs or are nearly glabrous. Growing 1½–3 feet high, it is found on wooded slopes and cliffs, is frequent, and is widely distributed.
Saxifragaceae (Saxifrage family) May–July

2.40 *Heuchera villosa*

ALUM-ROOT

As in no. 2.39, the stamens and style project beyond the perianth. In *H. villosa* the flowers have long hairs on the outside and are never oblique. The stems, 1–2 feet tall, and the petioles also have long spreading hairs. This species is widely distributed and frequent on wooded cliffs, one variety growing chiefly on limestone and another on sandstone.
Saxifragaceae (Saxifrage family)
July–September

H. longiflora and *H. pubescens* have oblique flowers and stamens shorter than the perianth. They are fairly frequent in eastern Kentucky and flower in May and June.

H. parviflora var. *rugelii,* with very thin leaves, is our smallest species, only 6–15 inches high. Flowering from July to September, it grows only on shaded sandstone cliffs in the area of the Pottsville escarpment in eastern and western Kentucky and in the Cumberland Mountains of southeastern Kentucky, where it is frequent.

2.41 *Euphorbia corollata*

FLOWERING SPURGE

Although the flowering spurge appears to have 5 white "petals," they are actually bracts which surround a minute cluster of flowers lacking sepals and petals, and the cluster is thus mistaken for a flower. The stem, which has milky juice, is 1½–3 feet tall; the branches of the inflorescence rise from a whorl of small leaves; other leaves are alternate and oblong. It is frequent in prairie patches and at the edge of dry open woods in most sections of the state.
Euphorbiaceae (Spurge family)
July–August

2.42 *Trautvetteria caroliniensis*

TASSEL-RUE, FALSE BUGBANE

This is a stout plant, 2–3 feet tall, with a compound inflorescence and palmately lobed and toothed leaves which are broader than long. The petioled basal leaves are 6–10 inches wide; the sessile stem leaves are smaller. The numerous stamens constitute the most conspicuous part of the white flowers, which are ¼–½ inch broad; there are no petals, and the sepals fall soon after the flower opens. The tassel-rue is fairly frequent, locally plentiful, near streams and in wet woods in southeastern and southern Kentucky; it is rare in a few other localities.
Ranunculaceae (Buttercup family) July

A small spring-flowering plant with a similar but solitary flower is *Hydrastis canadensis*, the goldenseal, which is illustrated in Series Seven, no. 1.3, because its sepals fall before the flower opens.

2.43 *Thalictrum dioicum*

EARLY MEADOW RUE

All species of meadow rue have somewhat ephemeral sepals, no petals, numerous showy stamens, much-divided leaves, and leaflets usually with 3 rounded lobes.

In the early meadow rue the pistil-bearing and stamen-bearing flowers are on separate plants. The staminate plants are more conspicuous, having numerous drooping flowers with yellow anthers; the fewer pistillate flowers, not drooping, are purplish green. This species, 1–2 feet tall, grows on wooded slopes. It is more frequent in calcareous than noncalcareous areas and is more frequent in central, northern, and southern Kentucky than in eastern and western Kentucky.
Ranunculaceae (Buttercup family) April

2.44 *Thalictrum polygamum*

TALL MEADOW RUE

Growing 3–7 feet tall, this meadow rue produces billowy masses of panicled flowers with white stamens. Most flowers are staminate, but some contain both stamens and pistils; the filaments are strongly dilated. This meadow rue, which grows in low ground, especially in flood-plain woods and thickets, is widely scattered in the state but is not frequent.
Ranunculaceae (Buttercup family)

July

Two other tall species of *Thalictrum* in Kentucky are *T. revolutum* and *T. dasycarpum,* both of which grow 3–5 feet tall and have stamens with slender, not dilated, filaments. *T. revolutum,* called the waxy meadow rue, also has gland-tipped hairs on the lower surfaces of the leaflets, and the margins are slightly rolled over.

2.45 *Thalictrum clavatum*

CLIFF MEADOW RUE

The cliff meadow rue is a delicate plant, 8–20 inches high, having a widely branched panicle with its few white flowers on long slender stalks. The filaments of the stamens are strongly dilated. This species is frequent on moist shaded sandstone cliffs in eastern and southern Kentucky.
Ranunculaceae (Buttercup family)

June

2.46 *Campanula divaricata*

SOUTHERN HAREBELL, PANICLED BELLFLOWER

Hanging from slender branches of the panicle, each pale blue flower, ¼–⅜ inch long with flaring corolla lobes and a protruding style, suggests a little bell complete with clapper. The plant, 1–2 feet high with lanceolate, sharply toothed leaves, grows in dry rocky woods in the Cumberland Mountains and the southeastern part of the Cumberland Plateau.

Campanulaceae (Bluebell family) August

2.47 *Laportea canadensis*

WOOD-NETTLE

This attractive plant makes especially verdant patches in rich moist woods but sharply stings any intruder who brushes against it. Growing 2–3 feet tall, it has gracefully branching inflorescences of tiny white flowers in the axils of broadly oval, alternate leaves 3½–5 inches long. It is common throughout the state.

Urticaceae (Nettle family) July

The nettles of the genus *Urtica* have opposite leaves; some species are native and one is a European weed found in waste places. Some relatives lack stinging hairs, such as the false nettle, *Boehmeria cylindrica*, which has non-branching axillary inflorescences, and the little annual clearweed, *Pilea pumila*, which has clear stems and opposite, thin, light green leaves.

2.48 *Xanthorhiza simplicissima*

SHRUB-YELLOWROOT

This is a low slender shrub, 1–2 feet tall, with erect stems bearing crowded terminal clusters of many racemes or panicles, and pinnate leaves with 5 toothed leaflets. The brownish or greenish purple flowers, ¼ inch across, have 5 sepals and no petals. It is fairly frequent in moist ground, especially stream margins, in the Cumberland Plateau and Cumberland Mountains.

Ranunculaceae (Buttercup family) April

2.49 *Arenaria patula*

SANDWORT, WILD BABY'S-BREATH

This delicate little annual, 4–10 inches high, has very slender stems and linear or hairlike opposite leaves; each flower has 5 notched petals ¼–⅜ inch long. It grows on dry limestone cliffs and ledges, and thus adds grace and daintiness to a harsh environment. It is frequent in the Bluegrass region and fairly frequent in the Mississippian Plateau.

Caryophyllaceae (Pink family) Late April–early May

2.50 *Galium concinnum*

SHINING BEDSTRAW

The species illustrated is a delicate and airy one. The much-branched stem is 6–18 inches high and the linear leaves, 6 in a whorl, are ½–⅝ inch long. The fruits are smooth, and the stems and leaves are only slightly rough. It grows in woods, is widely scattered in the state, and is apparently most frequent in central Kentucky.

Rubiaceae (Madder family) June–July

Kentucky has 11 species of *Galium*, all called bedstraw. All have slender square stems, whorled leaves, and very small flowers in clusters. In the flowers the ovary is below the attachment of the corolla, which has 4 white or purplish lobes; the fruit is a pair of small spheres joined together, prickly in some species, smooth in others.

Of the 11 species, only *G. aparine*, called cleavers as well as bedstraw, is an obnoxious weed, a pest in shady places. Both leaves and weak stems, 2–4 feet long, are rasping with down-curved prickles, and the fruits are also prickly.

2.51 *Houstonia lanceolata*
HOUSTONIA

All houstonias have opposite sessile leaves. Kentucky has 6 species with white or pale purplish, funnel-shaped, clustered flowers, ¼–⅜ inch long, each with 4 spreading corolla lobes. The lance-leaved species, illustrated, grows chiefly in central and western Kentucky.
Rubiaceae (Madder family) June–July

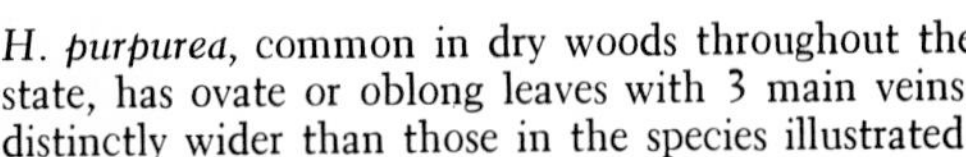

H. purpurea, common in dry woods throughout the state, has ovate or oblong leaves with 3 main veins, distinctly wider than those in the species illustrated.

The following 3 species have linear leaves: *H. tenuifolia,* with the narrowest leaves, found in southeastern Kentucky; *H. nigricans,* with sessile flowers, found especially on limestone cliffs in central Kentucky; and *H. longifolia,* which is more frequent in the Knobs than elsewhere.

H. canadensis, which has a basal rosette of small lanceolate or oblong leaves bearing marginal hairs, is frequent in dry woods in most of the state but rare in the Bluegrass region.

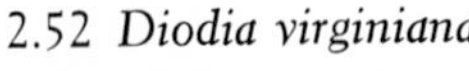

2.52 *Diodia virginiana*
BUTTONWEED

This buttonweed, with reclining stems 8–20 inches long, has narrowly elliptic leaves, linear stipules, and axillary, sessile flowers. The white or pale pink corolla is tubular, about ⅜ inch long, with 4 spreading lobes. This species grows in wet ground in eastern, southern, and western Kentucky but is not frequent.
Rubiaceae (Madder family) July–August

D. teres, the annual buttonweed, which has smaller flowers, narrower leaves, and bristle-like stipules, is characteristic of leached and eroded fields and is often called "poor Joe." It is distributed in all regions of the state and is more frequent than *D. virginiana.*

2.53 *Gaultheria procumbens*

TEABERRY, WINTERGREEN

Technically a dwarf creeping shrub about 4 inches high, the teaberry has lustrous, leathery, evergreen leaves containing oil of wintergreen. The urn-shaped flowers, about ¼ inch long, are followed by red berry-like fruits. It is frequent in oak-pine woods in acid soil in eastern and southern Kentucky.

Ericaceae (Heath family) July

2.54 *Euonymus obovatus*

RUNNING STRAWBERRY-BUSH

This prostrate shrub with a trailing stem and upright 4-angled branches 4–10 inches high has opposite, oblong, petioled leaves, inconspicuous flowers, and showy fruits. The flat greenish-purple flowers, ¼–⅜ inch across, are borne in the leaf axils. The fruits are 3-lobed and each seed has a bright red covering. Growing on moist wooded hillsides, it is frequent in the Bluegrass and other areas of central Kentucky and infrequent in the rest of the state.

Celastraceae (Staff-tree family) Flowers: May
Fruit: September

2.55 *Sedum ternatum*

STONECROP

Leaves of the stonecrop are rounded at the apex and fleshy, and the inflorescence, usually 3-forked, bears flowers on the upper side. The flowers are built on a pattern of either 4s or 5s: the sepals, petals, and pistils each 4 or 5 and the stamens twice as many. The stonecrop grows 4–6 inches high, often making a mat on mossy banks, ledges, and boulders in woods. It is frequent throughout the state.

Crassulaceae (Orpine family) April–May

2.56 *Sedum pulchellum*

WIDOW'S-CROSS, PINK STONECROP

The young plants of this winter annual are bright green in late winter and early spring. It has narrowly cylindrical leaves and rose-pink flowers in a flat-topped, forking inflorescence with 4–7 branches. It grows only on limestone, either wet or dry, and the height of the plant, from 4 to 15 inches, varies with the amount of moisture. It is fairly frequent in the Bluegrass region and the Mississippian Plateau.

Crassulaceae (Orpine family) June

2.57 *Apocynum cannabinum*

HEMP DOGBANE, INDIAN HEMP

This dogbane is called Indian hemp because of its fibrous stems. Growing 2–4 feet high, it contains milky juice and has opposite, elliptic, smooth-margined leaves. Flowers are greenish white and urn-shaped, less than ¼ inch long; the narrowly cylindrical fruit is 4–5 inches long. This species is common in old fields, at the edge of woods, and in clearings throughout the state.

Apocynaceae (Dogbane family)

June–July

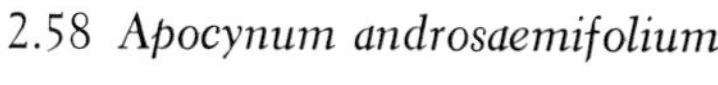

2.58 *Apocynum androsaemifolium*

SPREADING DOGBANE

This species differs from the preceding chiefly in its fragrant, pale pink, bell-shaped flowers about 1/3 inch long, which are marked inside with deep rose. Growing 1–2 feet high, it is found at the edge of woods but is very infrequent in Kentucky.

Apocynaceae (Dogbane family) July

2.59 *Valerianella* spp.

CORN-SALAD, LAMB'S-LETTUCE

Corn-salad is a smooth, tender, succulent annual or biennial, usually 10–20 inches high, with a forking stem and opposite, sessile, oblong leaves. The small white flowers in compound clusters are funnel-shaped and 5-lobed. In the Bluegrass region it is common in wet sunny ground at the edge of creeks and on alluvial flats. The species are separated largely by technical characters of the fruit; those most frequently found are *V. intermedia* and *V. patellaria.*

Valerianaceae (Valerian family)

May

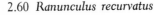

2.60 *Ranunculus recurvatus*

HOOKED CROWFOOT

The plant, bearing 3-lobed leaves, is 10–20 inches high and usually hairy. Each flower, about ⅜ inch across, has pale yellow petals and recurved sepals and produces several one-seeded fruits, each with a hooked beak. This species grows in moist ground in wooded valleys and is frequent and widespread throughout the state.

Ranunculaceae (Buttercup family) May

Two smaller species of crowfoot which are common throughout the state are R. *abortivus* and R. *micranthus*, both called small-flowered crowfoot. These are 8–18 inches high with basal leaves which are roundish, heart-shaped at the base, and often lobed, and with stem-leaves which are divided into 3–5 linear or lanceolate segments; their flowers are less than ¼ inch across. R. *micranthus* is hairy, and R. *abortivus* is glabrous. Both flower in April.

2.61 *Linum virginianum*

SLENDER YELLOW FLAX

This is a very slender plant with a forking stem 1–1½ feet tall. The flowers, about 1/3 inch across, have 5 sepals, 5 petals, 5 stamens, and 5 styles; the fruit is a nearly spherical capsule. This species grows in dry open woods and clearings, especially on hillsides, is frequent in the Knobs, and is fairly frequent in other sections with the exception of the Bluegrass.

Linaceae (Flax family) June–July

Kentucky has 3 other native species of *Linum*, of which the most frequent is the stiff yellow flax, *L. medium*, with stiffly erect branches, which is often found on eroded hillsides.

The cultivated flax, *L. usitatissimum*, a larger plant with larger blue flowers, is occasionally found on roadsides and in waste places.

2.62 *Portulaca oleracea*

PURSLANE

In this prostrate, much-branched, mat-forming annual the stems are often reddish, and the leaves are thick, fleshy, and spatulate. The yellow flowers are sessile and about 1/3 inch across. Purslane is a common garden weed which is also found in waste places.

Portulacaceae (Purslane family)

Summer

2.63 *Anagallis arvensis*

SCARLET PIMPERNEL

This dainty little annual weed with pretty flowers has somewhat reclining stems 4–10 inches long. The leaves are oval, opposite, sessile, and smooth, and the flowers are axillary. The pinkish orange or pale scarlet corolla has 5 widely spreading lobes. This European immigrant is fairly frequent in gardens and waste places.

Primulaceae (Primrose family)

August–September

2.64 *Houstonia patens*

SMALL BLUETS

This tiny annual, 2–4 inches tall, has purple flowers solitary on slender stalks. The corolla is about ¼ inch across the 4 lobes, which spread from a tubular base. This species is frequent in open areas in western Kentucky.

Rubiaceae (Madder family)

Late April–early May

A larger and paler species of bluets, *H. caerulea*, is illustrated as no. 1.86.

Series Five: **Dicotyledons (2)**

Dicotyledons having bilaterally symmetrical flowers with 4 or 5 petals or corolla lobes and net-veined leaves.

Bilateral symmetry

(Two-sided. Only 1 plane of cutting will divide it into 2 equal halves)

ARRANGEMENT OF PLATES

Group 1. Flowers pea-shaped: that is, the uppermost and largest petal is erect and called the "standard"; 2 small lateral petals are called "wings"; and the 2 lowermost petals are more or less united to form a "keel." All are members of the legume family (Leguminosae) 1.1–1.24

Pea-shaped flower

Group 2. Corolla 2-lipped, suggesting a mouth: that is, from a united and tubular base it separates into distinctly upper and lower portions, each of which may or may not be lobed 2.1–2.40

Two-lipped flower

Group 3. Flowers bilaterally symmetrical and of various shapes but neither pealike nor 2-lipped 3.1–3.41

1.1 *Stylosanthes biflora*

PENCIL-FLOWER

Leaves with 3 bristle-tipped leaflets are borne on wiry stems 6–15 inches long, which may be spreading, ascending, or reclining. The leaflets may be broad at the apex and ½–⅝ inch long, or narrowly lanceolate and over 1 inch long. The golden pea-like flowers are about ⅜ inch long. The pencil-flower grows in dry open woods, dry woodland borders, and sunny shaly slopes; it is frequent in the Knobs and fairly frequent in most other regions except the Bluegrass.

July

1.2 *Lotus corniculatus*

BIRDFOOT TREFOIL

Clusters of golden pea-shaped flowers, each ½ inch long, are borne terminally on an erect branch. The main stem is usually reclining, 6–24 inches long, and has leaves with 5 leaflets. This is a native of Europe which is occasionally found on roadsides and in pastures.

July–August

1.3 *Baptisia leucophaea*

CREAM WILD INDIGO

The flowers are about 1 inch long in a raceme 5–8 inches long with conspicuous bracts; the leaves have 3 leaflets and a pair of large stipules. This species, 15–30 inches high, with widely spreading branches, is frequent in dry open woods in southwest Kentucky.

May

B. leucantha, with white flowers about 1 inch long, grows 2–3 feet high with ascending branches and has small bracts and stipules which fall early. Though infrequent, it is widely scattered in the state. *B. tinctoria,* a bushy plant, has leaflets less than 1 inch long and yellow flowers about ½ inch long. It is found in the southeastern mountains.

1.4 *Baptisia australis*

BLUE FALSE INDIGO

This is a stout plant 3–5 feet tall, with compound leaves having 3 firm obtuse leaflets, each 1–3 inches long. The blue flowers, about 1 inch long, are in large, erect racemes. The plant grows in moist woods and thickets, especially on river banks, in northern, central, and southern Kentucky but is infrequent.

May–June

1.5 *Amphicarpa bracteata*

HOG-PEANUT

The hog-peanut is a twining plant with very slender stems and thin trifoliate leaves. The leaflets are ovate and rounded at the base; the terminal one is usually 1–2 inches long. The flowers, which are in axillary racemes, are slender, white or purplish, and ½–¾ inch long. It is common in moist woods, especially on wooded stream banks, throughout Kentucky.

August

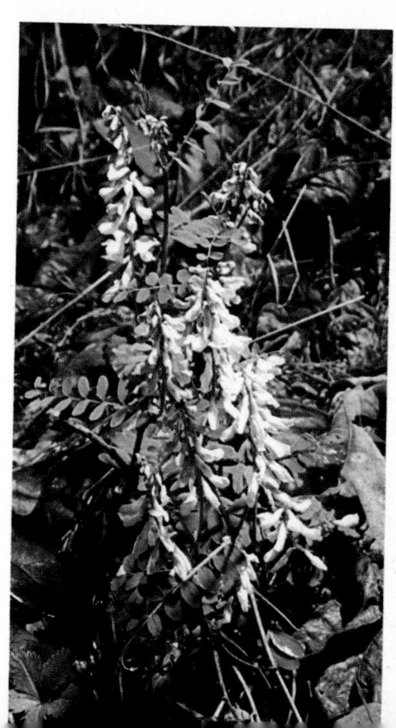

1.6 *Vicia caroliniana*

WOOD VETCH

Our only native vetch, this species has pinnate leaves with 5–9 pairs of narrow leaflets; tendrils terminate the leaves and suggest the common name "devil's shoestring." Slender white flowers, ⅜–½ inch long, are borne in racemes. The wood vetch, 15–30 inches high, may be found in open oak woods in most regions of the state but is more frequent in the eastern two-thirds than in the western third.

April

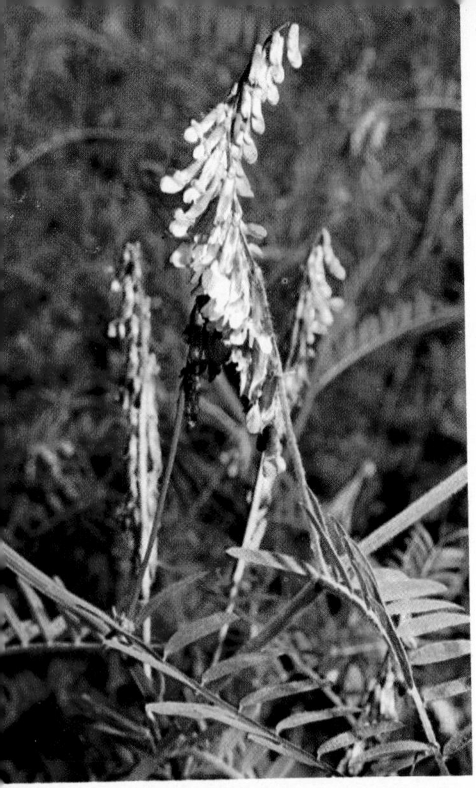

1.7 *Vicia villosa*

HAIRY VETCH

This weak-stemmed winter annual, 2–3 feet high, has flowers ½–¾ inch long in one-sided racemes. As in all vetches, the leaves are pinnate and terminated by tendrils. This species, commonly planted with small grain as a winter cover in cultivated fields, frequently escapes to roadsides and other open weedy places.

June

Other blue-flowered species of vetch are similarly but less frequently used.

Alfalfa, *Medicago sativa*, has purple flowers in headlike racemes, trifoliate leaves, erect stems, and no tendrils. It is frequently planted for forage and occasionally escapes.

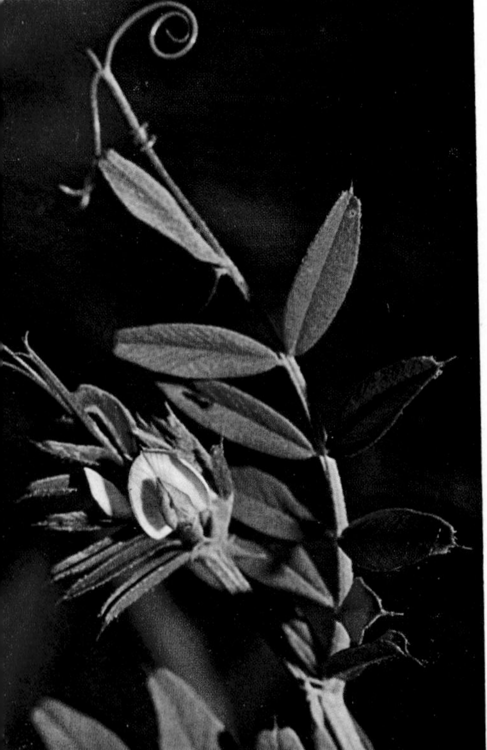

1.8 *Vicia sativa*

SPRING VETCH

The rose-purple flowers, ¾–1 inch long, are borne singly or in pairs in the axils of the leaves, which have notched leaflets. This European annual, having been cultivated for forage, escapes to various open places.

June

1.9 *Trifolium pratense*

RED CLOVER

Clovers, belonging to the genus *Trifolium,* have leaves with 3 leaflets and flowers in dense headlike spikes. Flowers in the various species are white, pink, pinkish purple, yellow, and crimson. They have been introduced from Europe and are valuable for forage and for soil enrichment. This species escapes to roadsides and waste places more frequently than the others.

June–July

The sweet clovers, of the genus *Melilotus* (not illustrated), also with 3 leaflets, are tall straggling plants having yellow or white flowers in open spikes.

1.10 *Coronilla varia*

CROWN VETCH

The crown vetch has umbels of pink and white flowers, each about ½ inch long, pinnate leaves with many small leaflets, and creeping stems which form a carpet. It is extensively planted along highway cuts and embankments, and occasionally escapes.

June

1.11 *Psoralea psoralioides*

SCURF-PEA

This plant is sometimes called Sampson's snakeroot, a name also applied to a species of gentian to which it is unrelated, an example of confusion in the use of common names.

The scurf-pea is a slender plant, 1–2½ feet tall, having long-stalked spikes of pale violet flowers ¼ inch long, and leaves with 3 linear-oblong leaflets each 2–2½ inches long. It grows in dry open woods in noncalcareous soil; it is frequent in the Knobs and also occurs in west-central and southern Kentucky.

June

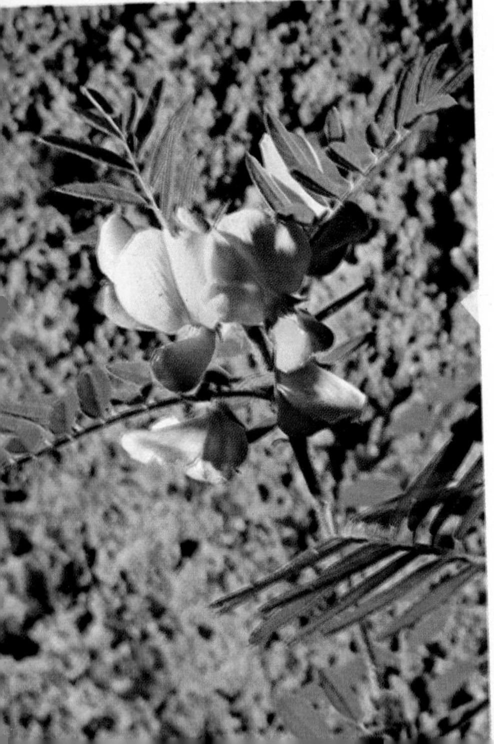

1.12 *Tephrosia virginiana*

GOAT'S-RUE

Beautiful and sometimes called wild sweet pea, the goat's-rue has bicolored flowers with the standard about ½ inch across. The pinnate leaves and stem, 1–2 feet high, are covered with silky hairs. It is frequent in dry open oak and oak-pine woods in noncalcareous soil and occurs in every region of the state except the limestone areas of the Bluegrass.

June

1.13 *Clitoria mariana*

BUTTERFLY-PEA

The large pale blue flower of the butterfly-pea is strikingly beautiful with a standard 1¼–2 inches long. The stems are 1–3 feet long, trailing, twining, or ascending. The plant grows on open oak and pine uplands and, though infrequent, is scattered across the state, occurring in most regions except the Bluegrass.

July

1.14 *Strophostyles umbellata*

TRAILING WILD BEAN

The pink flowers, turning greenish with age and ⅜–½ inch long, are in compact racemes borne on long stalks. Leaflets of the trifoliate leaves are oblong or narrowly ovate. This trailing or twining plant grows in moist or dry ground in sunny situations; it is fairly frequent in the Mississippian Plateau and infrequent in most other regions.

July

A similar species, *S helvola,* in which the leaflets have a bulge on the margin and are sometimes nearly lobed, is fairly frequent in the Knobs and southwest Kentucky and infrequent elsewhere.

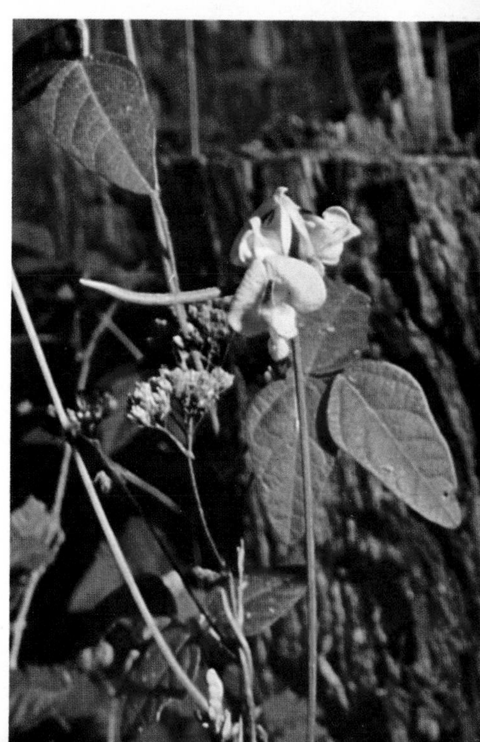

1.15 *Apios americana*

GROUNDNUT

A rootstock consisting of a string of tuberous enlargements is responsible for the common name. The plant, which climbs over bushes, has leaves with 5–7 leaflets and short racemes on long stalks. The flowers are purplish brown, ½ inch broad, and fragrant. It is fairly frequent in moist thickets and is widely distributed in the state.

July

1.16 *Galactia volubis*

MILK-PEA

The twining stem and trifoliate leaves are conspicuously hairy; the purplish pink flowers, 1/3 inch long, are borne in axillary racemes. The milk-pea grows in dry open woods, borders, and thickets on uplands and is fairly frequent in the Knobs and across southern Kentucky.

July–August

1.17 *Phaseolus polystachios*

WILD BEAN

This species is our only wild representative of the genus that includes the cultivated beans. The stem is twining, the leaves are trifoliate, and the flowers are in racemes. The flowers, which are purplish pink and ⅜–½ inch long, have a spirally coiled keel-petal. Growing in mesophytic woods and moist thickets, the wild bean is widely distributed through the state but is not frequent.

August

The Genus *Desmodium*, the Tick-trefoils

Sixteen species of *Desmodium* occur in Kentucky. All have trifoliate leaves and pinkish purple flowers, about ⅜ inch long, in racemes. The most significant distinguishing feature is a flat pod with several constrictions covered with hooked hairs which cling to clothing. For this reason they are often called "sticktights."

1.18 *Desmodium glutinosum*

POINTED-LEAF TICK-TREFOIL

This species has leaves crowded around the top of a short stem from which the long-stalked inflorescence rises to a height of 2½–4 feet. It is frequent in woods and woodland borders throughout the state.

July–August

D. nudiflorum, the naked-flowered tick-trefoil, has all leaves basal and a leafless flower-stem. It is common in dry open woods, apparently in all regions of the state except the Inner Bluegrass.

1.19 *Desmodium rotundifolium*

ROUND-LEAF TICK-TREFOIL

Since this is our only prostrate species of *Desmodium* and the only one with round leaflets, it is easily recognized. It is frequent in open oak woods throughout the state.

August

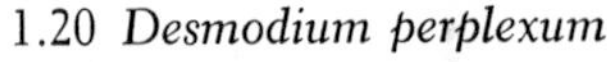

1.20 *Desmodium perplexum*

TICK-TREFOIL, STICKTIGHTS

Like several other species, not illustrated, this is a bushy, much-branched plant 2–4 feet high, with racemes borne in the upper axils. The stem and leaves are hairy, the leaflets are elliptic or ovate, and the stipules are small and lance-shaped. This species is common in old fields and borders of woods and thickets throughout the state.

August–September

One of the most common of other similar species, separated from *D. perplexum* by somewhat technical characters, is *D. canescens*. The narrow-leaf tick-trefoil, *D. paniculatum*, which has petioled leaves with lanceolate or narrowly oblong leaflets, is also common. *D. sessilifolium*, with narrow leaflets but no petioles, is less common.

The Genus *Lespedeza*, the Bush-clovers

The bush-clovers have trifoliate leaves, flowers ¼–⅜ inch long (pinkish purple, creamy yellow, or white), and small one-seeded pods. In addition to 9 native species of *Lespedeza*, several species have been introduced from Asia for forage and for erosion control.

1.21 *Lespedeza intermedia*

BUSH-CLOVER

The stems are stiffly erect, 1–2½ feet tall, the leaflets are elliptic, and the stalks of the flower clusters are shorter than the leaves. Growing in dry open woods, it is fairly frequent in most regions of the state with the probable exception of the Bluegrass.

August

A tall, erect, hairy plant with elliptic leaves and creamy yellow flowers is *L. hirta,* which is frequent in dry open woods.

1.22 *Lespedeza repens*

CREEPING BUSH-CLOVER

We have 2 trailing species which are similar: *L. procumbens* has very hairy stems, and *L. repens* has nearly glabrous stems. Both have leaflets usually ½–⅝ inch long. Both are frequent in dry open woods throughout the state.

August–September

1.23 *Lespedeza cuneata*

SILKY LESPEDEZA

This species is often called *L. sericea,* which is not a valid name. The stem is erect, 2–4 feet tall, wandlike, and very leafy. The wedge-shaped leaves, which are ½–1 inch long, have a short sharp point on the truncate tip and silky hairs beneath. Flowers are axillary, about ⅜ inch long. This native of Asia has been used in soil conservation projects to reduce erosion on difficult slopes and to build up the soil in leached and eroded fields; it has escaped and become naturalized in several localities.

September

1.24 *Lespedeza stipulacea*

KOREAN CLOVER, KOREAN LESPEDEZA

This annual, 6–18 inches high, is extensively planted and frequently escapes. The flowers are subtended by leafy bracts which have bristly margins.

August–September

2.1 *Linaria vulgaris*

BUTTER-AND-EGGS

The yellow-and-orange flowers are 1 inch long with a spur at the base of the lower lip; the throat is closed as in the garden snapdragon. The leaves are pale green and linear, and the stem is 1–2 feet high. This naturalized European may be found along fences, in fields, and on roadsides.
Scrophulariaceae (Figwort family)
June–September

2.2 *Collinsonia canadensis*

HORSE-BALM, CITRONELLA

The horse-balm produces a panicle of yellow lemon-scented flowers, each ½–⅝ inch long with a slightly fringed lower lip and long stamens and pistil. The ovate leaves are 4–6 inches long. It is fairly frequent in rich woods in most sections of the state.
Labiatae (Mint family) August

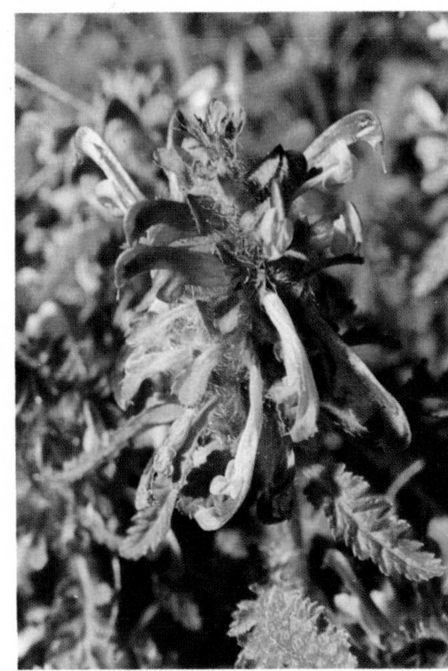

2.3 *Pedicularis canadensis*

WOOD-BETONY

In varying combinations of yellow, reddish, brownish red, and brownish purple, the hooded flowers, ¾–1 inch long, are borne in compact terminal spikes. This hairy plant, 6–15 inches high with pinnately cut leaves, is fairly frequent in woods in most regions of the state with the probable exception of the Inner Bluegrass.

Scrophulariaceae (Figwort family) Late April–May

2.4 *Lobelia cardinalis*

CARDINAL FLOWER

The cardinal flower is probably our most spectacular late summer wildflower, with brilliant red corollas 1½ inches long in a raceme 6–12 inches long on a stem 2–4 feet tall. There are 3 lobes in the lower lip and 2 in the upper; the stamen tube, united around the style as in all lobelias, stands between the 2 upper lobes and extends beyond them. Since the stigma does not mature until the pollen in that flower has been shed, only cross pollination can occur. The cardinal flower is a favorite of hummingbirds and is pollinated by them as the extended stamens and stigma are rubbed by the bird's head when it inserts its long beak deep into the flower. It grows in partial shade at the edge of slow streams and in wet meadows. Though widely distributed in the state, it is not frequent.

Lobeliaceae (Lobelia family) August

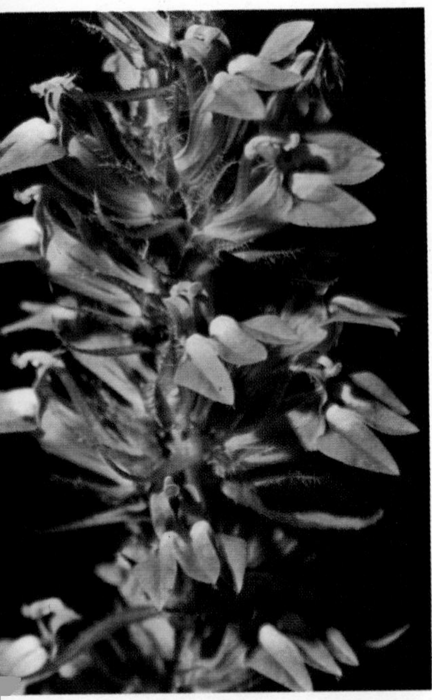

2.5 *Lobelia siphilitica*

GREAT BLUE LOBELIA

This is a robust plant 1½–3 feet tall with large, dense spikes and alternate lanceolate leaves tapering to a sessile base. The flower is about 1 inch long, and the stamen-ring and pistil are included within the corolla tube as in all blue lobelias. In this position pollination is accomplished by bees which light on the lower lip and crawl into the tube, in contrast to the cardinal flower (no. 2.4), which is pollinated by hummingbirds. The great lobelia grows especially on streamsides and is frequent throughout the state.

Lobeliaceae (Lobelia family)

August–September

2.6 *Lobelia puberula*

DOWNY LOBELIA

The plant is 1–3 feet tall and finely downy; the leaves are oblong, and the flowers, about ¾ inch long, are in somewhat open, often one-sided, spikes. This species is widespread in a variety of wet and dry habitats throughout the state and is fairly frequent.

Lobeliaceae (Lobelia family)

August–September

2.7 *Lobelia spicata*

PALE SPIKED LOBELIA

This lobelia, 1–2 feet tall, has a slender spike of pale blue or white flowers, 3/8–1/2 inch long, and sessile, oblong or lanceolate leaves. It is frequent on oak-wooded hillsides and red cedar slopes in the Knobs and Mississippian Plateau but is infrequent elsewhere.

Lobeliaceae (Lobelia family)

June

2.8 *Lobelia inflata*

INDIAN TOBACCO

The "inflated" capsules account for the species ephithet; the common name results from the tradition that Indians smoked and chewed the dried leaves. As in all lobelias, the plant contains a narcotic poison. It grows 1–2 feet high and is usually branched. The flowers are pale blue, 3/8 inch long. It is frequent in open woods, thickets, and old fields in all sections of Kentucky.

Lobeliaceae (Lobelia family)

July–August

2.9 *Synandra hispidula*

SYNANDRA

The white flowers, about 1¼ inches long, are borne in the axils of sessile bracts in a terminal spike; they have a concave upper lip and a 3-lobed lower lip, which is marked with purple on the inside. The leaves are thin, broadly ovate, heart-shaped, and long-petioled. The plant, 1–2 feet high, grows in the deep humus of rich moist woods. It is scattered in several regions of the state but is most frequent in central and northern Kentucky.

Labiatae (Mint family) May

2.10 *Chelone glabra*

TURTLEHEAD

Large white flowers, 1–1¼ inches long, are borne in spikes on a stem 18–30 inches high. The thick 2-lipped corolla, having the lips barely separated, suggests a turtle's head with a just-open mouth. The leaves are opposite, lanceolate, and toothed. It grows in wet ground, such as streamsides, swamps, and springy places, and is more frequent in the eastern half of the state than the western.

Scrophulariaceae (Figwort family) August–September

2.11 *Monarda fistulosa*
BERGAMOT

The spicy-aromatic bergamots, of the genus *Monarda*, have slender 2-lipped corollas about 1 inch long densely aggregated in terminal clusters subtended by conspicuous bracts. In this species the corolla is pale lavender; the leaves are ovate and petioled. In one variety the stem and lower leaf-surfaces have long hairs, and in another they are velvety. This species is common in old fields, thickets, and borders throughout the state.

Labiatae (Mint family) July

2.12 *Monarda russeliana*
WHITE BERGAMOT

In this species the corolla is white, dotted with purple; the leaves are lance-shaped, glabrous, and sessile or nearly so. In Kentucky it is known to occur only in the eastern Knobs, where it is fairly frequent in oak and mesophytic woods.

Labiatae (Mint family)

Late May–June

Other species of *Monarda* with whitish flowers are as follows: *M. bradburiana*, which grows in western Kentucky, differs from the species illustrated in having ovate toothed leaves which are hairy beneath. The leaves of *M. clinopodia* are ovate and have petioles ½–1¼ inches long. This species, flowering in June and July, is fairly frequent in woods throughout the state.

2.13 *Penstemon digitalis*

FOXGLOVE BEARD-TONGUE

All species of beard-tongue have 4 fertile stamens plus a large, fuzzy, sterile one which is the source of the common name; the genus name also refers to the odd fifth stamen.

This species is smooth, lustrous, and 3–4 feet tall. The white corolla, about 1 inch long and sometimes marked with purple inside, is abruptly dilated from a smaller tubular base into a wide-open throat. It grows in open woods, borders, and grassy areas; though scattered over the state, it is only fairly frequent.
Scrophulariaceae (Figwort family)

June

2.14 *Penstemon tenuiflorus*

SLENDER-FLOWERED BEARD-TONGUE

In the slender white flowers of this beard-tongue the lower lip arches up in the middle, touching the upper lip and thereby closing the throat. The plant is 15–30 inches high. It is frequent in cedar barrens and dry open woods in calcareous areas of western Kentucky.
Scrophulariaceae (Figwort family)

May

2.15 *Penstemon hirsutus*

HAIRY BEARD-TONGUE

This beard-tongue is more like the slender-flowered species (no. 2.14) than any other of the 9 species of *Penstemon* in Kentucky; these two are the only ones with the lower lip forming a "palate" which closes the throat. The flowers of *P. hirsutus,* however, are violet on the outside instead of white. Growing on sunny rocky, especially limestone, slopes, it is common in the Bluegrass and fairly frequent in other areas from the eastern Knobs westward across the state.

Scrophulariaceae (Figwort family)

May

2.16 *Penstemon brevisepalus*

SHORT-SEPAL BEARD-TONGUE

This species is very similar to *P. canescens,* the gray beard-tongue, from which it differs not only in having shorter and less pointed sepals but also in having the corolla less abruptly dilated from the tubular base. Both have a pale pinkish purple corolla in which the lower lip projects much farther than the upper, both have the bearded sterile stamen characteristic of all species of beard-tongue, and both are 15–30 inches tall. They grow especially in woodland borders and are distributed throughout the state. *P. canescens* is frequent, and *P. brevisepalus* is fairly frequent.

Scrophulariaceae (Figwort family)

May–June

2.17 *Collinsia verna*

BLUE-EYED MARY

The bright blue and white flowers, about ½ inch long, are borne in whorls from the upper nodes of weak stems 6–18 inches tall. The middle lobe of the lower lip, concealed beneath the other 2 lobes, is folded lengthwise and encloses the stamens. Leaves are opposite, ovate, and chiefly sessile. This spectacular little annual is fairly frequent and locally plentiful on rich, open wooded slopes in the Inner Bluegrass; there are isolated occurrences in other regions from central Kentucky westward.

Scrophulariaceae (Figwort family) May

2.18 *Meehania cordata*

MEEHANIA

The handsome blue flowers, 1–1¼ inches long, are borne in 1-sided, leafy spikes. The plant is trailing with erect flowering stems 4–8 inches high and heart-shaped petioled leaves. It grows in damp ground in rich woods (such as lower ravine slopes), where it sometimes forms large patches. It is frequent in eastern Kentucky but rare in other sections.

Labiatae (Mint family) May

2.19 *Mimulus ringens*

MONKEY-FLOWER

In this species flowers on long stalks are borne in the axils of opposite sessile leaves. The 2-lipped corolla, usually pale violet but sometimes pinkish or nearly white, is 1–1¼ inches long, and the "mouth" is closed. The 4-angled stem is 1–3 feet tall. This monkey-flower is fairly frequent on margins of ponds and streams and in swamps in the eastern two-thirds of the state.

Scrophulariaceae (Figwort family)

July–August

Another species of monkey-flower, *M. alatus,* has petioled leaves, flowers on short stalks, and winged margins on the angles of the stem. Growing in the same type of habitat as no. 2.19, it is, however, frequent throughout the state.

2.20 *Physostegia virginiana*

FALSE DRAGONHEAD

A spike of pinkish violet flowers, each about 1 inch long, terminates the 4-angled stem, which is 1–3 feet tall. The leaves are lance-shaped, sharply toothed, and opposite. This species, also called "obedient plant," is found in open woods and thickets, principally in eastern, south-central, and southern Kentucky, but is infrequent.

Labiatae (Mint family)

August–September

The Genus *Scutellaria*, the Skullcaps

The unusual calyx is the principal distinguishing feature of these attractive blue flowers. It is 2-lipped, as well as the corolla, and the upper lip bears a protuberance on the top which makes the whole calyx suggest a Roman soldier's helmet, a resemblance most pronounced in the flower buds and the developing fruit. The upper lip of the corolla is strongly arched over the 4 stamens. These plants are not aromatic as are most other members of the mint family. Kentucky has 10 species of *Scutellaria.*

2.21 *Scutellaria integrifolia*

LARGE-FLOWERED SKULLCAP

The flowers are about 1 inch long, the stem is 1–2 feet high, and the leaves are lanceolate, untoothed, and tapering to a sessile base. This beautiful species is infrequent in fields, woods, and thickets in eastern and southern Kentucky.
Labiatae (Mint family) June

2.22 *Scutellaria lateriflora*

MAD-DOG SKULLCAP

The stems are 1–2½ feet high, and the flowers are about ¼ inch long in numerous axillary racemes. This species is frequent on stream and pond borders and in alluvial bottomlands throughout the state.
Labiatae (Mint family) August

2.23 *Scutellaria incana*

DOWNY SKULLCAP

This species, 2–3 feet tall, is finely whitish-velvety, especially in the upper parts of the plant. The leaves are ovate and petioled. A colony of these plants with their full panicles of flowers, each ¾–⅞ inch long, makes a handsome display. They are fairly frequent in open woods, borders, and thickets, usually in moist ground, in most regions of the state.

Labiatae (Mint family) July

S. ovata, the heart-leaved skullcap, is similar, with a varying degree of hairiness, but is not whitish-velvety, and has somewhat heart-shaped leaves. Flowering in June and July, it is fairly frequent in woods throughout the state.

S. elliptica, the hairy skullcap, has elliptic leaves and is hairy throughout. It is 1–2 feet tall, usually unbranched, with a small terminal panicle of flowers each 2/3 inch long. Flowering in June, it is frequent in dry woods and borders throughout Kentucky.

2.24 *Scutellaria nervosa*

VEINY SKULLCAP

The slender stem is 6–18 inches tall and the axillary flowers are about 1/3 inch long. The leaves are distantly round-toothed, thin, and veiny; those subtending the flowers are progressively reduced in size. This skullcap is frequent in open woods from the eastern Knobs westward through the state.

Labiatae (Mint family) May

S. parvula, the small skullcap, 3–12 inches high, has smaller, thicker, less toothed, and less veiny leaves, and those subtending the flowers are not much smaller than the lower leaves. It has the same range as *S. nervosa* but is infrequent.

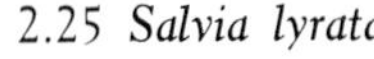

2.25 *Salvia lyrata*

LYRE-LEAVED SAGE

Blue flowers, borne in whorls in an interrupted spike, are about 1 inch long with the upper lip much smaller than the lower. The stem, 12–20 inches high, rises from a basal rosette of irregularly pinnately lobed leaves. The lyre-leaved sage is common in woodland borders, meadows, and parks throughout the state.

Labiatae (Mint family) May

2.26 *Blephilia ciliata*

DOWNY WOOD-MINT

Flowers in the wood-mints are whorled in short thick spikes, with each whorl subtended by a circle of ovate, acute bracts. The corolla, ½ inch long, has an erect upper lip and a spreading 3-lobed lower lip.

In this species, which is 1–1½ feet high, the flower is usually pale blue with purple spots; stem leaves are downy beneath and nearly sessile, and those on runners, which often form a considerable mat, are broadly oval and petioled. It is frequent in dry open woods and thickets, principally on limestone, from the eastern Knobs westward, and is most frequent in central Kentucky.

Labiatae (Mint family) June

The hairy wood-mint, *B. hirsuta,* is 1½–3 feet tall and hairy throughout. Its stem leaves are petioled and its flowers are whitish with purple spots. It is widely scattered but infrequent

2.27 *Prunella vulgaris*

HEAL-ALL, SELF-HEAL

Flowers and bracts are crowded in dense headlike spikes. The bracts are broadly ovate, abruptly pointed, and ⅔ inch long. Each flower, ½–⅝ inch long and usually purple, has a hoodlike upper lip. The stem is 6–18 inches tall and the petioled leaves are lanceolate or elliptic. Growing principally in old fields in moist ground, it is common throughout the state.

Labiatae (Mint family) July–August

2.28 *Cunila origanoides*

DITTANY

Wiry stems 1–1½ feet high, widely spreading branches, opposite ovate leaves 1–1½ inches long, small purple flowers clustered terminally and in the leaf axils, and 2 long stamens and the pistil protruding from the corolla—these characterize the dittany. It is frequent in dry oak woods in noncalcareous areas throughout the state but is apparently absent from the limestone regions.

Labiatae (Mint family) August

2.29 *Hedeoma pulegioides*

AMERICAN PENNYROYAL

This very pungently aromatic little annual, 4–16 inches high, sometimes called "pennyrile," has given its name to a major part of the Mississippian Plateau, popularly called "the Pennyroyal." The pale violet flowers, only ⅛–¼ inch long and scarcely surpassing the calyx, are in clusters in the leaf axils. The elliptic leaves are ½–1 inch long. It is common in dry fields throughout the state.
Labiatae (Mint family)
August–September

2.30 *Lamium amplexicaule*

HENBIT

The leaves are rounded with scalloped margins, the lower ones petioled and the upper sessile. Slender reddish purple flowers, ½–¾ inch long, are in the upper axils. This little European annual, which is 3–12 inches high, is established as a common weed in gardens, in fields, and on roadsides throughout the state.
Labiatae (Mint family)
March–April

L. purpureum, the purple dead-nettle, has all leaves petioled; the upper leaves, often purplish, overlap. Flowers in a leafy spike are paler than those of *L. amplexicaule.* It is also a common annual weed.

2.31 *Glechoma hederacea*

GROUND-IVY

The ground-ivy is a creeping plant with flowering stems 4–10 inches tall. The blue-violet flowers, whorled in the axils of round leaves, are ½–¾ inch long. Though ground-ivy is a problem in lawn or garden, it makes an attractive ground cover, especially the large-flowered variety, in damp thickets. Naturalized from Europe, it is common throughout the state.
Labiatae (Mint family)
April–May

2.32 *Stachys riddellii*

RIDDELL'S HEDGE-NETTLE

Flowers in the hedge-nettles are pale pinkish purple with a 3-lobed lower lip and an upper lip somewhat arched over the 4 stamens. This species is 1½–3 feet tall and hairy. Its flowers, ⅜ inch long, are whorled in a slightly interrupted spike; the leaves are heart-shaped at the base, petioled, and ovate. It grows in woods and, though widely scattered in the state, is not frequent. *S. clingmanii* is a similar, infrequent species.

Labiatae (Mint family) July

2.33 *Stachys tenuifolia*

NARROW-LEAVED HEDGE-NETTLE

This species differs from no. 2.32 in being glabrous and in having chiefly lanceolate leaves and a much interrupted spike. It is fairly frequent in moist wooded bottomlands, especially in the Knobs and in central and western Kentucky.

Labiatae (Mint family) July

2.34 *Nepeta cataria*

CATNIP

Catnip, a strongly aromatic plant, is much branched, 2–3 feet high, and whitish-downy throughout. The leaves are triangular and coarsely toothed; the flowers, ½ inch long, are whitish with purple spots. It is a common weed naturalized from Europe.
Labiatae (Mint family)
July–August

2.35 *Agastache nepetoides*

GIANT HYSSOP

This branching plant 3–5 feet tall bears dense erect spikes resembling candles in a candelabrum. The flowers are pale yellow or creamy, and the leaves are ovate, coarsely toothed, and petioled. It is found in thickets and woodland borders, chiefly in limestone areas, and is most frequent from northern through central Kentucky southwestward.
Labiatae (Mint family) August

2.36 *Pycnanthemum pycnanthemoides*

HOARY MOUNTAIN-MINT

The clusters of very small flowers, whitish and purple-dotted, are made conspicuous by the whitened upper leaves. This pleasingly aromatic plant is 1–3 feet tall and has ovate, toothed leaves. It is frequent in woodland borders and meadows in most regions of the state.
Labiatae (Mint family) July–August

P. incanum, also called hoary mountain-mint, is very similar and not easily distinguished from *P. pycnanthemoides.*

2.37 *Pycnanthemum flexuosum*

SLENDER MOUNTAIN-MINT

This species, which also has a pungent odor, is 1½–2½ feet high and full of linear leaves and short axillary branches. The heads of small flowers are numerous in a compact inflorescence. It grows in grassy meadows, most commonly in noncalcareous clay soils, and occurs in all regions of the state except apparently the Inner Bluegrass.
Labiatae (Mint family) July–August

2.38 *Justicia americana*

WATER-WILLOW

Slender willow-like leaves plus an aquatic habitat suggest the common name for this plant which is 1½–3 feet tall. The flowers are in headlike clusters on long stalks from the axils of the upper leaves. The corolla, which is about ½ inch long, pale violet or white with purple spots, has a 3-lobed lower lip and an undivided or notched upper lip; there are only 2 stamens. The water-willow is common in shallow water of slow streams throughout the state.

Acanthaceae (Acanthus family)

July–August

2.39 *Phryma leptostachya*

LOPSEED

Slender pale lavender flowers, ¼–⅜ inch long, are opposite in a slender spike, and the developing fruits bend down against the stem. The stem is 1–3 feet tall, usually unbranched but branched in large specimens; the leaves are ovate, toothed, and opposite. It is frequent in mesophytic woods and borders throughout the state.

Phrymaceae (Lopseed family)

July

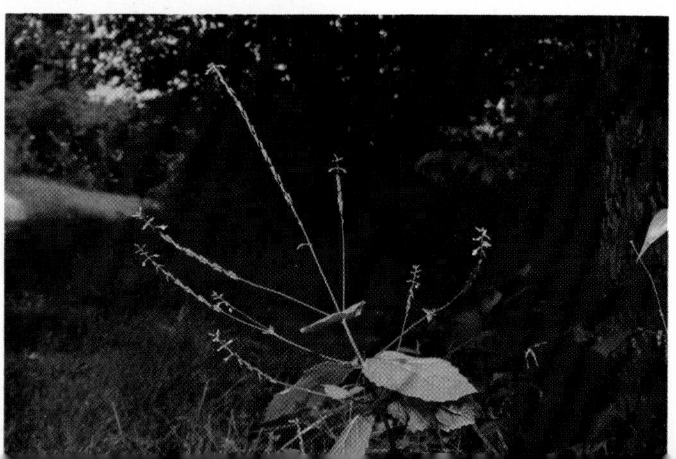

3.1 *Cassia marilandica*

WILD SENNA

Clusters of yellow flowers are borne in the axils of pinnate leaves. The 5 separate petals, each about ½ inch long, are only slightly unequal; the pod is flat, with segments wider than long. The plant, 3–5 feet tall, is fairly frequent in fields and along roadsides in most regions of the state.

Leguminosae (Legume family)
July-August

A similar but less frequent species of wild senna is *C. hebecarpa,* in which the segments of the pods are longer than wide.

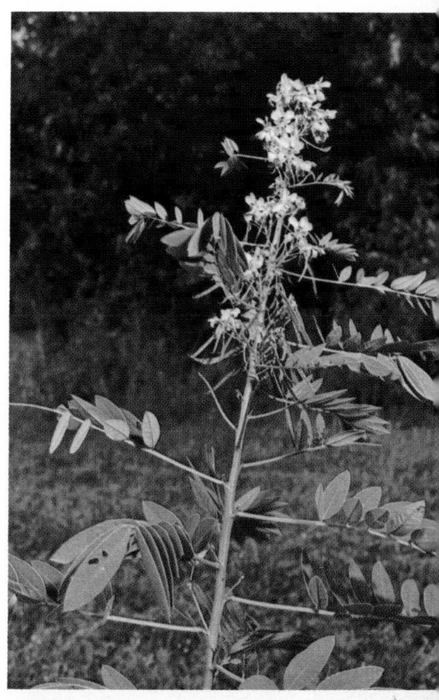

3.2 *Cassia fasciculata*

PARTRIDGE-PEA

An annual 1–2 feet high, the partridge-pea has flowers in small axillary clusters and pinnate leaves with linear-oblong leaflets slightly sensitive to touch. The petals, ½–¾ inch long, are nearly equal but the stamens are very unequal. It grows in dry soil at the edge of woods and in old fields; it occurs in most regions of the state but in varying frequency: from common in the Knobs and Mississippian Plateau to rare in the Bluegrass.

Leguminosae (Legume family) July

The small-flowered sensitive plant, *C. nictitans,* only 6–15 inches high, with smaller leaflets and flowers ¼ inch long, is more sensitive to touch. It is widely distributed over the state in noncalcareous soil in old fields and on open slopes.

The Genus *Impatiens*, the Jewelweeds

Since the seed capsules break open when touched, these annual plants are also called touch-me-nots.

The leaves have a delicate texture, and the stems are juicy and nearly translucent. The juice is effective in preventing and alleviating irritation from poison ivy. The biggest part of the flower, which dangles on a slender stalk, consists of 1 large saclike sepal with a "tail" at one end. There are 2 other small sepals and 3 petals, 2 of which are 2-lobed.

Both species are frequent in moist shady soil, especially along streams, throughout the state.

Balsaminaceae (Touch-me-not family) July–August

3.3 *Impatiens capensis*

SPOTTED JEWELWEED

The spotted jewelweed has flowers ¾–1¼ inches long and stems 2–5 feet tall.

3.4 *Impatiens pallida*

PALE JEWELWEED

The pale jewelweed has flowers 1–1½ inches long and stems 3–6 feet tall.

The Genus *Aureolaria*, the False Foxgloves

Kentucky has 7 species of *Aureolaria.* All have yellow flowers over 1 inch long with a bell-shaped corolla tube and 5 corolla lobes, only slightly oblique. They grow in oak woods where they are semiparasitic on the roots of oak trees.

3.5 *Aureolaria virginica*

FALSE FOXGLOVE

In this species the flowers are about 1½ inches long. The stems are hairy; the lower leaves have one or two pairs of lobes though the upper leaves are unlobed. It is frequent from the eastern Knobs to west-central and southern Kentucky.

Scrophulariaceae (Figwort family)

July

A. *laevigata,* in which the stems are glabrous and the leaves unlobed, is frequent in the Cumberland Plateau and the eastern Knobs. A. *flava,* 3–6 feet tall, which has glabrous gray-green stems and deeply pinnately lobed leaves, is widely scattered but most frequent in the western half of the state.

3.6 *Aureolaria pedicularia*

FERNLEAF FALSE FOXGLOVE

The leaves are cleft to the midrib and have toothed segments. The corolla is 1–1½ inches long on a stalk ¾–1 inch long. This much-branched annual grows in dry upland woods in southeastern, southern, and southwestern Kentucky but is infrequent.

Scrophulariaceae (Figwort family) August

A similar species, also found in southern Kentucky, is A. *pectinata,* 1–2 feet high, with more sharply cut leaves and with flower stalks less than ½ inch long.

3.7 *Dasistoma macrophylla*

MULLEIN FOXGLOVE

This is a large much-branched plant 3–5 feet tall. The lower leaves are 6–12 inches long and deeply pinnately lobed; the upper leaves, with flowers in their axils, are lance-elliptic and greatly reduced in size. The flowers, ½–¾ inch long, have 5 corolla lobes and are woolly inside the corolla tube. The mullein foxglove is frequent in open woods and thickets in northern, south-central, and western Kentucky, and is most frequent in the Outer and Inner Bluegrass regions.
Scrophulariaceae (Figwort family)

July

3.8 *Verbascum blattaria*

MOTH MULLEIN

The white or yellow flowers, about 1 inch across and borne in a raceme, are almost radially symmetrical, but a slight difference between the 3 lower and 2 upper corolla lobes places it in this series. The buds are button-like, and in the open flower the stamens with purple hairs and a bent-down style suggest the antennae and proboscis of a moth. This foreign weed, smooth and 1–3 feet high, is common on roadsides and in waste places.
Scrophulariaceae (Figwort family)

June–July

The woolly or common mullein, *V. thapsus*, 3–6 feet high, which has gray-woolly stem and leaves and a dense spike of yellow flowers, is a very common weed.

3.9 *Triosteum angustifolium*

YELLOW HORSE-GENTIAN

In all horse-gentians the flowers are in the axils of opposite leaves, and the corolla flares into 5 nearly equal lobes. The corolla and long slender calyx lobes are attached above the ovary, which develops into an orange-red fruit topped by the persistent calyx.

In this species the flowers are pale yellow, about ½ inch long, the lance-elliptic leaves taper at both ends, and the stem is bristly-hairy, 1–2 feet high. It is fairly frequent in rocky woods and is widely scattered in the state.

Caprifoliaceae (Honeysuckle family) Flowers: May
Fruit: July

3.10 *Triosteum aurantiacum*

HORSE-GENTIAN

This species, which grows 2–3 feet high, has leaves abruptly narrowed into a winged, sessile, slightly clasping base, and purplish red flowers about ¾ inch long. The plant, more or less hairy, grows in dry woods; it is frequent in the Bluegrass and infrequent elsewhere.

Caprifoliaceae (Honeysuckle family)
Flowers: May
Fruit: July

T. perfoliatum, also with purplish red flowers, has its pairs of leaves joined together at the base. It is found in south-central Kentucky but is infrequent.

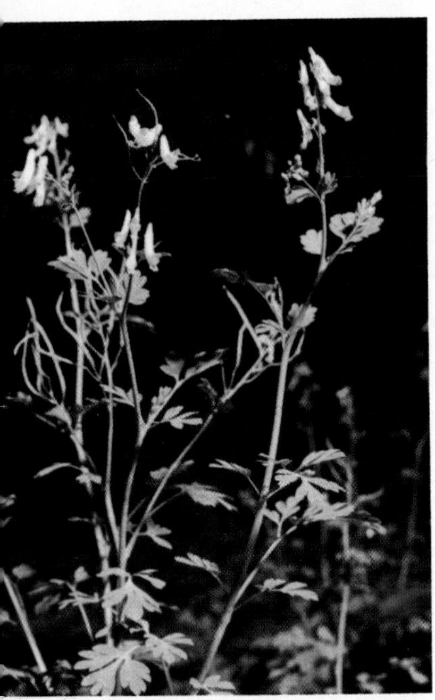

3.11 *Corydalis sempervirens*

PINK CORYDALIS

In *Corydalis* the flowers have 4 petals, 2 much longer than the others and 1 of the larger pair with a saclike spur at the base. The bluish gray-green leaves are compound and much divided.

This species has flowers ½–¾ inch long, pink with yellow tips, and a stem 12–30 inches high. In Kentucky it is restricted to the southeastern section and is locally plentiful on sandstone on Pine Mountain.

Fumariaceae (Fumitory family)

May

3.12 *Corydalis flavula*

YELLOW CORYDALIS

Flower structure and leaf form are as described under the preceding species. This corydalis has pale yellow flowers ¼–⅝ inch long in short racemes on a stem 6–12 inches tall. It grows in thickets and woodland borders in most regions of the state but is most frequent in central and northern Kentucky.

Fumariaceae (Fumitory family)

April

3.13 *Dicentra cucullaria*

DUTCHMAN'S-BREECHES

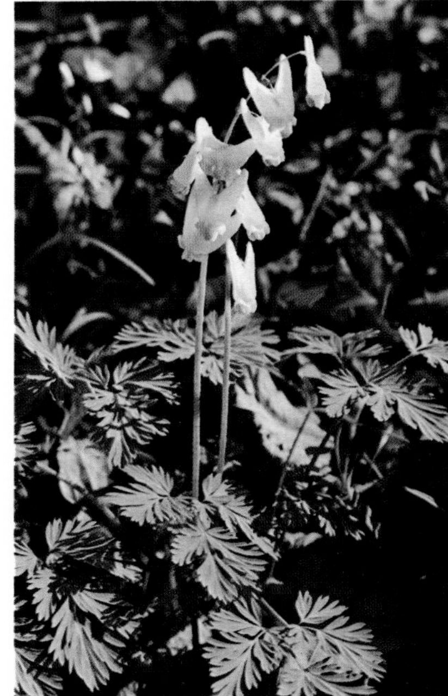

Pendent 2-spurred flowers in a 1-sided raceme suggest a Dutch boy's pantaloons hanging "ankles up" on a line. The flowers, ½–¾ inch long, have 2 scale-like sepals and 4 petals, 2 of which are prolonged into spurs at the base. Leaves of this species can scarcely be distinguished from those of the next species. Growing in deep humus in rich mesophytic woods on well-drained slopes, both may be found in any region of the state and may be locally plentiful, but such habitats are becoming too few.

Fumariaceae (Fumitory family)

Early April

3.14 *Dicentra canadensis*

SQUIRREL-CORN

The flowers differ from those of the Dutchman's-breeches in being heart-shaped, having short spurs that are not divergent, and in being fragrant.

As in the Dutchman's breeches, the leaves are all basal, gray-green, and finely cut. Both species, delicate fragile plants 6–10 inches tall having the same habitat requirements, are among the most attractive wildflowers of early spring. The squirrel-corn is less frequent than the Dutchman's-breeches.

Fumariaceae (Fumitory family)

April

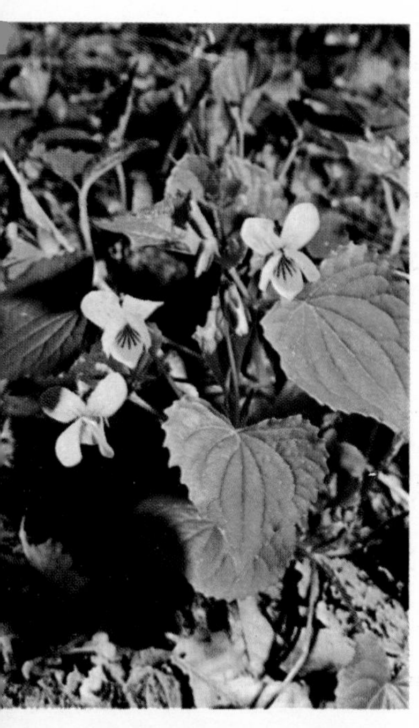

3.15 *Viola pensylvanica*

SMOOTH YELLOW VIOLET

Our most frequent and widely distributed species of yellow violet has a smooth, upright leafy stem 4–12 inches high, and 1–3 basal leaves. It grows in mesophytic woods throughout the state.

Violaceae (Violet family) April

A similar species, *V. pubescens*, the downy yellow violet, lacks basal leaves (or occasionally may have 1), and the upper stem and young leaves are hairy. It is also widely distributed but is less frequent.

The roundleaf yellow violet, *V. rotundifolia*, has all leaves basal, lacking a stem above ground, and it flowers before the leaves are fully developed. It grows in sandy acid soil in woods of eastern, especially southeastern, Kentucky but is not frequent.

3.16 *Viola hastata*

HALBERD-LEAVED YELLOW VIOLET

This species, with an erect stem 4–10 inches high, has long-triangular leaves which usually show an interesting pattern of light and dark. The yellow petals are often slightly purplish on the outside. It grows on moist wooded slopes, often under hemlocks, in eastern and southeastern Kentucky but is not frequent.

Violaceae (Violet family) April

3.17 *Viola blanda*

SWEET WHITE VIOLET

This is a delicate little plant 2–4 inches high having all leaves basal and lacking a leafy stem. The fragrant flowers are only about ½ inch long. The dark green, satiny leaves are heart-shaped with a very narrow space between the lobes, which sometimes even overlap. The sweet white violet is frequent in moist, shaded acid soils, especially in cool ravines, in eastern and southern Kentucky.
Violaceae (Violet family) April-May

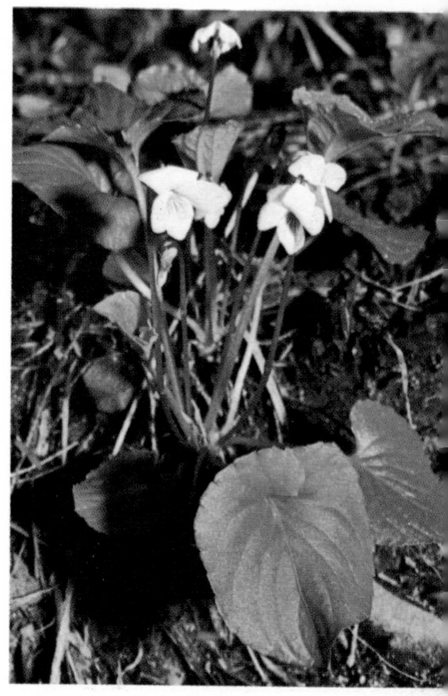

3.18 *Viola primulifolia*

SWAMP WHITE VIOLET

The principal leaves of this species are ovate-oblong, rounded or truncate at the base or tapering into the petiole; only the earliest leaves are heart-shaped; all leaves are basal. The plant, 3–8 inches high, grows in flat, wet, poorly drained ground in the Cumberland Plateau and the eastern and southern Knobs; in such situations it is frequent.
Violaceae (Violet family) April-May

The lance-leaved violet, V. *lanceolata,* with narrow leaves, is a closely related but less frequent species growing in the same type of habitat.

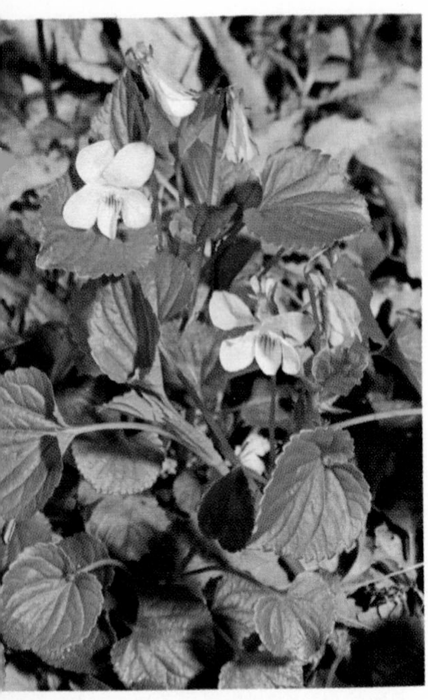

3.19 *Viola striata*

WHITE VIOLET

In this species the flowers are bright white and especially conspicuous. The stem is upright, leafy, and 6–12 inches high. The stipules are small, with toothed margins. This species is common and widespread in low woods and thickets, especially along stream banks, and in alluvial soil where it sometimes grows in profusion.
Violaceae (Violet family) April-May

3.20 *Viola canadensis*

CANADA VIOLET

The Canada violet has a leafy stem 10–18 inches tall. The whitish flowers have a tinge of purple on the back side of the upper petals, and the small stipules have straight, uncut margins. It grows in the deep humus of mesophytic woods in the eastern two-thirds of the state and is most frequent in the Cumberland Plateau and Cumberland Mountains.
Violaceae (Violet family) April-May

3.21 *Viola rafinesquii*

FIELD PANSY

This perky little annual, 3–8 inches high, sometimes called Johnny-jump-up, belongs to the pansy section of the genus *Viola*. All pansies are characterized by erect leafy stems and very large stipules usually more conspicuous than the leaf blades. In this species the blades are spatulate and the stipules are cut into narrow segments. The jaunty flowers are whitish or pale blue, ½–⅝ inch long. It is common in fields, meadows, and woodland borders throughout the state.
Violaceae (Violet family) April

3.22 *Viola rostrata*

LONG-SPURRED VIOLET

The distinguishing mark of this species is a slender spur about ½ inch long, much longer than that of any other violet. The pale blue flowers with dark purple lines are borne on leafy stems which are 4–8 inches high. It grows in mesophytic woods and is frequent in eastern and southern Kentucky.
Violaceae (Violet family) April-May

A similar but infrequent species, the dog violet (V. *conspersa*), has spurs less than ⅜ inch long.

3.23 *Viola papilionacea*

COMMON BLUE VIOLET

Our most common violet, also called meadow violet, grows in large tufts, often forming extensive colonies. Attached to a thick underground stem, the long-petioled heart-shaped leaves are somewhat coarse and veiny in comparison with other violets. Occasionally the flowers are pale lilac. Throughout the state it is abundant in meadows, on roadsides, in thickets, and near dwellings; it is a serious problem when it invades a lawn.
Violaceae (Violet family) April

3.24 *Viola cucullata*

MARSH BLUE VIOLET

This lovely slender violet stands high above its leaves (6–10 inches tall) and is our last species to flower. It is widely scattered in the state and is fairly frequent near springs and seepage areas and in wet meadows.
Violaceae (Violet family) May

3.25 *Viola sororia*

WOOLLY BLUE VIOLET

Densely soft-hairy, this species has broadly heart-shaped leaves. It is frequent in dry open woods on slopes in most sections of the state and infrequent in mesophytic situations.

Violaceae (Violet family) April

In *V. hirsutula* the upper surface of leaves is hairy; otherwise the plant is glabrous. The veins are purple and the leaf is often mottled.

3.26 *Viola triloba*

THREE-LOBED VIOLET

Although the earliest leaves are glabrous, unlobed, and rounded, the later principal leaves are soft-hairy and 3-lobed, with a variable amount and depth of cutting in the lobes. (When it sometimes appears to be 5-lobed, a careful examination will show that it has a basically 3-lobed pattern with the 2 lateral lobes further divided.) This purple-flowered species is frequent in dry open woods in most regions of the state.

Violaceae (Violet family) April

V. palmata has all leaves (including the earliest) truly palmate with 5–11 lobes. *V. palmata* is less frequent and requires rich mesophytic woods.

3.27 *Viola sagittata*

ARROW-LEAVED VIOLET

This species differs from other purple-flowered, so-called "stemless" violets in having oblong-lanceolate leaves lobed or incised at the base. It is usually found in wet meadows or woods in flat lowlands, but sometimes occurs in dry upland woods; it is frequent in the Knobs and fairly frequent in eastern, southern, and western Kentucky.

Violaceae (Violet family)

April

3.28 *Viola pedata*

BIRDFOOT VIOLET

The leaves cleft into narrow segments suggest a bird's foot. Although the plant is rarely over 6 inches high, the flowers are larger than most violets, often 1–1¼ inches across. One variety has flowers uniformly colored and one variety has the 2 upper petals seemingly made of dark purple velvet. This beautiful species is fairly frequent and locally plentiful in dry open pine or oak woods, especially on slopes, in most regions of the state except the Bluegrass.

Violaceae (Violet family) April

Note: There are 9 other species of blue or purple violets in Kentucky. They are either less frequent than those included here or are distinguished by somewhat technical characters. Hybridization between different species sometimes occurs.

3.29 *Delphinium tricorne*

DWARF LARKSPUR

Beautiful though poisonous to cattle, the larkspurs have calyx and corolla colored alike. There are 5 sepals, one of which is prolonged into a spur; this species has 4 petals, 2 of which extend into the calyx-spur.

The dwarf larkspur, 8–18 inches high, has purple, lavender, or white flowers about 1 inch long and leaves cleft into many segments. Most common in calcareous areas, it grows nevertheless throughout the state in woods and thickets, both dry and moist, and transforms many a woodland into a flower garden.

Ranunculaceae (Buttercup family)

April

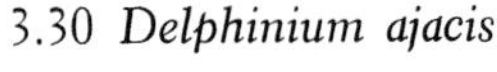

3.30 *Delphinium ajacis*

ROCKET LARKSPUR

This annual species is 1–3 feet tall and has finely cut leaves. The flowers may be purple, pink, or white. Instead of 4 petals, as in the dwarf larkspur, this species has only 2 and these are united. Introduced from Europe, it has escaped from gardens into sunny rocky fields and other open places.

Ranunculaceae (Buttercup family)

June

3.31 *Echium vulgare*

BLUEWEED

Sometimes called viper's bugloss, this plant, 1–2½ feet tall, has its stem and slender leaves covered with bristly hairs. The inflorescence presents an interesting color combination, with freshly opened flowers bright blue, stamens reddish, old flowers purple, and buds pink. Each flower is ½–¾ inch long. Found in sunny rocky fields, pastures, and other open places, this native of Europe is locally plentiful, especially in a few northern and central Kentucky counties, but is not widespread. Biennial.

Boraginaceae (Borage family) June–July

3.32 *Trichostema dichotomum*

BLUE CURLS

A flower of the blue curls has 4 long bluish, curled stamens; the blue corolla, ¼–⅜ inch long, has 4 lobes ascending and 1 lobe deflexed. The opposite leaves have smooth margins. This much-branched annual, 6–24 inches high, grows in woodland borders, clearings, and meadows, and, though widely scattered in the state, is infrequent.

Labiatae (Mint family)

August–September

3.33 *Teucrium canadense*

GERMANDER, WOOD-SAGE

The stamens extend through a cleft in the upper part of the corolla and the 5 corolla lobes spread beneath. The pale purplish pink flowers, ½–¾ inch long, are in a crowded spike terminating an unbranched stem 1–3 feet high, which bears opposite leaves. Growing in thickets, meadows, and fencerows in somewhat moist ground, it is found in most regions of the state and is usually common.

Labiatae (Mint family) July

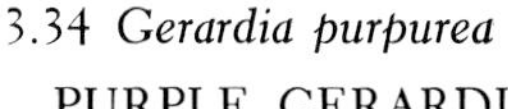

3.34 *Gerardia purpurea*

PURPLE GERARDIA

The pinkish purple flowers about 1 inch long are nearly radially symmetrical with only slightly unequal lobes. Lasting but a day, they are borne in the axils of the upper leaves. The leaves are linear and the slender stem, 1–3 feet tall, is usually branched. This annual, which is semi-parasitic on grass roots, grows in wet ground such as pond margins, ditches, and wet meadows in acid soil. Though scattered in various sections of the state, it is not frequent.

Scrophulariaceae (Figwort family) September–October

G. tenuifolia, the slender gerardia, has flowers ½ inch or less on little axillary stalks ½ inch or more long. It grows principally in the western half of the state.

3.35 *Veronica persica*

BIRD'S-EYE

The bright blue flowers, 3/8–1/2 inch across with 4 unequal lobes, are borne on slender stalks in the axils of bracts which are alternate although the leaves are opposite. This little annual, 4–8 inches high, was introduced from Asia and has escaped to roadsides, lawns, and other open places, but is not frequent.
Scrophulariaceae (Figwort family)
April–May

3.36 *Veronica officinalis*

COMMON SPEEDWELL

The creeping stems, 4–10 inches long and ascending at the tips, form a dense mat. The opposite, elliptical leaves are toothed, thick, and hairy, and the erect spikes have pale blue flowers not over 1/4 inch long with 4 unequal lobes. The common speedwell is found on dry banks in open woods and woodland borders and in old fields; it is frequent in the Knobs and infrequent in eastern and southern Kentucky.
Scrophulariaceae (Figwort family)
May

Several small annual European speedwells with tiny flowers are troublesome weeds in lawns.

3.37 *Veronicastrum virginicum*

CULVER'S-ROOT

Standing 3–6 feet high with whorled, sharply toothed leaves, the culver's-root bears several long, dense spikes of white or pale purplish flowers. The corolla is tubular, about ⅜ inch long with lobes almost radially symmetrical, and the stamens and style extend far out. The culver's-root grows in woods and openings, usually in moist ground, and, though infrequent, is widely scattered in all regions of the state.

Scrophulariaceae (Figwort family)

August

3.38 *Polygala senega*

SENECA SNAKEROOT

Our species of *Polygala* have minute flowers, the structure of which can be observed only with magnification. Two sepals, larger than the other 3 and colored like the petals, are called "wings." The 3 petals, 1 of which is keel-shaped, are united with each other and with the stamen-tube.

The Seneca snakeroot has clustered unbranched stems 10–18 inches tall, each bearing a white spike ¾–1½ inches long and lance-elliptic alternate leaves. It is frequent in woods on limestone slopes in the Bluegrass and infrequent elsewhere.

Polygalaceae (Milkwort family)

June

3.39 *Polygala sanguinea*

FIELD MILKWORT

The rose-purple flowers overlap in a dense headlike inflorescence which is about ½ inch thick. (Flower structure in *Polygala* is described in no. 3.38.) The leaves are linear and the stem grows 6–12 inches high. This species is frequent in moist, acid, infertile meadows in the Knobs and in eastern, southern, and western Kentucky.

Polygalaceae (Milkwort family) July

3.40 *Petalostemum purpureum*

PURPLE PRAIRIE-CLOVER

Thick dense spikes 1–2 inches long bear rose-purple flowers. The corolla consists of a single petal called the standard, and besides 5 fertile stamens there are 4 sterile ones resembling small petals. The leaves are pinnate, usually with 5 linear leaflets, and the stem is 1–3 feet tall. This prairie species reaches the eastern limit of its range in the western half of Kentucky, where it is infrequent.

Leguminosae (Legume family) July

The white prairie-clover, *P. candidum*, also occurs infrequently in the same area of the state.

Series Six: **Dicotyledons (3), Composites**

In the Composite family, that which may at first glance seem to be a flower is actually an inflorescence or cluster, of the type botanists call a *head.* Such a head is composed of many minute flowers inserted on the expanded end of a flowering stem, called a *receptacle,* which is surrounded by a compact arrangement of many small bracts collectively called the *involucre.*

In these heads 2 basic flower-types are possible: radially symmetrical, with a tubular corolla and 5 tiny lobes or teeth at the apex, and bilaterally symmetrical, in which the corolla is strap-shaped or tongue-shaped. Both types may occur in the same head, as in the familiar daisy. In such a head hundreds of radially symmetrical tubular flowers form the disk and are therefore called *disk flowers;* these are surrounded by a circle of radiating strap-shaped flowers which accordingly are called *ray flowers.* Other composite heads, such as the thistles, have all flowers of the tubular, disk type. Still others—for example, the common dandelion—have all flowers of the strap-shaped, ray type.

Two other features of composite flower structure, significant in classification and identification, should be explained. The calyx, which is so much modified that it is given the special name *pappus,* may consist of hairs, spiny teeth, or scales, or may be absent. From the ovary of the flower with its single ovule a small, dry, 1-seeded fruit called an *achene* develops; the pappus remains attached to the top of the achene.

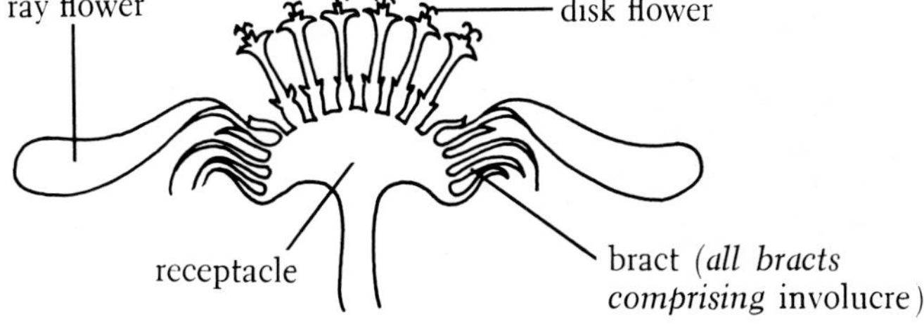

Section through a composite head

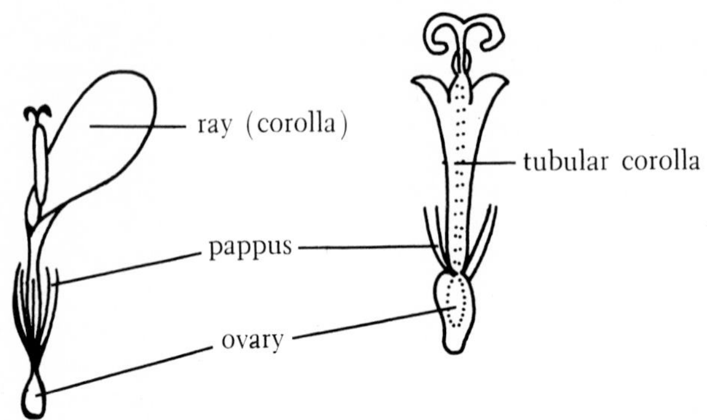

Individual composite flowers

ARRANGEMENT OF PLATES

Group 1. Heads composed of tubular flowers only; rays absent

- Flowers white, greenish white, or grayish white 1.1–1.7
- Flowers pinkish, purple, rose-purple, or blue 1.8–1.17

Group 2. Heads composed of strap-shaped flowers only; disk absent 2.1–2.5

Group 3. Heads composed of both disk flowers and ray flowers

- Rays yellow; disk yellow or brown
  - Goldenrods, having minute heads clustered in compound inflorescences 3.1–3.11
  - Heads ½–3½ inches across, in sequence as follows:
    - Heads 1 inch or less 3.12–3.14
    - Heads 1–2½ inches 3.15–3.24
    - Heads 2–3½ inches 3.25–3.35
- Rays white, pink, violet, or purple; disk yellow, purplish, or rusty 3.36–3.54

1.1 *Antennaria solitaria*

PUSSY-TOES

Kentucky has 6 species of *Antennaria,* all known as "pussy-toes." All have basal rosettes of leaves, lower leaf-surfaces and runners covered with soft, white, silky down, involucral bracts usually white and papery, and pappus of soft hairlike bristles; stems are usually 4–12 inches high; all grow in dry, open, rocky woods. This is the only species with a solitary head. *A. solitaria* and *A. plantaginifolia,* which has several heads on a stem and broader basal leaves, are the most frequent and widespread species in the state.

Late March–early April

1.2 *Gnaphalium obtusifolium*

EVERLASTING, CUDWEED, CATFOOT

The numerous fragrant heads with white papery involucre are "everlasting" when dry. Stems and lower leaf-surfaces are usually white-felty; leaves are 1–2 inches long and wavy; plants are 1–3 feet tall, much branched above the base, and biennial. The everlasting is common in old fields, pastures, and open woods throughout the state.

September–October

A smaller, less branched, less white species is the purple cudweed, *G. purpureum,* which is also common.

1.3 *Cacalia atriplicifolia*

PALE INDIAN-PLANTAIN

The pale Indian-plantain is more noticeable for its stature and its paleness than for any feature of the few-flowered heads. It grows 5–7 feet tall, with a broad, flat-topped inflorescence of greenish white heads; stems and lower leaf-surfaces are somewhat whitened. Lower leaves are 4–6 inches broad, broader than long, with large teeth; upper leaves are much smaller, and longer than broad. This species is frequent in open woodland throughout Kentucky.

July–August

1.4 *Eupatorium rugosum*

WHITE SNAKEROOT

The fluffy snow-white flowerheads in a flat-topped inflorescence make the white snakeroot an attractive plant of autumn. Each head is about ¼ inch long; leaves are opposite, long-petioled, ovate, and sharply toothed. The foliage is poisonous to sheep and cattle, and to man through milk. The plant grows 2–4 feet tall, and is common in woods, thickets, and woodland borders in rich moist ground throughout the state.

September

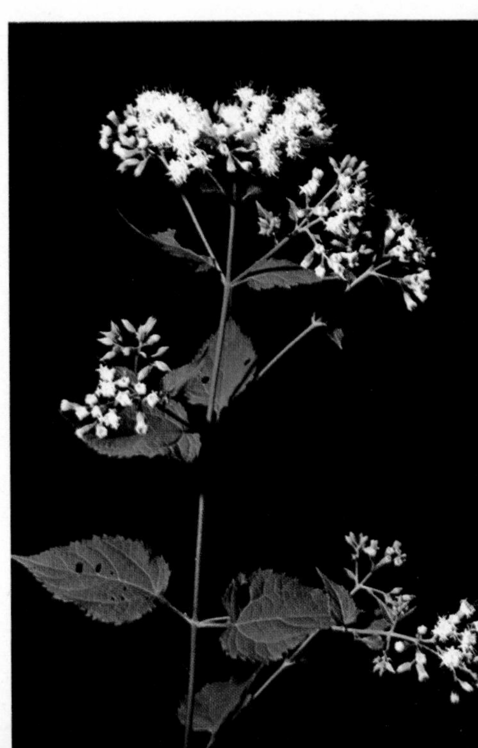

1.5 *Eupatorium serotinum*

LATE THOROUGHWORT

This species, 4–6 feet tall, is more weedy and aggressive than the other species of *Eupatorium* shown. Branches of the upper stem are gray-green and flowers are grayish white; leaves are opposite, lanceolate, coarsely toothed, and long-petioled. It is common in borders of woods, clearings, and old fields throughout the state.

September

1.6 *Eupatorium perfoliatum*

BONESET

This coarse-looking plant, 3–5 feet tall, warrants attention because of its perfoliate leaves and because of a tonic our forefathers made from the dried leaves. Leaves are dull green and wrinkled; flower-heads are drab white. It is frequent in sunny wet ground throughout the state.

August

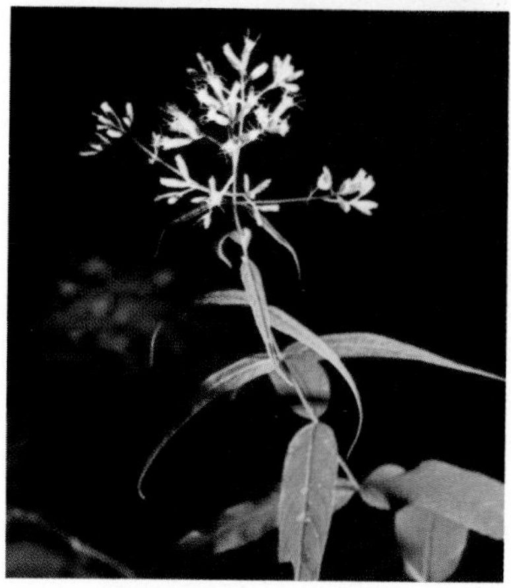

1.7 *Eupatorium sessilifolium*

UPLAND BONESET

Leaves are thin, bright green, sessile, lanceolate, rounded at the base, and long-pointed at the tip. Flowers are white. Standing 2–4 feet tall, this boneset grows in open woods in all sections of the state but is infrequent.

August–September

Kentucky has 10 other species of white-flowered *Eupatorium*, some fairly frequent and widespread, others more restricted in range and habitat.

1.8 *Eupatorium coelestinum*

MISTFLOWER

The flowers are blue or blue-violet, the heads in dense, flattish clusters. This beautiful native species, 1–3 feet high, is sometimes cultivated and is often called "hardy ageratum" because of its resemblance to the cultivated *Ageratum*, a smaller introduced annual. The mistflower is common in wet meadows, alluvial flats, and borders of woods and thickets in low ground throughout the state.

Late August–October

E. incarnatum is a small species with lilac or purplish pink flowers in heads that are somewhat sparse on scattered branches. The stem is slender, weak, and sometimes straggling, 1–4 feet long. It grows in moist thickets, ditches, and woodland borders in calcareous soil. In Kentucky it is frequent only in the Bluegrass, but also grows in the Mississippian Plateau. It flowers in September and October.

1.9 *Eupatorium fistulosum*

JOE-PYE WEED

The Joe-Pye weed is a stately plant 5–10 feet high, aptly called also "queen-of-the-meadow," with a dome-shaped inflorescence of many slender purplish pink heads. The stem of this species is purple and hollow, and the leaves, with blunt teeth, are usually in whorls of 4–6. This plant is frequent in meadows and other sunny moist areas throughout the state.

August–September

A shorter Joe-Pye weed, *E. purpureum*, is also frequent in Kentucky. It has a green solid stem, sharply toothed leaves in whorls of 3 or 4, and very pale pinkish flowers. It grows in open woods.

1.10 *Liatris spicata*

BLAZING STAR, GAYFEATHER

Heads of feathery rose-purple flowers are arranged in a spike terminating an unbranched wandlike stem 2–5 feet tall, which bears numerous narrow, rigid leaves. The top heads bloom first, contrary to the usual pattern in a spike. The involucre is purple-tinged, slender, and considerably longer than broad. This beautiful plant grows at the base of wooded slopes and in other slightly moist and partially sunny areas in eastern and western Kentucky, but is infrequent.

July–August

1.11 *Liatris squarrosa*

BLAZING STAR, GAYFEATHER

Heads are few, stalked, many-flowered, and as broad as long. Involucral bracts have stiff, abruptly spreading tips; leaves are narrow and firm. This species of *Liatris,* growing 1–2 feet tall, is fairly frequent in dry open woods and clearings, on clay banks, and on red cedar slopes in scattered sections of the state.

July–August

Kentucky has 3 other species of *Liatris,* including 2 rare ones and *L. scariosa,* which is fairly frequent. The latter is a tall species with broad, many-flowered, stalked heads with bracts not turning out at the tips. It has wider leaves than the 2 species shown.

1.12 *Vernonia altissima*

IRONWEED

Ironweed is an erect plant 4–7 feet tall with heads of deep red-purple flowers in a flat-topped inflorescence. Leaves are alternate, sessile, and sharply toothed. It grows along roadsides, in old fields, and especially in pastures, where livestock avoid it. Although there are 4 species of ironweed in Kentucky, this is the only one common and widespread.

August–September

V. *missurica,* a prairie species, is found only in the Jackson Purchase region but is frequent there. V. *fasciculata,* another prairie species, ranges as far east as central Kentucky but is rare. V. *noveboracensis* grows in moist places in southern Kentucky.

1.13 *Carduus nutans*

NODDING THISTLE, MUSK THISTLE

Heads are large (1½–2½ inches across), solitary, long-stalked, and nodding; outer involucral bracts have rigid, spreading, spiny tips. Stems are stout, 2–4 feet tall, and prickly-winged; lobes of leaves are also prickly-pointed. This troublesome biennial European weed is found principally in waste ground but has spread into farmland, where it has become common.

June

1.14 *Cirsium vulgare*

COMMON THISTLE, BULL THISTLE

This aggressive weed from Europe has more spiny armor than any of our native thistles. Prickly-pointed wings run down the stem from the bases of the prickly leaves, and all the involucral bracts have rigid prickles. The leaves also have stiff hairs and may be gray-woolly beneath. Heads are 1¼–2 inches across. A biennial growing 3–5 feet tall, it is a common, widely established pest in fields, pastures, roadsides, and waste places.

August–September

Several other European weedy thistles are spreading in Kentucky. These are species of *Cirsium*, *Carduus*, and *Onopordum*.

1.15 *Cirsium discolor*

FIELD THISTLE

This native thistle has no wings on the stem. The leaves are densely white-woolly beneath, lobed nearly to the midrib, and prickly; the involucral prickles are weak and are confined to the outer bracts; the heads are 1¼–2 inches across. This biennial plant grows 3–7 feet tall. It is common throughout the state at the edge of woods, in thickets, fields, and pastures, and along roadsides, especially in rich moist ground. Though troublesome in farmland, it is not as pernicious as the foreign species of thistles.

August–September

C. altissimum, the tall thistle, is a native species growing up to 10 feet tall. Its leaves, white-woolly beneath, as in *C. discolor*, are merely toothed or shallowly lobed.

1.16 *Cirsium muticum*

SWAMP THISTLE

Though the flower-heads of most thistles are beautiful, many persons fail to see beauty in obnoxious weeds. The native swamp thistle, however, combines beauty with no bad habits. Involucral bracts, which make an interesting, checkered pattern, are glutinous and without prickles; heads are approximately 1½ inches across. Leaves are somewhat thin, deeply lobed, pale and cobwebby beneath; leaf prickles are few, weak, and harmless. The stem, soft and hollow, is branched and 3–6 feet tall. This species, a biennial, grows in moist or wet ground in open woods and at the edge of woods. In Kentucky it is known from only a few localities in the Cumberland Plateau.

June–September

1.17 *Centaurea maculosa*

STAR THISTLE, KNAPWEED

The stem is slender, wiry, bushy-branched, and 1–3½ feet high; the leaves are divided into narrow segments. The flower-heads are about 1 inch across; the involucre is ½ inch high and the involucral bracts have dark triangular tips which are fringed. This European biennial, which has no prickles, is found on roadsides, in pastures, and in waste places, and has become locally abundant in scattered parts of the state.

June–August

2.1 *Cichorium intybus*

CHICORY

The lovely blue of chicory by the roadside adds beauty to a morning drive, but by noon on a sunny day the flowers have withered and the blue is gone. Flower-heads, 1–1½ inches across, appear stalkless on a stiff, furrowed stem; leaves are chiefly basal. The chicory root is sometimes ground and mixed with coffee. This European weed is common along roadsides throughout most of the state, less common in waste places.

June–September

2.2 *Taraxacum officinale*

DANDELION

Bright golden flower-heads make the dandelion showy, a deep taproot makes it hard to eradicate, and the fluffy ball of achenes, each with a parachute-like pappus, entices a small child to blow and help the wind disseminate more dandelion plants. All these features, plus its use as edible greens, contribute to the dandelion's being probably the best known European weed in the United States. It is common in lawns and on roadsides.

April–May

2.3 *Krigia biflora*

DWARF DANDELION, CYNTHIA

This native plant is bluish green and completely smooth. Its flower-stalks are few, each bearing a solitary orange-yellow head about 1½ inches across. Stem-leaves are few and clasping; principal leaves are basal. This so-called dwarf dandelion (1–2 feet high and hardly a dwarf) is found especially in open woods on slopes and at the edge of woods; it is frequent in most sections of the state, though apparently absent from the Inner Bluegrass.

May

Kentucky has 2 other species of dwarf dandelion: *K. dandelion* and *K. virginica*, both of which have basal rosettes of leaves and leafless flower-stalks.

2.4 *Hieracium venosum*

HAWKWEED, RATTLESNAKE-WEED

Any *Hieracium* can be called hawkweed. This species, sometimes called rattlesnake-weed, has leaves chiefly basal and a branched inflorescence of several small heads, each ½ inch across. It can be distinguished from other hawkweeds by the reddish purple veins in the leaves. Growing 1–2 feet high, it is frequent in dry open oak and oak-pine woods in the hilly sections of the state, especially the Knobs and the Cumberland Plateau.

June

Some of the half-dozen species of hawkweed in Kentucky have more leaves on the stem, but all bear several or numerous small heads in a branched inflorescence.

2.5 *Prenanthes altissima*

RATTLESNAKE-ROOT,
TALL WHITE LETTUCE

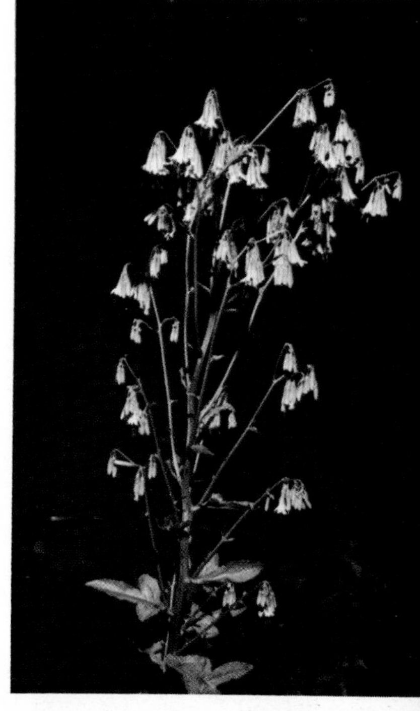

The flower-heads when open resemble little bells hanging in loose clusters from the branches of the inflorescence, which stands 4–6 feet tall. The flowers are greenish white or cream-colored, only 5 or 6 per head in this species, and the pappus of copious, soft, capillary bristles is also creamy. The leaves are highly variable in shape, from deeply lobed to undivided, often triangular or arrow-shaped; the lower leaves are long-petioled, with a blade 2-6 inches long; the upper leaves are much smaller and short-petioled. The rattlesnake-root is frequent in oak woods on hillsides and uplands in most sections of the state.

August–September

Our 5 other species of *Prenanthes* have more than 6 flowers per head, and, with one exception, are smaller plants.

The Genus *Solidago*, the Goldenrods (Numbers 3.1–3.11)

Unfortunately the goldenrods have been accused of causing much hay fever. Goldenrod pollen is heavy, sticky, and not produced in great quantity, and is transported by insects, not by wind; a person sensitive to goldenrod pollen would therefore have to be close to the plant in order to experience an allergic reaction. Most of the hay fever ascribed to goldenrod is caused by ragweed, which flowers inconspicuously at the same time, producing tremendous quantities of light pollen borne far and wide by the wind.

Goldenrods have minute heads clustered in large compound inflorescences of various shapes. Some species of these beautiful and unduly maligned plants spread a cloth of gold over old fields in the autumn while others, growing in lesser abundance in woodlands, contribute bright spots on the forest floor. Although a species of goldenrod can easily be recognized as such, it is not always easy to distinguish some species from others with certainty, for they are separated on technical characters which are not readily evident. Augmenting the problem, species often hybridize.

Kentucky has 31 species of goldenrods; obviously not all can be included here. The ones selected are grouped according to the shape and branching of the inflorescence, and within each of these categories the most common (or the most outstanding for some other reason) are pictured; others frequent in the state are described in a general way.

Numbers 3.1–3.2, and others described under them, have a full and somewhat plume-like inflorescence, with heads borne only on the upper side of the branches of the inflorescence.

In numbers 3.3–3.5 the inflorescence has only a few divergent branches, with heads on only 1 side.

Numbers 3.6–3.10 have heads spirally arranged, not 1-sided. Of these, numbers 3.6–3.8 have prominent axillary as well as terminal clusters; numbers 3.9–3.10 have terminal, erect panicles.

Number 3.11 is flat-topped.

3.1 *Solidago altissima*

TALL GOLDENROD

The "tall goldenrod," 3–6 feet high but not our tallest species, is both our most abundant species and one of the most showy and graceful. The panicle is large and pyramidal with recurved branches. The stem is gray-downy, especially on the upper part; the leaves, rough above and finely downy beneath, have 3 main veins and a few blunt marginal teeth toward the apex. In all parts of the state this species is abundant in fencerows and old fields.

September

3.2 *Solidago juncea*

EARLY GOLDENROD

Flowering in midsummer, this species, which grows 2–4 feet high, has basal tufts of large toothed leaves 7–14 inches long, which taper into margined petioles. Both stem and leaves are smooth and without hairs. Widespread in the state, it is fairly frequent in open woods and woodland borders.

July–August

The group of goldenrods bearing heads only on the upper side of the branches of a plume-like inflorescence, as illustrated by the 2 preceding species, contains not only the largest number of species but also the species most difficult to identify with certainty. Some of the others are as follows:

S. gigantea, the great goldenrod, sometimes called late goldenrod though no later than most species, is 3–7 feet tall with stems smooth, purplish, and glaucous (except in the inflorescence). Leaves, with 3 main veins, are sharply toothed, especially toward the tip; hairs are either absent or confined to the veins of the lower surface. It is fairly frequent in moist ground in thickets and woodland borders. (August–September)

S. canadensis, the Canada goldenrod, is closely related to *S. altissima* (no. 3.1) but differs from it in appearing more leafy (leaves numerous and crowded, narrowly lance-shaped, and sharply toothed) and in having smaller heads (involucres measuring only about 1/10 inch or 2–2.5 mm. high as contrasted with ⅛–¼ inch or 3–5 mm. in *S. altissima*). The stem, 2–5 feet tall, is minutely downy on the upper part and without hairs on the lower part; the leaves show 3 main veins. It is fairly frequent in fields and on roadsides and dry slopes. (September)

S. nemoralis, the gray goldenrod, has gray-downy stems 1–3 feet tall. The lowest leaves are broadest and toothed near the apex and tapered at the base, and have 1 main vein; the upper leaves are progressively smaller. It is common in poor soil of old fields and dry slopes at the edge of woodland; it is found in all sections of the state except the Inner Bluegrass. (August–September)

S. odora, the sweet goldenrod, has narrow leaves which are anise-scented when crushed. It is found in sandy soil.

S. arguta and *S. bootii* both have strongly toothed, broadly oval basal leaves, pointed at the apex and tapering at the base, with 1 main vein; upper leaves are smaller. They may have widely divergent branches of the panicle, suggesting the next group. They grow in open woods.

3.3 *Solidago ulmifolia*

ELM-LEAVED GOLDENROD

The inflorescence consists of slender, elongate, recurved leafy branches; there may be either a single one with some small secondary branches or a few widely spreading ones. Leaves are elliptic, the principal ones coarsely toothed and tapering to a margined petiole, the upper ones sessile and without teeth. The stem, without hairs except in the inflorescence, is 1½–4 feet tall. This goldenrod is frequent in dry open woods throughout the state.

August–September

3.4 *Solidago rugosa* var. *celtidifolia*

ROUGH GOLDENROD

The variety pictured has greatly prolonged, distant, and divergent branches. Both this and var. *aspera* are very rough and harsh; their leaves are thick and appear wrinkled and veiny. (Other varieties have thinner leaves that are less rough and wrinkled.) All varieties of *S. rugosa* in Kentucky are tall (2–6 feet) and hairy; upper leaves are toothed, lanceolate to oval, numerous and crowded; lower leaves are deciduous before flowering time. The species as a whole is fairly frequent in low, wet ground in meadows, thickets, and woodland borders.

September

3.5 *Solidago sphacelata*

FALSE GOLDENROD

The presence of basal tufts of large, broadly heart-shaped, petioled leaves, 3–5 inches long and more numerous than the flowering stems, sets this species apart from other goldenrods. The inflorescence has few widely spreading branches. It grows especially on open-wooded limestone cliffs; hence it is frequent in the Inner Bluegrass region and the Mississippian Plateau and infrequent on other rock in other sections.

September

3.6 *Solidago caesia*

WREATH GOLDENROD, BLUE-STEMMED GOLDENROD

The stem is slender, flexible, and glaucous, 1–3 feet high and gracefully arching. Small clusters of heads are borne in the axils of lance-shaped leaves. This is a very frequent species in woods throughout the state.

September–October

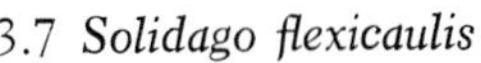

3.7 *Solidago flexicaulis*

BROAD-LEAF GOLDENROD, ZIGZAG GOLDENROD

Leaves are broadly elliptic and pointed at both ends; the stem is zigzag, 1–3 feet tall. Clusters of heads are terminal and in the upper axils. This species is frequent in mesophytic woods in eastern and central Kentucky, less frequent in western Kentucky.

September

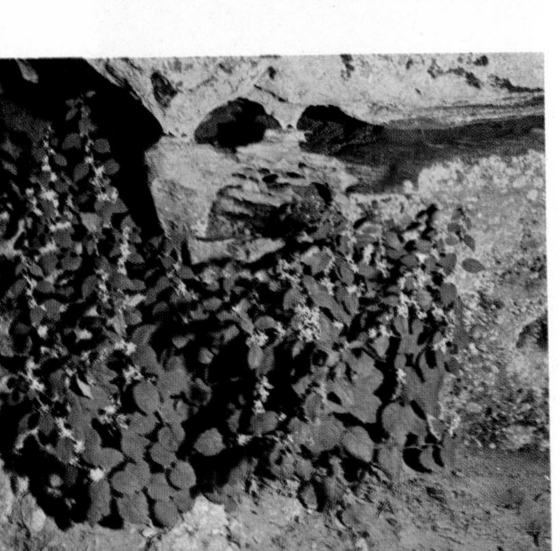

3.8 *Solidago albopilosa*

WHITE-HAIRED GOLDENROD, ROCKHOUSE GOLDENROD

This species is covered with long, white, soft hairs and is only 8–24 inches high. It is an endemic species which grows in dense shade under overhanging sandstone-conglomerate cliffs in the Cumberland Plateau. It is urgent that it be protected.

September

3.9 *Solidago erecta*

ERECT GOLDENROD, SLENDER GOLDENROD

This is an example of a group of goldenrods having a compact, erect arrangement of clusters of flower-heads.

In this species, which is 1–3 feet tall, smooth, and essentially without hairs, the inflorescence is usually narrow, but in robust individuals it may be branched. It is frequent in dry open oak and oak-pine woods in most sections of the state except the Bluegrass region.

September

S. hispida, the hairy goldenrod, resembles the species above except for being hairy. *S. bicolor*, the white goldenrod, resembles the hairy goldenrod except for having white flowers. These species have the same habitat as the erect goldenrod but are less frequent.

3.10 *Solidago speciosa*

SHOWY GOLDENROD

This tall and stout species (2–6 feet high) suggests an oversize version of the erect goldenrod (no. 3.9). The inflorescence is a broad, dense, and stiff panicle; leaves are firm, the basal ones 4–10 inches long. It grows on open-wooded slopes in eastern Kentucky but is infrequent.

September

3.11 *Solidago graminifolia*

GRASS-LEAVED GOLDENROD

This species, also called fragrant goldenrod, is easily distinguished from all others by its flat-topped inflorescence. The plant stands 2–4 feet tall; its leaves are narrowly lance-shaped. It is widely distributed in the state and is common in low ground.

August–September

3.12 *Senecio aureus*

GOLDEN RAGWORT

All species of *Senecio* may be called ragwort, groundsel, or squaw-weed. All have small yellow-rayed heads in flat-topped clusters; stem leaves are pinnately cleft and smaller than the stalked basal leaves.

S. aureus, 1–2½ feet tall, has heads about ¾ inch across and heart-shaped basal leaves. It grows in moist ground, including ravines and seepage areas in woods. It is widely distributed in the state and is frequent in all sections except the Bluegrass region.

April–early May

S. obovatus, the round-leaved ragwort, differs in having basal leaves which are rounded and broadest at the apex and which taper at the base into a petiole. It grows in woods and borders, often dry, and flowers in April. It is most frequent in the calcareous soil of the Bluegrass, less frequent in eastern Kentucky, and least frequent in western Kentucky.

S. smallii, Small's ragwort, has linear-oblong basal leaves. Flowering in May, it grows in open woods and clearings, especially in eastern and southern Kentucky and in the Knobs.

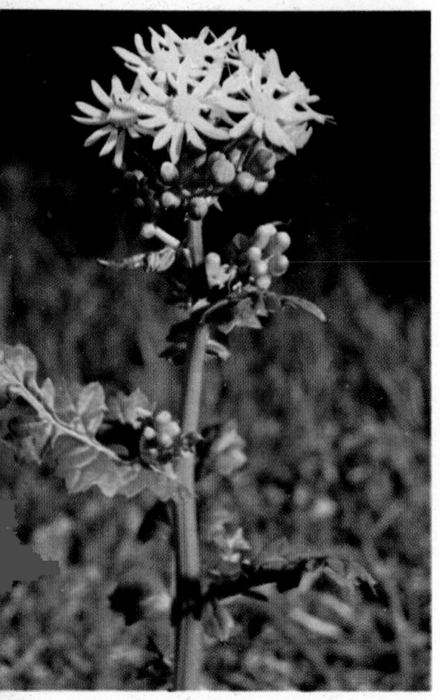

3.13 *Senecio glabellus*

BUTTERWEED

The butterweed has fleshy hollow stems 2–3 feet tall. Heads are about ¾ inch across. Basal leaves are deeply pinnately lobed, with the terminal lobe largest; stem leaves are similar but very much smaller. An annual or biennial, it is common in wet meadows and wet open woods in western Kentucky.

Late April–early May

3.14 *Chrysopsis mariana*

MARYLAND GOLDEN ASTER

This bright golden aster has several heads, each about 1 inch across, terminating the stem, which is about 1–2 feet high. Leaves are alternate, oblong, without teeth on the margin. It is frequent in dry open oak and oak-pine woods in eastern and southern Kentucky.

September

A golden aster with parallel-veined leaves is illustrated in Series Seven, no. 2.7.

3.15 *Bidens cernua*

NODDING BUR-MARIGOLD, STICKTIGHT

The genus name *Bidens* ("two teeth") refers to the pappus, which usually has the form of 2 barbed spines (but occasionally may be rudimentary or lacking in some species); this feature also accounts for the common names "sticktight" and "tickseed." In this genus the outer involucral bracts are green and usually longer than the inner membranous ones.

This annual bur-marigold is distinguished by heads 1–1½ inches across (nodding in age) and opposite lance-shaped leaves meeting around the stem. The plant is 1–3 feet high, much branched or unbranched. It is frequent on pond and stream margins and in marshy ground, especially in northern, central, and eastern Kentucky.

September–October

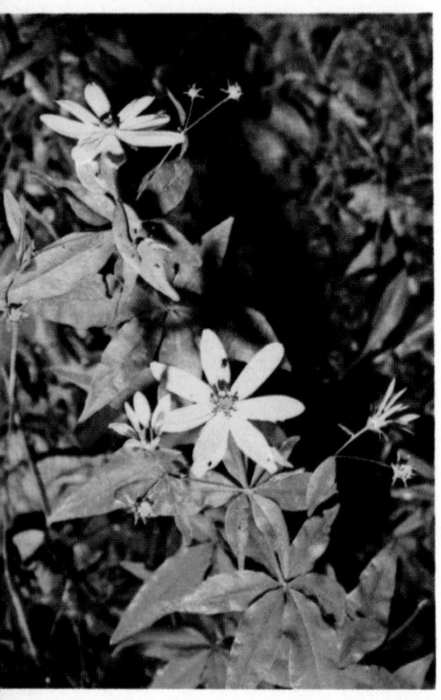

3.16 *Bidens aristosa*

TICKSEED SUNFLOWER

See the discussion of the genus *Bidens* under no. 3.15.

Dense, bushy, 2–4 feet tall, and laden with golden flower-heads, this is a very showy species. Heads usually are 1½–2 inches across, rarely more; leaves are opposite and pinnately compound, having leaflets deeply cut with large teeth. It grows in wet meadows, pond borders, and other sunny wet places; it is a common and widely distributed annual or biennial.

September–October

We have 2 other species of tickseed sunflowers: *B. polylepis*, similar to the preceding species, is separated from it by somewhat technical characters. *B. coronata* differs from both of these in having the segments of the compound leaves lance-linear with few teeth.

Other species of *Bidens* in the state are more weedy and less showy.

3.17 *Coreopsis major*

LARGE COREOPSIS, TICKSEED

A pair of opposite, sessile leaves, each composed of 3 leaflets, make it appear that 6 "leaves" encircle the stem at each node. This feature, together with heads 1–2 inches across on a plant 2–3 feet tall, will easily distinguish this species, which is common in open oak woods in all sections of the state except the Bluegrass region.

Late June–July

A small coreopsis, *C. auriculata*, 8–20 inches high, has heads 1½–1¾ inches across, solitary or few on long stalks. The leaves, which are chiefly basal, have a pair of earlike lobes at the base of the oval blade. It is fairly frequent in woods in the Knobs and the Mississippian Plateau. May

3.18 *Coreopsis tripteris*

TALL COREOPSIS, TICKSEED

The stem of the tall coreopsis, smooth and glaucous, stands 4–9 feet high bearing numerous heads in an openly branched inflorescence. Heads are 1–1½ inches across, with disks brownish when mature. Leaves are opposite, petioled, each with 3 narrow leaflets 2–4 inches long. The species is frequent in thickets, woodland borders, and meadows throughout most of the state but is infrequent in the Bluegrass region.

July–August

3.19 *Helenium autumnale*

AUTUMN SNEEZEWEED, YELLOW-HEADED SNEEZEWEED

The sneezeweeds are not purveyors of hay fever, as the name might indicate, since the heavy sticky pollen cannot be carried by the wind, but the dried powdered leaves inhaled as snuff will cause sneezing. Having a globe-like disk, wedge-shaped lobed rays, and winged stems, they are easily distinguished from other yellow composites flowering in summer and fall.

The autumn sneezeweed is 1–4 feet high; its heads, which have yellow disks, are ¾–1 inch across. It is frequent in moist ground such as stream margins, flood plains, and wet ground in meadows, and is widely distributed over the state.

September–October

3.20 *Helenium nudiflorum*

PURPLE-HEADED SNEEZEWEED

The globe-like purplish brown disk, the wedge-shaped rays, and the winged stems clearly differentiate this plant from the "black-eyed Susans" (nos. 3.24, 3.25). The plant is 18–36 inches high; it is widely distributed and frequent in moist ground in meadows and old fields.

July

3.21 *Actinomeris alternifolia*

WINGSTEM,
YELLOW IRONWEED

This is a coarse plant 3–7 feet tall, with rough leaves, the bases of which continue down as wings on the stem. The heads, which are numerous in an open inflorescence, have a globe-shaped, loosely flowered disk and irregular rays (½–1¼ inches long) which become deflexed. It is common in lowland thickets and borders throughout the state.

August–September

3.22 *Verbesina helianthoides*

SUNFLOWER CROWNBEARD

The specific epithet *helianthoides* means "like *Helianthus*" or "like a sunflower." The crownbeards can be distinguished from true sunflowers by their winged stems; this species can be distinguished from other wingstems and crownbeards by its larger heads (1¼–2½ inches across). It is fairly frequent in openings in dry woods and at the edge of woods from central Kentucky westward.

August

3.23 *Helianthus microcephalus*

SMALL-HEADED SUNFLOWER, SMALL WOOD SUNFLOWER

All other sunflowers have larger heads and are illustrated from no. 3.32 through no. 3.35.

In this species heads about 1¼ inches across with light yellow rays are borne on numerous slender spreading branches of the inflorescence. The stem is slender, smooth, and 3–6 feet tall; leaves are rough, lance-ovate, long-pointed, and usually opposite. The small-headed sunflower is frequent in open woods in all sections of the state.

August–September

3.24 *Rudbeckia triloba*

THIN-LEAVED CONE-FLOWER, BROWN-EYED SUSAN

All species of coneflower have an enlarged, somewhat conical receptacle to which the disk flowers and rays are attached.

This species is a bushy-branched plant 2–4 feet high bearing heads 1¼–2¼ inches across. It has some 3-lobed leaves as well as many undivided leaves. It can be distinguished from other small coneflowers also by the sharp, stiff-pointed chaff extending beyond the disk flowers on the receptacle. It grows in thickets, old fields, and woodland borders but is unevenly distributed: most common in the Bluegrass region and least frequent in eastern Kentucky. It may be annual, biennial, or perennial.

July–August

3.25 *Rudbeckia hirta*

BLACK-EYED SUSAN

Large heads (2–3½ inches across) are borne on long slender stems 1–2½ feet high. Stems and leaves are bristly-hairy. Black-eyed Susans are frequent throughout most of the state in dry open woods, in old fields, and on roadsides, but are infrequent in the Bluegrass region.

July–August

3.26 *Rudbeckia laciniata*

WILD GOLDENGLOW, TALL CONEFLOWER

Growing 4–10 feet high and much branched, the tall coneflower has heads with reflexed rays 1¼–2¼ inches long and a greenish yellow center which elongates with age. Leaves are deeply cut, 3- to 7-lobed, and petioled. It is frequent on creek banks, alluvial ground along rivers, and in other rich moist places throughout the state.

August

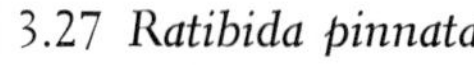

3.27 *Ratibida pinnata*

PRAIRIE CONEFLOWER, GRAY-HEADED CONEFLOWER

The prairie coneflower resembles the preceding species in many ways but is rarely over 3 or 4 feet tall. The plant is hairy, whereas the tall coneflower is without hairs, and its pinnately divided leaves have more slender segments. Its broadly columnar disk is grayish at first, becoming brownish with age, and has an anise-like fragrance when crushed. It is found in grassy areas and on roadsides, especially in calcareous soil, and is fairly frequent except in eastern Kentucky.

July

3.28 *Polymnia uvedalia*

YELLOW LEAF-CUP, BEAR'S FOOT

This is a stout, coarse plant 4–9 feet tall, having large leaves 6–10 inches long with angular lobes and winged petioles. Heads, 1½–3 inches across, are relatively few, in terminal clusters. The involucre is green and cuplike. It is fairly frequent in thickets, openings in woods, and borders of woods in low ground in most sections of the state.

July–August

3.29 *Silphium perfoliatum*

CUP-PLANT, INDIAN CUP

The distinguishing feature of the cup-plant is the manner in which the uppermost pair of leaves join and form a cup in which water collects around the flowering stalks. This is a monstrous herb, often 6–8 feet high, with a stout 4-angled stem and coarsely toothed leaves 6–12 inches long, which join in pairs. Heads are 2–3 inches across. In the Bluegrass region it is frequent on creek banks and in thickets and woodland borders in bottomlands; it is widely scattered and infrequent elsewhere in the state.

July–August

3.30 *Silphium trifoliatum*

WHORLED ROSINWEED

As in all species of *Silphium,* the outer involucral bracts are broad, stiff, and green. The plant is slender, 3–7 feet tall; the stem is smooth, usually glaucous; leaves are petioled and rough, some in whorls of 3 or 4, some opposite or alternate. This species is fairly frequent in dry open woods and woodland borders in most sections of the state.

July–August

A rosinweed of western Kentucky is *S. integrifolium,* which has sessile leaves either opposite or alternate.

Another species, in Kentucky found only in the west, is the compass plant, *S. laciniatum,* a large coarse plant with deeply pinnately cut leaves.

The prairie dock, *S. terebinthinaceum,* which has basal leaves a foot or more long and only reduced leaves on the 3–8 foot flowering stem, occurs in both western and eastern Kentucky.

3.31 *Heliopsis helianthoides*

FALSE SUNFLOWER, OX-EYE

The following features of general appearance should be noted in recognizing this sunflower-like plant: golden yellow heads 1½–2¾ inches across, flowering earlier than most sunflowers; leaves opposite, petioled, toothed, and rough or smooth; stem smooth, 3–5 feet tall. Technically its fertile, seed-producing ray flowers distinguish it from *Helianthus,* the true sunflowers, in which rays are sterile. Widely distributed in the state and especially frequent in the Bluegrass, it grows in woodland borders and thickets in low ground.

July–early August

The Genus *Helianthus*, the Sunflowers

"Sunflower" to many persons means only the large annual, *Helianthus annuus*, which is cultivated and which often escapes to roadsides and waste places. However, Kentucky has 17 species of native perennial sunflowers, plus another introduced and escaped perennial. Five representative species are pictured. (*H. microcephalus*, the small-headed sunflower, is included above as no. 3.23.)

3.32 *Helianthus divaricatus*

WOODLAND SUNFLOWER

Leaves are somewhat stiff, rough, sessile, and opposite, a pair spreading widely apart. Heads average about 2 inches in diameter; the stem is smooth, 2–6 feet tall. This sunflower is frequent in dry open woods throughout the state.

Late July–August

H. hirsutus, the stiff-haired sunflower, is a similar species, equally frequent, differing mainly in having stiff hairs on the stem.

3.33 *Helianthus strumosus*

ROUGH-LEAVED SUNFLOWER

Leaves are thick and firm, very rough on the upper surface (with short stiff hairs having enlarged bases), downy on the lower surface; tapering to a short petiole, they are chiefly opposite (upper ones may be alternate). Heads are 1¾–2¾ inches across; the stem is smooth, often glaucous on the lower part. This species, found in dry open woods, is widely scattered over the state and fairly frequent.

Late July–August

3.34 *Helianthus decapetalus*

THIN-LEAVED SUNFLOWER

Leaves in this species are thin and slightly rough; the principal ones are ovate, abruptly narrowed into winged petioles, and opposite (upper leaves may be alternate). Heads average 2½ inches in diameter. The stem is smooth, 2–5 feet high. It is fairly frequent at the edge of woods and thickets in moist ground.

Late July–August

3.35 *Helianthus tuberosus*

JERUSALEM ARTICHOKE

Not related either to Jerusalem or to the true artichokes, this is our largest indigenous sunflower. It was cultivated by the Indians for its edible tubers, which may still be used as food by man and which always provide valuable food for herbivorous animals.

It has a rough stem 5–10 feet tall, thick leaves as rough as sandpaper (upper ones alternate, lower opposite), and numerous panicled golden heads 2–3½ inches across. It grows in moist soil, especially along streams and bottomlands, and is frequent throughout the state.

Late August–September

Of the remaining species of sunflowers in Kentucky, the one most frequent and most easily recognized is *H. mollis*, the downy sunflower. The entire plant is downy or whitish-hairy; leaves are sessile, the principal ones with a heart-shaped clasping base.

3.36 *Echinacea purpurea*

PURPLE CONEFLOWER

A unique color combination of pinkish purple rays and a rust-colored cone-shaped center, together with considerable size, make a very striking plant. The rays, 1½–2½ inches long, are downswept at maturity. The sharply toothed leaves are 4–7 inches long and the plant stands 3–4½ feet tall. Though the purple coneflower is found infrequently in openings on wooded slopes in the Cumberland and Mississippian plateaus, it is usually plentiful where it is established.

July

Another species of purple coneflower, *E. pallida,* is found in the Mississippian Plateau but is less frequent. Its leaves are without teeth and its rays are usually shorter, less deflexed, and sometimes paler.

3.37 *Chrysanthemum leucanthemum* var. *pinnatifidum*

OX-EYE DAISY, FIELD DAISY

The ox-eye daisy is a European immigrant which has been very successful in establishing itself in abundance throughout the United States. A field full of daisies in flower is beautiful although it may displease a farmer. The flower-heads, 1½–2 inches across, are borne at the end of slender stems 1–2 feet high, which make them adaptable for bouquets. The leaves are lobed with large, blunt teeth. This plant is abundant in fields, meadows, and waste places throughout the state.

June

3.38 *Astranthium integrifolium*

WESTERN DAISY

This is a delicate native daisy, smooth, 6–16 inches high, and not at all weedy. Rays are pale violet, heads are ¾–1¼ inches across, and leaves are spatulate or narrowly elliptic. The western daisy, an annual, grows in the Bluegrass region and the Mississippian Plateau, where it is fairly frequent in moist, usually calcareous soil in sun or partial shade.

Late May–early June

3.39 *Achillea millefolium*

YARROW, MILFOIL

Individual heads of the yarrow are so small that close examination is required to show that the rays are not little petals and that there are very minute disk flowers in the center. The heads are in a flat-topped cluster; leaves are gray-green and finely cut into very narrow segments. This European weed, 1–3 feet high, grows in fields, in waste ground, and on roadsides, and is common in all sections of the state. A rose-colored form is infrequent.

June

The Genus *Erigeron*, the Fleabanes

Fleabanes differ from asters chiefly in the character of the involucral bracts. In the fleabanes they are narrow, of the same length, and in a single circle; in asters they are in several rows, usually overlapping like shingles on a roof.

3.40 *Erigeron pulchellus*

ROBIN'S-PLANTAIN

This species of fleabane has a close cluster of few heads, each ¾–1½ inches across, with pale pink or pale violet rays. Principal leaves are basal, and the plant, 8–20 inches tall, is soft-hairy. It grows on open wooded slopes and is fairly frequent in most sections of the state.

May

3.41 *Erigeron philadelphicus*

PHILADELPHIA FLEABANE

The stem, bearing clasping leaves, is much branched, with heads terminating the branches. The heads are ¾–⅞ inch across, with pale violet or pale pink rays, and the buds are nodding. The plant, 1½–2½ feet tall, is slightly hairy or nearly smooth. It is common in fields and thickets throughout Kentucky.

May

Two large weedy species of fleabane with white rays, which are often called white-top, *E. annuus* and *E. strigosus*, grow abundantly in old fields throughout the state and flower in June and July.

The Genus *Aster* (Numbers 3.42–3.53)

Flowering in September and October, asters contribute much to the autumn beauty of field and forest. They bear panicles or corymbs of flower-heads with blue, violet, purple, or white rays. Involucral bracts are in several overlapping rows, and the pappus is composed of soft hairs.

Numbers 3.42–3.48 have blue, violet, or purple rays. Of these, numbers 3.42–3.44 have lower leaves that are petioled and heart-shaped at the base; numbers 3.44–3.47 have leaves which clasp around the stem. Numbers 3.49–3.53 have white rays.

Altogether, 28 species of *Aster* occur in Kentucky, 19 with predominantly blue or violet rays and 9 with all white rays. It should be noted that many species of blue and violet asters may occasionally produce white-flowered forms. If you do not find the identity of a white aster among the species always white, check those which are predominantly blue or violet.

3.42 *Aster shortii*

SHORT'S ASTER

This aster was discovered on the cliffs of the Kentucky River by Dr. Charles Wilkins Short, Professor of Materia Medica and Medical Botany at Transylvania University, and was named for him in 1834. (The species occurs in most of the eastern United States.)

The flower-heads are violet-blue, ¾–1 inch across, in large open panicles on somewhat arching stems. Leaves are toothless or nearly so; the lower ones are narrowly heart-shaped and slender-petioled. Growing 2–4 feet tall, Short's aster is frequent in dry woods from the eastern Outer Bluegrass region westward through the state, and is scarce in the Cumberland Plateau and eastern Knobs.

Late September–October

3.43 *Aster cordifolius*

HEART-LEAVED ASTER, BLUE WOOD ASTER

This aster, 1½–3 feet tall, has a full panicle of densely arranged blue-violet heads, each ½–¾ inch across. Its principal leaves, which have slender petioles, are heart-shaped at the base and sharply toothed. It grows in woodlands in most sections of the state, but is more frequent in mesophytic than in dry woods and in the eastern two-thirds of the state than in the western part.

October

Other violet-flowered asters which have heart-shaped leaves and which are fairly frequent in Kentucky are as follows:

A. *lowrieanus,* Lowrie's aster, which has leaves with winged petioles, is smooth and glaucous, even feeling almost greasy. It is 2–3 feet high and the heads are ¾–1 inch across. It is found in open woods and borders of woods in October.

A. *sagittifolius,* the arrow-leaf aster, has lower leaves narrowly ovate or arrow-shaped with winged petioles and blunt teeth. The plant is strictly erect and 2–4 feet tall, with a steeple-shaped panicle of pale blue-violet heads ½–¾ inch across. It grows in dry, open woods in September and October.

A. *macrophyllus,* the large-leaf aster, differs from other asters in its extensive patches of large, rough, heart-shaped leaves (4–6 inches across) and few flowering stems (2–5 feet tall) with small leaves and pale violet flowers. It is fairly frequent on wooded slopes in the Knobs and in eastern and southern Kentucky in August and September.

3.44 *Aster undulatus*

WAVY-LEAF ASTER

This is a blue-violet aster which grows somewhat stiffly upright, 1–3 feet tall. Its leaves are rough, wavy-edged, or slightly toothed; the lowest ones, with a heart-shaped blade, have the petiole dilated at the base and clasping; principal stem-leaves have winged petioles which usually clasp the stem; uppermost leaves are sessile and not clasping. This species is frequent in dry open woods in the hilly sections of the state but is apparently absent from the Bluegrass region.

September–October

3.45 *Aster prenanthoides*

CROOKED-STEM ASTER

Stems are often zigzag, 1–2½ feet tall; the heads, with pale violet-blue rays, are ¾–1 inch across; the leaves are slender and contracted into long winged petioles which are abruptly dilated at their strongly clasping bases. This aster is frequent in wet ground, such as stream margins, ditches, and wet meadows, especially in the eastern half of the state.

September

3.46 *Aster patens*

SPREADING ASTER

The plant is slender, 1–3 feet tall, with a few widely spreading flowering-branches; the rays are purple or violet in heads about 1 inch across. The leaves are oblong-oval, each with a pair of basal earlike lobes which almost meet around the stem. It is fairly frequent in dry open woods throughout the state.

September

The smooth aster, A. *laevis,* which stands stiffly upright, 2–4 feet high, is very smooth and often glaucous. Its leaves are firm and usually without teeth, the upper ones sessile and clasping the stem and the lower ones tapering into petioles. It grows in open woods in scattered sections of the state but is not frequent.

3.47 *Aster novae-angliae*

NEW ENGLAND ASTER

This is probably our handsomest aster: 2–6 feet tall and dense with deep, rich purple flower-heads, each about 1¼ inches across. The stem is stout; the leaves are lance-shaped, rough, and clasping at the base. The New England aster grows especially in moist rich ground in meadows; it is fairly frequent throughout the state, most common in the northern part of the Outer Bluegrass region.

October

3.48 *Aster oblongifolius*

AROMATIC ASTER

A bushy-branched plant 8–24 inches tall, this species has brittle wiry stems and crisp, dry-textured, oblong, toothless leaves. Heads, about 1 inch across, are violet-purple, each at the end of a leafy branchlet. Growing on limestone cliffs and ledges, it is infrequent but locally abundant, especially in the Inner Bluegrass region.

October

Among the blue-violet asters not pictured and not described in connection with a previous species, the following are fairly frequent:

A. *surculosus*, the creeping aster, has erect stems 8–24 inches high rising from a horizontal stem. Leaves are narrowly elliptic; involucral bracts are stiff with rigidly out-turned tips. It is frequent in dry, open, rocky woods in the Knobs and Cumberland Plateau.

A. *linariifolius*, the stiff-leaf aster, has stiffly erect stems growing in bunches, usually 12–18 inches high. Leaves are linear and rigid, and the heads are in flat-topped corymbs. It is frequent in dry rocky ground in the Cumberland Plateau, Knobs, and Mississippian Plateau.

A. *sericeus*, the silky aster, has slender erect stems with stiff branches. Leaves are lance-shaped, hard, and silvery-silky. In Kentucky it is confined to dry red cedar slopes in the Mississippian Plateau.

3.49 *Aster pilosus* var. *demotus*

FROST-WEED ASTER

Blanketing many an acre with white, this is perhaps the most abundant of all species characteristic of old fields in Kentucky. This aster and the tall goldenrod, *Solidago altissima* (no. 3.1), are dominant species of the perennial weed stage in the returning of fields to woody vegetation; they follow annual weeds and are followed by shrubs (blackberries and others) which, in turn, are succeeded by woodland.

The plant, 2–5 feet tall, has widely spreading branches bearing heads especially on the upper side. Since the heads are dense and the leaves are small and linear, little green shows when the plant is in full flower.

Late September–October

3.50 *Aster simplex*

PANICLED ASTER

This is an upright plant 3–5 feet high, in which the branches of the panicle are not wide-spreading. Leaves are lance-shaped; heads, with white rays, are about ¾ inch across. The panicled aster grows in damp thickets, meadows, and borders of woods on flood plains and is common throughout the state.

September–October

3.51 *Aster lateriflorus*

CALICO ASTER

The common name refers to the pattern resulting when the disks of the crowded heads turn from yellow to purplish as they mature. Heads are ½–¾ inch across, arranged on the upper side of the widely spreading branches. Leaves are lance-shaped, and the plant grows 1–3 feet high. It is frequent in thickets, in open woods, and at the edge of woods in most sections of the state.

Late September–October

A. *vimineus*, the small white aster, 2–4 feet tall, has smaller, densely crowded heads with 15–30 rays (the calico aster has 9–15 rays).

3.52 *Aster infirmus*

CORNEL-LEAF ASTER

The slender stem, 1–2½ feet tall, is divergently branched, making a flat-topped arrangement of heads, each about ¾ inch across. There are 5–10 creamy white rays, fewer than in other white asters shown. Leaves, widest above the middle and toothless, have stiff hairs on the margins and on the veins beneath. It is frequent in dry open woods throughout eastern Kentucky, infrequent in the Mississippian Plateau, and apparently absent from the Bluegrass and western Kentucky.

August

A. *umbellatus*, the flat-topped aster, is 1½–5 feet tall with lanceolate leaves and numerous heads in a wide flattish inflorescence. It grows in wet ground in woods, thickets, and meadows. Though more widely distributed than A. *infirmus*, it is only fairly frequent.

3.53 *Aster divaricatus*

WHITE WOOD ASTER

Leaves are heart-shaped, sharply and coarsely toothed, and petioled. Stems are slightly zigzag, 1–2½ feet high. Heads, ¾–1 inch across, with white rays and brownish disk, are in a somewhat flat-topped inflorescence. The white wood aster is common on wooded hillsides and ravine slopes in the Cumberland Plateau, the southeastern mountains, and the Knobs, and less common in other sections of the state.

September

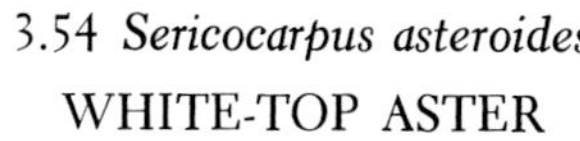

3.54 *Sericocarpus asteroides*

WHITE-TOP ASTER

In this aster-like species the heads, which are in flat-topped clusters, have only 4 or 5 rays. Both disk and rays are creamy white and the stiff involucral bracts are whitish with green tips. The leaves are spatulate and toothed near the apex. The plant, 10–20 inches tall, is frequent in dry open woods, especially in the Cumberland Plateau and the Knobs.

July–August

S. linifolius, the narrow-leaved white-top aster, differs in having firm linear leaves.

Series Seven: **Dicotyledons (4)**

Dicotyledons which are exceptions to the typical combination of net-veined leaves and perianth parts in fours or fives.

ARRANGEMENT OF PLATES

Group 1. Dicotyledons lacking a perianth 1.1–1.3

Group 2. Dicotyledons having perianth parts in threes or sixes with typical net-veined leaves, and those having distinctly parallel-veined leaves with typical "dicot" flowers 2.1–2.7
("Dicots" with narrow leaves which do not clearly show a vein-pattern should be sought in the regular series, IV, V, and VI.)

Group 3. Dicotyledons lacking green leaves
Cactus: a plant having broad, flattened, green, fleshy stems, and leaves reduced to spines 3.1
Saprophytic and parasitic plants lacking chlorophyll 3.2–3.26

1.1 *Saururus cernuus*

LIZARD'S-TAIL

The lizard's-tail has a graceful white spike with a nodding tip and pointed heart-shaped leaves on a stem 2–4 feet tall. Though the individual flowers are minute, a colony of these plants is a beautiful sight in swamps and at the edge of ponds and quiet streams. The species is fairly frequent in shady wet ground throughout the state.

Saururaceae (Lizard's-tail family)

June

1.2 *Euphorbia commutata*

EARLY SPURGE

This species of spurge is a yellow-green annual or perennial 8–15 inches high, occasionally tinged with red. The leaves are numerous, sessile, and broad at the tip; those subtending the inflorescence are broader than long and tend to be joined together. The flowers are minute, lacking sepals and petals, and a cluster of flowers made conspicuous by crescent-shaped glands simulates a flower. The early spurge grows on wooded hillsides, chiefly calcareous, and is most frequent in the Bluegrass and Mississippian Plateau.

Euphorbiaceae (Spurge family)

April–May

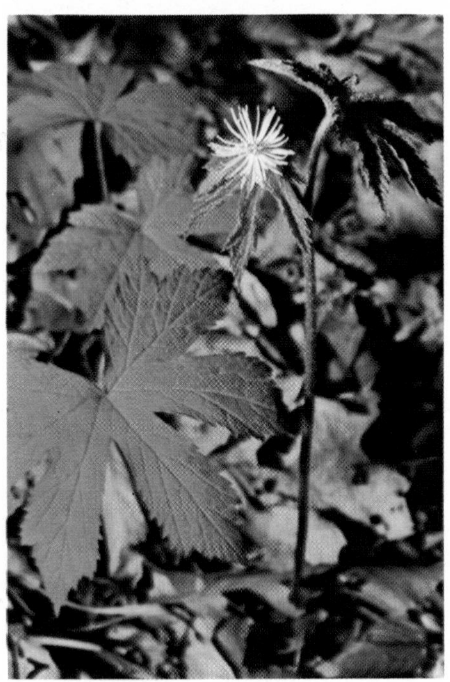

1.3 *Hydrastis canadensis*
GOLDENSEAL

Since the flower has no petals and the sepals fall as it opens, it appears to have no perianth, and the species is therefore placed in this group. The solitary flower consists of numerous conspicuous white stamens surrounding several separate pistils which later become a head of red berries. The leaves are palmately 5- to 7-lobed, veiny, and broader than long; they continue to enlarge after flowering time, eventually becoming 6–8 inches across. This species, formerly frequent in rich moist woods throughout the state, has almost been exterminated by digging of the rootstock for medicinal purposes. All the plants that are to be used medicinally should be cultivated, and the few remaining wild plants should be zealously protected.
Ranunculaceae (Buttercup family) May

Some related species (*Trautvetteria* and *Cimicifuga*) are placed in Series Four (nos. 2.42 and 2.10) because, in their large inflorescences, buds showing sepals would occur with opened flowers that have lost them.

2.1 *Asarum canadense*

WILD GINGER

A spicy aromatic rootstock is responsible for the common name. The heart-shaped petioled leaves, which have a silky sheen, are borne in a pair, with a solitary flower in the fork between the 2 petioles. The flower, at ground level and nearly concealed by leaf litter, has a brownish purple cup-shaped calyx with 3 pointed lobes and no petals. The shape and pointing of the lobes vary, and several varieties have been named. The beautiful pattern and symmetry to be observed within the cup make it worthwhile to brush aside dead leaves in order to marvel at a beauty that usually goes unseen. Wild ginger grows in rich woods and is especially frequent on ravine slopes throughout the state.

Aristolochiaceae (Birthwort family) April

2.2 *Asarum arifolium*

LITTLE BROWN JUG

The leaves are arrow-shaped, petioled, and evergreen. Each underground stem annually produces a single flower at ground level and adds 1 new leaf, the old leaves persisting. The flower, ¾–1¼ inches long, has a jug-shaped calyx which turns brown with age, and no corolla. This species grows in upland woods in the southeastern quarter of the state.

Aristolochiaceae (Birthwort family) April–May

2.3 *Rumex verticillatus*

SWAMP DOCK, WATER DOCK

This is an attractive and "innocent" relative of some common and obnoxious weeds, such as the red sorrel and sour dock. The plant is 2–4 feet tall, having 1 main stem and short axillary branches; leaves are lance-shaped with a smooth margin. Flowers, with 6 sepals and no petals, are small and whorled in panicles. The plant is more showy in fruit, when the drooping flower-stalks have elongated and the calyx has enlarged to ⅛–¼ inch. The swamp dock grows in shallow water of shady pools, swamps, and sluggish streams; it is widely scattered and infrequent.

Polygonaceae (Buckwheat family)

Fruit: June–August

2.4 *Caulophyllum thalictroides*

BLUE COHOSH

The flowers of the blue cohosh have 6 greenish or purplish petal-like sepals, 6 rudimentary petals, and 6 stamens. Less than ½ inch across, they are borne in a small panicle and are followed by blue berry-like seeds which are beautiful but poisonous. The gray-green plant bears at midstem a large compound leaf with 3-lobed leaflets 1–2 inches long. This species is restricted to rich mesophytic woods but geographically is widely distributed.

Berberidaceae (Barberry family)

Flowers: April
Seed: July

2.5 *Lythrum lanceolatum*

PURPLE LOOSESTRIFE

The purple flowers, about ½ inch across with 4–6 (usually 6) separate petals, are borne in the axils of the upper lanceolate leaves. The stem is 4-angled and 1½–3 feet tall. This loosestrife grows in swamps and other wet ground; it is fairly frequent in western Kentucky and rare in other regions. The closely related *L. alatum* is also infrequent in Kentucky.

Lythraceae (Loosestrife family)

July–August

Note: Several other dicotyledons which have a variable number of perianth parts may sometimes have 6, 9, or 12. These plants, such as *Anemonella* (rue anemone), *Hepatica,* and *Podophyllum* (may-apple), are placed in Series Four.

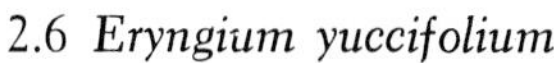

2.6 *Eryngium yuccifolium*

RATTLESNAKE-MASTER

This is a stiff plant 1½–3½ feet high with linear, strictly parallel-veined, spiny-edged, yucca-like leaves, the lowest of which are 1–2 feet long. Minute flowers, each with 5 bluish or whitish petals, are in dense heads ½–1 inch in diameter. This eryngo grows in open woods and prairie patches in southern and western Kentucky.

Umbelliferae (Parsley family)

August

2.7 *Chrysopsis nervosa*

GRASS-LEAVED GOLDEN ASTER

This interesting composite with yellow rays and disk is also called silkgrass because of the soft, white, silky hairs on the grasslike leaves, which are truly parallel-veined. It grows 1–2 feet high and is fairly frequent in dry, sandy open woods and clearings in eastern Kentucky.
Compositae (Composite family)
August–September

3.1 *Opuntia humifusa*

PRICKLY PEAR

Stems are green, fleshy, flattened, and jointed; leaves are reduced to spines; flowers are showy, 2–3 inches across. This cactus lives in a desert-like microclimate: in only an inch or two of soil on rock (usually limestone) in full sunlight. In Kentucky it is found from the Bluegrass region westward and southwestward.
Cactaceae (Cactus family) June

3.2 *Monotropa uniflora*

INDIAN PIPE

Both this species and the following obtain their food via fungi which decompose organic matter on the forest floor. Inside the flower in both species the most conspicuous feature is the large disk-shaped stigma atop a columnar style.

The Indian pipe, 3–10 inches high, is white with a solitary flower ½–1 inch long, resembling an upside-down pipe, nodding but becoming erect in fruit. It is found in rich, humus-laden woods, and is infrequent though scattered in various sections of the state.

Pyrolaceae (Wintergreen family)

July

3.3 *Monotropa hypopithys*

PINESAP

This beautiful and colorful plant, 4–12 inches high, has a raceme of flowers which are at first nodding but later erect. It is found in pine and oak as well as more mesic woods in various parts of the state but is not frequent.

Pyrolaceae (Wintergreen family)

September

3.4 *Epifagus virginiana*

BEECH-DROPS

This nongreen flowering plant has a branching stem 6–18 inches high, scattered leaf-scales, and 2-lipped flowers. It is parasitic on roots of beech trees and is frequent wherever beech trees grow.
Orobanchaceae (Broom-rape family)
July–September

3.5 *Conopholis americana*

SQUAWROOT, CANCER-ROOT

The squawroot, 3–8 inches high, has a crowded spike of flowers and a stout unbranched stem covered with numerous fleshy leaf-scales. It is parasitic on several species of trees, especially oaks, but is less frequent than the beech-drops.
Orobanchaceae (Broom-rape family)
May–June

Part III. Systematic List of Included Families, Genera & Species

INCLUDED FAMILIES

The numbers refer to the sequential arrangement of families in Part III.

INTRODUCTION

The plates have been arbitrarily grouped for ease in identification; therefore, in order to show how the species illustrated and described are related, they are here listed by families and genera.

In classification the *species* is the unit. Closely related species are grouped in a *genus;* related genera are placed together in a *family;* related families make up an *order;* orders are grouped into *classes,* and classes into *divisions,* which are the major classification categories of the kingdom. Thus the plant kingdom of more than 350,000 species has an orderly scheme of classification, one which ideally should show relationship. In some species with considerable variation and wide geographic range we use subspecific categories, such as *variety* and *forma.*

Instead of giving a complete classification it seems adequate in this list to begin with families, which are listed in the sequence followed in the Eighth Edition of *Gray's Manual of Botany* by M. L. Fernald. Within a family genera are listed alphabetically and within a genus species are listed alphabetically. Following the names of the species are the names (or abbreviations) of the person(s) responsible for the binomial. If the scientific name used in this book differs from that in *Gray's Manual,* Eighth Edition, the latter name is given in brackets. The numbers given refer to the series (roman numeral) and species number found in Part II. Species mentioned in Part II but not illustrated are indicated by asterisks.

FAMILIES OF FERNS & "FERN ALLIES": THE LOWER VASCULAR PLANTS

These plants have roots, stems, and leaves, all containing specialized cells for conduction, but do not produce flowers or seeds. The producing of spores (single asexual cells which are borne in spore-cases called sporangia) is the conspicuous method of reproduction and the means of species dispersal.

1 *Equisetaceae* (Horsetail family)

This family is characterized by jointed stems, leaves reduced to toothed sheaths, and cone-like structures which bear sporangia on cone scales. Only about 25 species in the family are left in the world today, relicts of a great group of plants which lived millions of years ago and were partly responsible for the formation of coal.

Equisetum arvense L. Field horsetail I, 4.1
E. hyemale L. var. *affine* (Engelm.) A.A. Eat. Scouring rush I, 4.2

2 *Lycopodiaceae* (Clubmoss family)

The common names applied to members of this family, such as clubmoss and groundpine, are misleading since they are neither mosses nor pines but relatives of the ferns. Leaves are small, evergreen, numerous, and overlapping on the stem. Slender cones, in which sporangia are borne in the axils of the cone scales, are present in all but a few species, which have sporangia in the axils of the upper leaves. These small plants, none over a few inches high, are our only modern representatives of a group that produced the largest trees in the swamp forests which flourished millions of years ago and formed our coal.

Lycopodium flabelliforme (Fernald) Blanch. [*L. complanatum* var. *flabelliforme*] Ground-cedar I, 4.5
L. lucidulum Michx. Shining clubmoss I, 4.3
L. obscurum L. Groundpine I, 4.6
L. porophilum Lloyd & Underw. Rock clubmoss I, 4.4
**L. tristachyum* Pursh Ground-cedar I, 4.5

3 *Ophioglossaceae* (Adder's-tongue family)

In this family a plant has a single leaf, either simple and undivided (and hence not looking "like a fern") or much divided and cut into "fernlike" segments; sporangia are borne in either a stalked spike or a panicle.

**Botrychium dissectum* Spreng. Cut-leaf grape-fern I, 1.2

B. obliquum Muhl. [*B. dissectum* forma *obliquum*] Common grape-fern I, 1.2
B. virginianum (L.) Sw. Virginia grape-fern I, 1.1
Ophioglossum engelmanii Prantl Adder's-tongue fern I, 1.3
**O. vulgatum* L. Adder's-tongue fern I, 1.3

4 *Osmundaceae* (Flowering fern family)

Although no fern bears flowers, the common name of this group results from the fact that the fertile, spore-bearing fronds are unlike the green sterile ones, and in some are very showy.

Osmunda cinnamomea L. Cinnamon fern I, 1.5
O. claytoniana L. Interrupted fern I, 2.2
O. regalis L. var. *spectabilis* (Willd.) Gray Royal fern I, 2.1

5 *Schizaeaceae* (Curly-grass family)

Genera in this family are placed together on the basis of the structure and arrangement of sporangia (in double rows on narrow divisions of the frond). The only one in Kentucky has twining fronds with palmate leaflets; the one responsible for the family name has linear curly leaves.

Lygodium palmatum (Bernh.) Sw. Climbing fern I, 2.3

6 *Hymenophyllaceae* (Filmy fern family)

The frond is composed of a single layer of cells; sporangia are borne at the bases of tiny bristles, each of which emerges from a marginal, cuplike structure.

Trichomanes boschianum Sturm Filmy fern, Bristle-fern I, 3.2

7 *Polypodiaceae* (Fern family)

This is the largest and most typical family of the true ferns, that is, the "ferniest" of the ferns. They are grouped together because they all have the same anatomy in the sporangium, which is a basically important although microscopic feature.

In all but *Onoclea*, clusters of sporangia are borne on the blade and the fertile portions are similar to the sterile ones, although they may be smaller.

Asplenium, *Athyrium*, and *Camptosorus* are closely related genera having elongate, straight, or curved sporangium-clusters situated along diverging veins. They differ in size and amount of cutting of the frond.

Adiantum pedatum L. Maidenhair fern I, 3.14
**Asplenium bradleyi* D.C. Eaton Cliff spleenwort, Bradley's spleenwort I, 3.6
A. *montanum* Willd. Mountain spleenwort I, 3.3
A. *pinnatifidum* Nutt. Lobed spleenwort I, 3.5
A. *platyneuron* (L.) Oakes Ebony spleenwort I, 3.7
*A. *resiliens* Kunze Black-stemmed spleenwort I, 3.6
A. *ruta-muraria* L. var. *cryptolepis* Fernald Wall-rue I, 3.4
A. *trichomanes* L. Maidenhair spleenwort I, 3.6
Athyrium asplenioides (Michx.) Desv. [A. *filix-femina*] Lady-fern I, 3.19
A. *pycnocarpon* (Spreng.) Tidestr. Gladefern I, 3.18
A. *thelypterioides* (Michx.) Desv. Silvery gladefern I, 3.17
Camptosorus rhizophyllus (L.) Link Walking fern I, 3.8
Cheilanthes lanosa (Michx.) D.C. Eaton [C. *vistita*] Hairy Lipfern I, 3.12
Cystopteris bulbifera (L.) Bernh. Bulblet fern I, 3.13
C. *fragilis* (L.) Bernh. Fragile fern I, 3.12
Dennstaedtia punctilobula (Michx.) Moore Hay-scented fern I, 3.20
**Dryopteris goldiana* (Hook.) Gray Giant woodfern, Goldie's fern I, 3.22
D. *marginalis* (L.) Gray Marginal shield-fern, Marginal woodfern I, 3.22
D. *spinulosa* (O.F. Muell.) Watt. Spinulose shield-fern I, 3.21
Onoclea sensibilis L. Sensitive fern, Bead-fern I, 1.4
Pellaea atropurpurea (L.) Link Purple cliffbrake I, 3.10
Phegopteris hexagonoptera (Michx.) Fee [*Dryopteris hexagonoptera*] Beech fern I, 3.15

**Polypodium polypodioides* (L.) Watt. var. *michauxianum* Weatherby Gray polypody, Resurrection fern I, 3.1

P. virginianum L. Polypody, Rockcap fern I, 3.1

Polystichum acrostichoides (Michx.) Schott Christmas fern I, 2.4

Pteridium latiusculum (Desv.) Hier. [*P. aquilinum* var. *latiusculum*] Bracken I, 3.23

Thelypteris noveboracensis (L.) Nieuwl. [*Dryopteris noveboracensis*] New York fern I, 3.16

**Thelypteris palustris* Schott [*Dryopteris thelypteris*] Marsh fern I, 3.16

Woodsia obtusa (Spreng.) Torr. Blunt-lobed woodsia I, 3.11

FLOWERING PLANTS

The flowering plants, in botanical classification a class called *Angiosperms*, constitute all plants which bear seed enclosed in a fruit. In these plants the means of species dispersal is by seeds, each of which is an embryonic plant in a dormant stage with a protective covering and usually some stored food. In some it is the fruit, containing the seed, that is actually scattered; in others the seeds themselves are scattered.

Seeds develop from ovules after fertilization has occurred within them. In all flowering plants ovules are enclosed within a structure called a pistil, part of which develops into the *fruit* as the seeds develop. The term fruit has no reference to whether or not it is edible.

The term flower implies to the layman a beautiful and showy object. However, all that is required for a structure to be a *flower* is a pistil and/or a stamen. Nevertheless, this book has concentrated on the "flowery-looking" flowers.

In botanical classification there are 2 subclasses of flowering plants based on a very fundamental but inconspicuous character: whether the seed contains 1 cotyledon or 2. Fortunately there are accompanying features of each subclass that are obvious and far handier to use in identification.

FAMILIES OF MONOCOTYLEDONS

These plants have scattered vascular bundles in the stem and 1 cotyledon in the seed; usually they have parallel-veined leaves and flower-parts in multiples of 3.

8 *Typhaceae* (Cat-tail family)

The family contains a single genus of tall marsh plants. Flowers are minute and densely crowded; stamens and pistils are borne in different flowers; the perianth is composed of bristles.

**Typha angustifolia* L. Narrow-leaved cat-tail III, 2.1
T. latifolia L. Cat-tail III, 2.1

9 *Alismataceae* (Water-plantain family)

Members of this family are aquatic or marsh plants with smooth, firm, petioled leaves; their flowers, usually whorled in racemes or panicles, have 3 green sepals, 3 white petals, 6 or more stamens, and several pistils.

Alisma subcordatum Raf. Water-plantain III, 1.13
**Sagittaria australis* (J.G. Sm.) Small Arrowhead III, 1.14
S. graminea Michx. Grass-leaf arrowhead III, 1.15
S. latifolia Willd. Arrowhead, Duck-potato III, 1.14

10 *Gramineae* (Grass family)

The grass family is very large, having over 1,000 species in the United States alone, for example. It contains not only the lawn and pasture grasses but also the grains, and therefore is one of the most important plant families.

Grass flowers are minute, borne in the axils of dry, chaffy scales arranged in spikelets, which in turn are in either spikes or panicles. They are so highly specialized that an exclusive terminology, too complex to include here, is employed to describe them. Grass stems are round in cross section and usually hollow, and the leaves are in 2 rows, their bases sheathing the stem with split sheaths. It should be noted that many linear-leaved plants which have the word "grass" in their common names are not grasses at all; no plant with petals and a showy flower is a grass.

Only 3 species of grasses are included:

Hystrix patula Moench Bottle-brush grass III, 2.11
Poa pratensis L. Kentucky bluegrass III, 2.12
Uniola latifolia Michx. Spangle grass III, 2.10

11 *Cyperaceae* (Sedge family)

The sedges superficially resemble the grasses, but their flowers are not as specialized as grass flowers, and from an economic standpoint the family is not nearly as important as the grass family. Stems of sedges are usually triangular in cross section and solid; stem leaves, when present, are usually in 3 rows, and the leaf-sheaths are not split. *Carex*, having over 500 species on this continent, is the largest genus in the North American flora.

Only a few striking-looking sedges are included:

Carex crinita Lam. Drooping sedge III, 2.7
C. *lupulina* Muhl. Hop sedge III, 2.8
Cyperus strigosus L. Umbrella sedge III, 2.3
Scirpus atrovirens Willd. var. *georgianus* (Harper) Fernald Small bulrush III, 2.6
*S. *cyperinus* (L.) Kunth Wool-grass III, 2.5
S. *pedicellatus* Fernald Wool-grass III, 2.5
S. *validus* Vahl var. *creber* Fern. Great bulrush III, 2.4

12 *Araceae* (Arum family)

The arum family is much more extensively represented in the tropics than in temperate regions and contains, for example, the well-known calla (*Zantedeschia*) and *Philodendron* of greenhouses and window-gardens.

Although the individual flowers in this family are minute, possessing neither calyx nor corolla, the whole fleshy inflorescence is often made conspicuous by a large sheathing bract called a spathe.

Acorus americanus Raf. Sweet flag, American calamus III, 2.2

Arisaema atrorubens (Ait.) Blume Jack-in-the-pulpit III, 1.1
A. *dracontium* (L.) Schott Green dragon III, 1.2
*A. *triphyllum* (L.) Schott Jack-in-the-pulpit III, 1.1

13 *Commelinaceae* (Spiderwort family)

Members of this family have jointed stems, leaves sheathing at the base, 3 sepals, and 3 ephemeral petals.

Commelina communis L. Dayflower II, 2.1
**C. diffusa* Burm Dayflower II, 2.1
**Tradescantia ohiensis* Raf. Ohio spiderwort II, 1.32
T. subaspera Ker Zigzag spiderwort II, 1.32
T. virginiana L. Early spiderwort II, 1.31

14 *Juncaceae* (Rush family)

Many rushes superficially resemble sedges but are more closely related to the lily family. Flowers are small, dry, and chaffy, with 6 perianth segments which are brownish, greenish, or purplish; stamens are 3 or 6, and the pistil is above the attachment of the perianth.

Juncus effusus L. Common rush III, 2.9

15 *Liliaceae* (Lily family)

This large family contains many ornamental plants such as tulips, hyacinths, and lilies, economic plants such as onions and asparagus, and many woodland wildflowers.

Sepals and petals, 3 of each, are colored alike except in *Trillium,* and they may be either separate or united; there are 6 stamens and the pistil is entirely above the attachment of the perianth.

Aletris farinosa L. Stargrass, Colic-root II, 1.17
Allium canadense L. Wild garlic II, 1.23
A. *cernuum* Roth Nodding wild onion II, 1.22
A. *tricoccum* Ait. Wild leek, Ramp III, 3.1
*A. *vineale* L. Field garlic II, 1.23
Camassia scilloides (Raf.) Cory Wild hyacinth II, 1.30

Chamaelirium luteum (L.) Gray Fairy-wand II, 1.16
Clintonia umbellulata (Michx.) Morong White clintonia, Speckled wood-lily II, 1.11
Disporum lanuginosum (Michx.) Nicholson Yellow mandarin II, 1.20
D. maculatum (Buckl.) Britt. Spotted mandarin II, 1.19
Erythronium albidum Nutt. White trout-lily II, 1.10
E. americanum Ker Yellow trout-lily II, 1.9
Hemerocallis fulva L. Orange daylily, Common daylily II, 1.4
Lilium canadense L. Canada lily II, 1.2
**L. michiganense* Farw. Michigan lily II, 1.2
L. philadelphicum L. Wood lily, Philadelphia lily II, 1.3
L. superbum L. Turk's-cap lily II, 1.1
Maianthemum canadense Desf. Canada mayflower II, 1.13
Medeola virginiana L. Indian cucumber-root II, 1.24
Nothoscordum bivalve (L.) Britt. False garlic II, 1.14
Ornithogalum umbellatum L. Star-of-Bethlehem II, 1.15
Polygonatum biflorum (Walt.) Ell. Solomon's-seal II, 1.25
**P. canaliculatum* (Muhl.) Pursh Solomon's-seal II, 1.25
**P. pubescens* (Willd.) Pursh Solomon's-seal II, 1.25
Smilacina racemosa (L.) Desf. False Solomon's-seal, Solomon's-plume II, 1.12
**Smilax ecirrhata* (Engelm.) S. Wats. Erect carrion-flower III, 1.11
S. herbacea L. Carrion-flower III, 1.11
Trillium erectum L. Erect trillium III, 1.9
T. flexipes Raf. Bent trillium III, 1.10
T. grandiflorum (Michx.) Salisb. Large-flowered trillium III, 1.8
T. luteum (Muhl.) Harbison Yellow trillium III, 1.6
T. nivale Riddell Dwarf white trillium, Snow trillium III, 1.4
T. recurvatum Beck Recurved trillium III, 1.5
T. sessile L. Sessile trillium III, 1.3

T. undulatum Willd. Painted trillium III, 1.7
Uvularia grandiflora Sm. Large-flowered bellwort II, 1.6
U. perfoliata L. Bellwort II, 1.7

16 *Dioscoreaceae* (Yam family)

This chiefly tropical family with only 1 genus extending into our region has twining stems, net-veined leaves, and separate pistillate and staminate flowers.

Dioscorea quaternata (Walt.) Gmel. Wild yam III, 1.12
**D. villosa* L. Wild yam III, 1.12

17 *Amaryllidaceae* (Amaryllis family)

The amaryllis family resembles the lily family in many respects (radially symmetrical flowers with 3 sepals and 3 petals colored alike, and 6 stamens) but differs principally in having the ovary of the pistil below the perianth. Though not many representatives are wild in the northeastern quarter of the United States, the family contains many ornamental plants which are native to other parts of the world, such as *Narcissus* (in which a crown is added to the perianth), *Amaryllis*, and *Lycoris*.

Agave virginica L. False aloe II, 1.21
Hymenocallis occidentalis (LeConte) Kunth Spider-lily II, 1.18
Hypoxis hirsuta (L.) Coville Yellow stargrass II, 1.8

18 *Iridaceae* (Iris family)

The iris family differs from both the amaryllis and the lily family in having 3 stamens instead of 6, and differs from the lily family also in having the ovary below the perianth. As in these other 2 families, there are 3 petals and 3 sepals colored like petals. Leaves in the iris family are distinctive, sometimes described as being "astride" the stem; they are folded lengthwise, embracing in the fold the stem and a younger leaf. Many ornamental plants such as *Gladiolus* and *Crocus* as well as the garden irises belong to this family.

In the genus *Iris* sepals and petals spread in different planes, and the style branches into 3 petal-like segments which arch over and shelter the stamens.

Belamcanda chinensis (L.) DC. Blackberry-lily II, 1.5
Iris cristata Ait. Crested dwarf iris II, 1.26
I. verna L. Dwarf iris II, 1.27
I. virginica L. var. *shrevei* (Small) E. Anders. Southern blue flag II, 1.28
**Sisyrinchium albidum* Raf. White blue-eyed grass II, 1.29
S. angustifolium Mill. Blue-eyed grass II, 1.29

19 *Orchidaceae* (Orchid family)

In number of species throughout the world, the orchid family is one of the largest families of flowering plants. Tropical orchids, such as those cultivated by florists, are the most showy; nevertheless, some of our temperate species are striking, and even the inconspicuous ones are interesting in their complexity.

Orchid flowers are highly complex, particularly in their adaptations for pollination. They have 3 sepals and 3 petals and are bilaterally symmetrical. One petal, much larger than the other two, is modified as a "lip" which serves as a landing place for pollinating insects. In the center of the flower there is a "column" formed by the union of stamen and pistil. Most orchids have only 1 stamen.

Orchid seed are so minute that a mass of them resembles powder; tens of thousands of seed are produced in a single small capsule. However, relatively few germinate, and of those that do only a few survive. Since orchid roots require an association with certain fungi, the appropriate fungus must be present, and the soil must be suitable to the fungus as well as to the orchid itself. Many years' growth is necessary before any orchid is sufficiently mature to produce a flower. All these factors contribute to the scarcity of our native orchids, and wherever they are found they should be left in place and their habitat protected.

Aplectrum hyemale (Muhl.) Torr. Putty-root III, 3.3
Calopogon pulchellus (Salisb.) R. Br. Grass-pink, Swamp-pink II, 2.11

Cleistes divaricata (L.) Ames Spreading pogonia II, 2.10

**Corallorhiza odontorhiza* (Willd.) Nutt. Coral-root III, 3.5

C. wisteriana Conrad Coral-root III, 3.5

Cypripedium acaule Ait. Pink lady's-slipper, Stemless lady's-slipper II, 2.7

C. calceolus L. var. *pubescens* (Willd.) Correll Yellow lady's-slipper II, 2.6

Goodyera pubescens (Willd.) R. Br. Rattlesnake-plantain II, 2.3

**Habenaria blephariglottis* (Willd.) Hook. White fringed orchid II, 2.14

H. ciliaris (L.) R. Br. Yellow fringed orchid II, 2.15

**H. clavellata* (Michx.) Spreng. Green woodland orchis II, 2.14

H. flava (L.) R. Br. Pale green orchis II, 2.14

**H. lacera* (Michx.) Lodd. Ragged orchis II, 2.14

H. peramoena Gray Purple fringeless orchid, Fan-lip orchid II, 2.12

H. psycodes (L.) Spreng. Purple fringed orchid II, 2.13

Hexalectris spicata (Walt.) Barnh. Crested coral-root III, 3.4

Isotria verticillata (Willd.) Raf. Whorled pogonia II, 2.9

Liparis lilifolia (L.) Richard Lily-leaved twayblade II, 2.2

**Malaxis unifolia* Michx. Green adder's-mouth II, 2.2

Orchis spectabilis L. Showy orchis II, 2.8

Spiranthes cernua (L.) Richard Ladies'-tresses II, 2.5

**S. gracilis* (Bigel.) Beck Ladies'-tresses II, 2.4

**S. lucida* (H.H. Eaton) Ames Ladies'-tresses II, 2.4

**S. ovalis* Lindl. Ladies'-tresses II, 2.5

**S. tuberosa* Raf. Ladies'-tresses II, 2.4

**S. lucida* (H.H. Eaton) Ames Ladies'-tresses II, 2.4

Tipularia discolor (Pursh) Nutt. Cranefly orchid III, 3.2

FAMILIES OF DICOTYLEDONS

The dicotyledons have a cylindrical arrangement of vascular tissue in the stem and 2 cotyledons in the seed; usually they have net-veined leaves and flower-parts in 4s or 5s.

FAMILIES HAVING FLOWERS WITH SEPARATE PETALS OR NO PETALS (NUMBERS 20–55)

Flowers are radially symmetrical and complete, with the ovary above the attachment of other parts, unless stated otherwise.

20 *Saururaceae* (Lizard's-tail family)

This is a small family of swamp-dwelling plants which have jointed stems, broad alternate leaves, and slender spikes of small white flowers which have no perianth.

Saururus cernuus L. Lizard's-tail VII, 1.1

21 *Urticaceae* (Nettle family)

Some genera of the nettle family have stinging hairs and some do not. Minute greenish or whitish flowers, without petals and mostly unisexual, are borne in axillary inflorescences. This family of largely herbaceous plants, predominantly tropical, is closely related in the same order to the elm family.

**Boehmeria cylindrica* (L.) Sw. False Nettle IV, 2.47
Laportea canadensis (L.) Wedd. Wood-nettle IV, 2.47
**Pilea pumila* (L.) Gray Clearweed IV, 2.47
**Urtica* spp. Stinging nettle IV, 2.47

22 *Aristolochiaceae* (Birthwort family)

In the *Aristolochiaceae,* a family composed of herbs and twining vines, the calyx, usually reddish-purplish-brownish, is united around the "inferior" ovary and expands into 3 lobes; no petals are present. Stamens, 6 or 12 in most genera, are nearly joined to the fleshy style, which is topped by a lobed stigma.

Asarum arifolium Michx. Little brown jug VII, 2.2
A. *canadense* L. Wild ginger VII, 2.1

23 *Polygonaceae* (Buckwheat family)

A distinguishing characteristic of the buckwheat family is a stipular sheath surrounding the stem at each node. The leaves are chiefly alternate and simple; the flowers, usually small, numerous, and aggregated in inflorescences, have 4–6 petal-like sepals (petals are usually absent); the fruit is small, hard, single-seeded, and surrounded by the calyx. The family includes the edible buckwheat and rhubarb, many weeds such as the smartweeds and knotweeds, and a few ornamentals such as the silver-lace vine.

Rumex verticillatus L. Swamp dock, Water dock VII, 2.3

24 *Phytolaccaceae* (Pokeweed family)

This family, which is best represented in the American tropics, has but 1 species reaching into our range. Its flowers are characterized by separate sepals, no petals, a variable number of stamens, and an ovary composed of a ring of carpels which becomes a berry.

Phytolacca americana L. Pokeweed, Pokeberry IV, 2.7

25 *Portulacaceae* (Purslane family)

The members of the purslane family have succulent leaves. The flowers usually have 2 sepals and 5 petals. This family contains several species of cultivated ornamental plants, including the so-called moss-rose, *Portulaca grandiflora*.

**Claytonia caroliniana* Michx. Spring-beauty IV, 1.94
C. *virginica* L. Spring-beauty IV, 1.94
Portulaca oleracea L. Purslane IV, 2.62

26 *Caryophyllaceae* (Pink family)

The family *Caryophyllaceae* is a large one found primarily in north temperate regions. It contains beautiful wildflowers, weeds, and cultivated ornamentals, including the florists' carnations and numerous garden flowers. The family can be distinguished by stems swollen at the nodes bearing opposite (or whorled), chiefly sessile, entire-margined leaves. The flowers, usually complete, have 4–5 petals (rarely absent) and 5–10 stamens; sepals may be 4 or 5 and either separate or united into a tube.

Agrostemma githago L. Corn cockle IV, 1.59
Arenaria patula Michx. Sandwort, Wild baby's-breath IV, 2.49
Dianthus armeria L. Deptford pink IV, 1.58
Saponaria officinalis L. Bouncing bet, Soapwort IV, 1.93
Silene caroliniana Walt. var. *wherryi* (Small) Fernald Wild pink IV, 1.57
S. *rotundifolia* Nutt. Round-leaved fire pink, Round-leaved catchfly IV, 1.56
S. *stellata* (L.) Ait.f. Starry campion IV, 1.27
S. *virginica* L. Fire pink, Red catchfly IV, 1.55
**Stellaria media* (L.) Cyrill. Common chickweed IV, 1.28
S. *pubera* Michx. Star chickweed, Great chickweed IV, 1.28

27 *Nymphaeaceae* (Water-lily family)

The *Nymphaeaceae* are aquatic plants with long-petioled leaves and showy flowers solitary on long stalks. The flowers have an indefinite number of sepals, petals, and stamens, and several simple pistils or a single compound pistil.

Nelumbo lutea (Willd.) Pers. American lotus, Yellow nelumbo IV, 1.25
Nuphar advena (Ait.) Ait.f. Yellow pond-lily, Spatterdock IV, 1.24
Nymphaea odorata Ait. Fragrant water-lily IV, 1.26

28 *Ranunculaceae* (Buttercup family, Crowfoot family)

This is a large north-temperate family of herbaceous plants plus a few semiwoody climbers. They have numerous stamens and several or numerous pistils. Some have complete flowers, some lack petals and have petal-like sepals, and some are unisexual. The flowers are usually radially symmetrical although a few exceptions (such as *Delphinium*) have bilaterally symmetrical flowers. The family contains many plants grown as ornamentals.

Actaea pachypoda Ell. White baneberry IV, 2.9
Anemone quinquefolia L. Wood anemone IV, 1.32
A. *virginiana* L. Tall anemone, Thimbleweed IV, 1.33
Anemonella thalictroides (L.) Spach. Rue anemone IV, 1.30
Aquilegia canadensis L. Columbine IV, 1.53
Cimicifuga racemosa (L.) Nutt. Black snakeroot, Black cohosh IV, 2.10
**Clematis glaucophylla* Small Leather flower IV, 1.61
*C. *pitcheri* T. & G. Leather flower IV, 1.61
*C. *versicolor* Small Leather flower IV, 1.61
C. *viorna* L. Leather flower IV, 1.61
C. *virginiana* L. Virgin's-bower IV, 1.34
Delphinium ajacis L. Rocket larkspur V, 3.30
D. *tricorne* Michx. Dwarf larkspur V, 3.29
Hepatica acutiloba DC. Hepatica IV, 1.29, 1.91
*H. *americana* (DC.) Ker. Hepatica IV, 1.29
Hydrastis canadensis L. Goldenseal VII, 1.3
Isopyrum biternatum (Raf.) T. & G. False rue anemone IV, 1.31
**Ranunculus abortivus* L. Small-flowered crowfoot IV, 2.60
*R. *acris* L. Tall buttercup IV, 1.4
*R. *bulbosus* L. Bulbous buttercup IV, 1.4
R. *fascicularis* Muhl. Early buttercup IV, 1.4
R. *hispidus* Michx. Hairy buttercup IV, 1.3
*R. *micranthus* Nutt. Small-flowered crowfoot IV, 2.60
R. *recurvatus* Poir. Hooked crowfoot IV, 2.60
*R. *repens* L. Creeping buttercup IV, 1.4
*R. *septentrionalis* Poir. Swamp buttercup IV, 1.4
Thalictrum clavatum DC. Cliff meadow rue IV, 2.45
*T. *dasycarpum* Fisch. & Ave-Lall. Purple meadow rue IV, 2.44
T. *dioicum* L. Early meadow rue IV, 2.43

T. polygamum Muhl. Tall meadow rue IV, 2.44
**T. revolutum* DC. Waxy meadow rue IV, 2.44
Trautvetteria caroliniensis (Walt.) Vail. Tassel-rue, False bugbane IV, 2.42
Xanthorhiza simplicissima Marsh. Shrub-yellowroot IV, 2.48

29 *Berberidaceae* (Barberry family)

Though the family contains several genera of shrubs, the plants in our range are herbaceous. The flowers have 4–6 sepals, 6–9 petals (rudimentary in *Caulophyllum*), stamens as many as the petals (or twice as many in *Podophyllum*), and a single pistil with the style absent or short.

Caulophyllum thalictroides (L.) Michx. Blue cohosh VII, 2.4
Jeffersonia diphylla (L.) Pers. Twinleaf IV, 1.36
Podophyllum peltatum L. May-apple, Mandrake IV, 1.35

30 *Papaveraceae* (Poppy family)

These are herbaceous plants containing milky or colored latex. The showy flowers have 2–3 sepals which fall early, 4–12 petals, numerous stamens, and a single pistil. The family contains several cultivated ornamentals and the species which is the source of morphine and other narcotics.

**Chelidonium majus* L. Celandine IV, 1.1
Sanguinaria canadensis L. Bloodroot IV, 1.37
Stylophorum diphyllum (Michx.) Nutt. Celandine poppy, Wood poppy IV, 1.1

31 *Fumariaceae* (Fumitory family)

[Included as a subfamily under *Papaveraceae* by Fernald in *Gray's Manual*, Eighth Edition]

This is a family of herbaceous plants with finely divided leaves and flowers which are bilaterally symmetrical. Petals are in 2 pairs, with one or both of the outer pair having a sac or spur at the base.

Corydalis flavula (Raf.) DC. Yellow corydalis V, 3.12
C. sempervirens (L.) Pers. Pink corydalis V, 3.11
Dicentra canadensis (Goldie) Walp. Squirrel-corn V, 3.14
D. cucullaria (L.) Bernh. Dutchman's-breeches V, 3.13

32 *Cruciferae* (Mustard family)

The members of the mustard family, all herbaceous, have cross-shaped flowers with 4 sepals, 4 petals, and 6 stamens, and a pod containing a false partition. The family includes many vegetables such as cabbage, broccoli, spinach, radishes, and turnips, numerous weeds, and several ornamental garden flowers including candytuft and alyssum, as well as attractive woodland wildflowers.

Alliaria officinalis Andrz. Garlic-mustard IV, 2.3
**Arabis canadensis* L. Sicklepod IV, 2.6
A. laevigata (Muhl.) Poir. Smooth rock-cress IV, 2.6
Barbarea vulgaris R. Br. Winter cress, Yellow rocket IV, 2.2
Cardamine bulbosa (Schreb.) BSP. Spring cress IV, 2.5
C. douglassii (Torr.) Britt. Purple cress IV, 1.95
**C. rotundifolia* Michx. Mountain watercress IV, 2.5
Dentaria diphylla Michx. Crinkleroot, Two-leaved toothwort IV, 1.39
D. heterophylla Nutt. Slender toothwort IV, 1.40
D. laciniata Muhl. Cut-leaf toothwort IV, 1.38
Hesperis matronalis L. Dame's rocket IV, 1.60
Iodanthus pinnatifidus (Michx.) Steud. Purple rocket IV, 1.96
Nasturtium officinale R. Br. Watercress IV, 2.4

32 *Crassulaceae* (Orpine family)

A family of succulent plants with thick leaves, the *Crassulaceae* are most abundant in South Africa but are also numerous in Mexico and south-central Asia. Many species are cultivated indoors and in rock gardens. Sepals, petals, and pistils are usually 4 or 5 each and the stamens are as many or, more often, twice as many.

Sedum pulchellum Michx. Widow's-cross, Pink stonecrop IV, 2.56
S. ternatum Michx. Stonecrop IV, 2.55

34 *Saxifragaceae* (Saxifrage family)

This large family composed of several subfamilies contains both shrubs and herbs; it includes several ornamentals, such as hydrangea and mock-orange as well as saxifrage, and some bushfruits such as currants. Sepals and petals are usually 4 or 5 each, stamens are usually as many or twice as many, and the pistil is usually divided in two; in some, the ovary is partly beneath the attachment of other parts.

**Astilbe biternata* (Vent.) Britt. False goat's-beard IV, 2.37
Heuchera americana L. Alum-root IV, 2.39
**H. longiflora* Rydb. Alum-root IV, 2.40
**H. parviflora* Bartl. var. *rugelii* (Shuttlw.) Rosend., Butt., & Lak. Alum-root IV, 2.40
**H. pubescens* Pursh Alum-root IV, 2.40
H. villosa Michx. Alum-root IV, 2.40
Mitella diphylla L. Miterwort, Bishop's-cap IV, 2.12
Saxifraga virginiensis Michx. Early saxifrage IV, 2.38
Tiarella cordifolia L. Foamflower IV, 2.11

35 *Rosaceae* (Rose family)

The rose family is economically as well as aesthetically significant, for it includes not only roses but apples, peaches, cherries, and strawberries, and also many herbaceous wildflowers. The leaves usually have stipules, sepals and petals are usually 5 each, and stamens are usually numerous; pistils may be several and separate or single and either simple or compound. The family is worldwide in distribution.

Agrimonia parviflora Ait. Agrimony IV, 2.1
Aruncus dioicus (Walt.) Fernald Goat's-beard IV, 2.37
Duchesnea indica (Andr.) Focke Indian strawberry, Mock strawberry IV, 1.5
Fragaria virginiana Duchesne Wild strawberry IV, 1.41
Geum canadense Jacq. White avens IV, 1.43

Gillenia stipulata (Muhl.) Trel. American ipecac, Indian physic IV, 1.42
**G. trifoliata* (L.) Moench Bowman's-root IV, 1.42
Potentilla canadensis L. Dwarf cinquefoil, Early cinquefoil IV, 1.8
P. recta L. Rough-fruited cinquefoil, Sulphur cinquefoil IV, 1.7
**P. simplex* Michx. Old-field cinquefoil, Common cinquefoil IV, 1.8
Rosa carolina L. Carolina rose, Pasture rose IV, 1.62
**R. palustris* Marsh. Swamp rose IV, 1.62
**R. setigera* Michx. Prairie rose IV, 1.62
Spiraea tomentosa L. Steeple-bush, Hardhack IV, 2.36
Waldsteinia fragarioides (Michx.) Tratt. Barren strawberry IV, 1.6

36 *Leguminosae* (Legume family, Pea family)

The third largest family of flowering plants, worldwide in distribution and especially abundant in the tropics, the legumes altogether comprise about 13,000 species, including trees, shrubs, and herbs. The family contains many food and forage crops such as peas, beans, and clovers, many trees such as redbud and black locust, many other ornamentals such as sweet peas and wisteria, and some poisonous species. With their roots infected with nitrogen-fixing bacteria, they enrich the soil wherever they grow.

Their leaves are usually alternate and compound and have stipules. The flowers are usually bilaterally symmetrical, although some are nearly radially symmetrical. Usually there are 5 sepals, 5 petals, and 10 stamens, 9 of which are often united by their filaments; there is a single simple pistil forming in fruit a true pod or legume.

Amphicarpa bracteata (L.) Fernald Hog-peanut V, 1.5
Apios americana Medic. Groundnut V, 1.15
Baptisia australis (L.) R. Br. Blue false indigo V, 1.4
**B. leucantha* T. & G. White wild indigo V, 1.3
B. leucophaea Nutt. Cream wild indigo V, 1.3
**B. tinctoria* (L.) R. Br. Yellow wild indigo V, 1.3
Cassia fasciculata Michx. Partridge-pea V, 3.2

**C. hebecarpa* Fernald Wild senna V, 3.1
C. marilandica L. Wild senna V, 3.1
**C. nictitans* L. Sensitive plant V, 3.2
Clitoria mariana L. Butterfly-pea V, 1.13
Coronilla varia L. Crown vetch V, 1.10
Desmanthus illinoensis (Michx.) MacM. Prairie mimosa IV, 2.15
**Desmodium canescens* (L.) DC. Hoary tick-trefoil V, 1.20
D. glutinosum (Muhl.) Wood Pointed-leaf tick-trefoil V, 1.18
**D. nudiflorum* (L.) DC. Naked-flowered tick-trefoil V, 1.18
**D. paniculatum* (L.) DC. Narrow-leaf tick-trefoil V, 1.20
D. perplexum Schub. Tick-trefoil, Sticktights V, 1.20
D. rotundifolium DC. Round-leaf tick-trefoil V, 1.19
**D. sessilifolium* (Torr.) T. & G. Sessile-leaf tick-trefoil V, 1.20
Galactia volubis (L.) Britt. Milk-pea V, 1.16
**Lespedeza cuneata* (Dumont) G. Don Silky lespedeza V, 1.23
**L. hirta* (L.) Hornem. Hairy bush-clover V, 1.21
L. intermedia (S. Wats.) Britt. Bush-clover V, 1.21
**L. procumbens* Michx. Creeping bush-clover V, 1.22
L. repens (L.) Bart. Creeping bush-clover V, 1.22
L. stipulacea Maxim. Korean lespedeza V, 1.24
Lotus corniculatus L. Birdfoot trefoil V, 1.2
**Medicago sativa* L. Alfalfa V, 1.7
**Melilotus* spp. Sweet clover V, 1.9
**Petalostemum candidum* (Willd.) Michx. White prairie-clover V, 3.40
P. purpureum (Vent.) Rydb. Purple prairie-clover V, 3.40
Phaseolus polystachios (L.) BSP. Wild bean V, 1.17
Psoralea psoralioides (Walt.) Cory Scurf-pea V, 1.11
Schrankia microphylla (Dry.) Britt. Sensitive brier IV, 2.16
**Strophostyles helvola* (L.) Britt. Trailing wild bean V, 1.14

S. umbellata (Muhl.) Britt. Trailing wild bean V, 1.14
Stylosanthes biflora (L.) BSP. Pencil-flower V, 1.1
Tephrosia virginiana (L.) Pers. Goat's-rue, Rabbit's-pea V, 1.12
Trifolium pratense L. Red clover V, 1.9
Vicia caroliniana Walt. Wood vetch, Devil's shoestring V, 1.6
V. sativa L. Spring vetch V, 1.8
V. villosa Roth Hairy vetch V, 1.7

37 *Linaceae* (Flax family)

This relatively small family, of worldwide distribution nevertheless, is important because of the species of flax cultivated for fibers used to make linen. Most of the family are herbaceous with alternate, entire-margined leaves; the flowers usually have 5 sepals, 5 petals, 5 (or 10) stamens, and 5 styles.

**Linum medium* (Planch.) Britt. Stiff yellow flax IV, 2.61
**L. usitatissimum* L. Common flax IV, 2.61
L. virginianum L. Slender yellow flax IV, 2.61

38 *Oxalidaceae* (Wood-sorrel family)

Plants of this predominantly tropical family taste sour because of the presence of oxalic acid. Many species have trifoliate leaves which fold at night. The flowers have 5 sepals, 5 petals, 10 stamens united by their filaments in 2 series, and 5 styles.

**Oxalis corniculata* L. Yellow wood-sorrel IV, 1.2
**O. europaea* Jordan Yellow wood-sorrel IV, 1.2
O. grandis Small Large wood-sorrel IV, 1.2
O. montana Raf. True wood-sorrel, Wood-shamrock IV, 1.92
**O. stricta* L. Yellow wood-sorrel IV, 1.2
O. violacea L. Violet wood-sorrel IV, 1.64

39 *Geraniaceae* (Geranium family, Crane's-bill family)

The most distinctive feature of the geranium family is the fruit, which is a slender capsule with a long beak formed by the styles. The flowers are complete and have 5 petals and usually 10 stamens (5–15). The leaves, which are often lobed, have stipules and palmate venation. The well-known cultivated geraniums, often grown in pots and window boxes, belong to this family but are in the genus *Pelargonium* and not the genus *Geranium.*

Geranium maculatum L. Wild geranium, Spotted crane's-bill IV, 1.63

40 *Polygalaceae* (Milkwort family)

This family has bilaterally symmetrical flowers subtended by bracts. Of the 5 sepals, 2 are larger than the others and petal-like, suggesting wings, and the 3–5 petals are smaller. There are usually 8 stamens, united by their filaments, and 1 pistil.

Polygala sanguinea L. Field milkwort V, 3.39
P. senega L. Seneca snakeroot V, 3.38

41 *Euphorbiaceae* (Spurge family)

The *Euphorbiaceae* constitute a large family, usually with milky latex, most abundant in the tropics. Several tropical species are economically important as sources, for example, of rubber, tung oil, and tapioca; the family includes also the ornamental poinsettia. Most spurge flowers are small and lack a corolla (some also lack a calyx); sometimes bracts are conspicuous and the inflorescence may simulate a flower. Stamen and pistil, usually 1 each, are in separate flowers; the ovary is 3-lobed and the fruit splits into 3 segments.

Euphorbia commutata Engelm. Early spurge VII, 1.2
E. corollata L. Flowering spurge IV, 2.41

42 *Buxaceae* (Box or boxwood family)

Composed of evergreen herbs, shrubs, and trees, the box family is important because of its ornamental species, especially the boxwoods but also the Japanese spurge (*Pachysandra terminalis*). Its flowers lack petals but have sepals; stamens and pistils are in separate flowers in the same inflorescence. Predominantly an Old World family, it has but 1 species indigenous to eastern United States.

Pachysandra procumbens Michx. Mountain spurge, Allegheny spurge IV, 2.14

43 *Celastraceae* (Staff-tree family)

This family of woody plants with simple leaves and small flowers includes the well-known bittersweet (*Celastrus*) and several species of *Euonymus* in ornamental cultivation. Sepals and petals are 4 or 5 each; stamens, usually 4 or 5, are attached to a fleshy disk which surrounds the ovary and nearly fills the center of the flower. The seeds are enveloped by an appendage which is usually fleshy and brightly colored.

Euonymus obovatus Nutt. Running strawberry-bush IV, 2.54

44 *Balsaminaceae* (Touch-me-not family)

The touch-me-not family, which is most abundant in the tropics of Asia and Africa, is represented in the United States by only 2 indigenous species. They have succulent stems with bland, watery juice, thin leaves, and bilaterally symmetrical flowers. The sepals are petal-like; one of them, larger than the other sepals and the petals, is saclike and prolonged into a spur. The ripe capsules burst suddenly when touched.

Impatiens capensis Meerb. Spotted jewelweed, Spotted touch-me-not V, 3.3

I. pallida Nutt. Pale jewelweed, Pale touch-me-not V, 3.4

45 *Malvaceae* (Mallow family)

The mallow family, containing herbs and shrubs, is widely distributed in both temperate and tropical regions. It includes many well-known plants such as cotton, hollyhocks, several ornamental species of *Hibiscus*, and several weeds. The flowers are 5-petalled, and usually showy; the numerous stamens have their filaments united into a tube surrounding the style.

Hibiscus militaris Cav. Rose mallow IV, 1.65
**H. moscheutos* L. Swamp rose mallow IV, 1.65

46 *Hypericaceae* (St. John's-wort family)

Herbs and shrubs in the St. John's-wort family have leaves opposite or whorled, simple and untoothed, usually sessile, and bearing either translucent or black dots. Flowers, usually orange or yellow, have 4 or 5 petals and usually numerous stamens (few in some species) borne in clusters.

Ascyrum hypericoides L. St. Andrew's-cross IV, 1.10
Hypericum dolabriforme Vent. St. John's-wort IV, 1.12
**H. frondosum* Michx. Shrubby St. John's-wort IV, 1.9
H. perforatum L. Common St. John's-wort IV, 1.11
H. spathulatum (Spach) Steud. Shrubby St. John's-wort IV, 1.9
H. sphaerocarpum Michx. St. John's-wort IV, 1.13

47 *Violaceae* (Violet family)

The temperate representatives of the family are all herbaceous although the tropical members may be herbaceous or woody. The leaves are either basal or alternate on the stem; all leaves have stipules. The flowers are chiefly bilaterally symmetrical and complete. The lowest of the 5 petals is spurred or saclike at the base; filaments of the stamens are short and the anthers are close together. The mature capsule splits in thirds, dispersing the seeds. In addition to the petal-bearing flowers there are some late ones, lacking petals, which never open and are self-fertilized. The genus *Viola*, the largest one of the family, contains many cultivated violets and pansies as well as many well-known wildflowers.

Viola blanda Willd. Sweet white violet V, 3.17
V. canadensis L. Canada violet V, 3.20
**V. conspersa* Reichenb. Dog violet V, 3.22
V. cucullata Ait. Marsh blue violet V, 3.24
V. hastata Michx. Halberd-leaved yellow violet V, 3.16
**V. hirsutula* Brainerd Woolly blue violet V, 3.25
**V. lanceolata* L. Lance-leaved violet V, 3.18
**V. palmata* L. Early blue violet V, 3.26

V. *papilionacea* Pursh Common blue violet, Meadow violet V, 3.23
V. *pedata* L. Birdfoot violet V, 3.28
V. *pensylvanica* Michx. Smooth yellow violet V, 3.15
V. *primulifolia* L. Swamp white violet V, 3.18
*V. *pubescens* Ait. Downy yellow violet V, 3.15
V. *rafinesquii* Greene [V. *kitaibeliana* var. *rafinesquii*] Field pansy V, 3.21
V. *rostrata* Pursh Long-spurred violet V, 3.22
*V. *rotundifolia* Michx. Roundleaf yellow violet V, 3.15
V. *sagittata* Ait. Arrow-leaved violet V, 3.27
V. *sororia* Willd. Woolly blue violet, Downy blue violet V, 3.25
V. *striata* Ait. White violet, Striped violet V, 3.19
V. *triloba* Schwein. Three-lobed violet V, 3.26

48 *Passifloraceae* (Passion-flower family)

Principally vines climbing by tendrils, the passion-flowers bear alternate petioled leaves and axillary flowers. The flowers have a fringed crown in addition to the 5 sepals and 5 petals. The family, which contains several ornamental species, is predominantly tropical American; only 2 species occur in our range.

Passiflora incarnata L. Passion-flower IV, 1.97
P. lutea L. Yellow passion-flower IV, 1.98

49 *Cactaceae* (Cactus family)

This New World family is composed chiefly of fleshy thickened plants, usually with spines and usually without typical leaves. The flowers are solitary, sessile, and showy. The ovary is beneath the attachment of sepals, petals, and stamens, all of which are numerous.

Opuntia humifusa Raf. Prickly pear VII, 3.1

50 *Lythraceae* (Loosestrife family)

The loosestrife family contains both herbaceous and woody species. These plants usually have opposite or whorled simple leaves without marginal teeth. Sepals are 4–7, petals are of the same number or absent, and the stamens are usually as many or twice as many; these are all borne on a calyx tube which surrounds the ovary but is free from it. (Stamens are numerous in the cultivated crape-myrtle.)

**Lythrum alatum* Pursh Purple loosestrife VII, 2.5
L. lanceolatum Ell. Purple loosestrife VII, 2.5

51 *Melastomataceae* (Melastome family)

Plants of the melastome family, which is predominantly tropical, have opposite, prominently veined leaves with palmate, almost parallel, venation. The flowers are often showy; petals are 4 or 5 and stamens are usually twice as many.

**Rhexia mariana* L. Maryland meadowbeauty IV, 1.66
R. virginica L. Virginia meadowbeauty IV, 1.66

52 *Onagraceae* (Evening primrose family)

These are principally herbs of temperate regions, most abundant in North America, although they include a few tropical woody plants such as *Fuchsia* in ornamental cultivation. The calyx lobes, petals, and stamens are usually 2 or 4 each (5 in *Jussiaea*), and the ovary is conspicuously below the other parts of the flower.

Circaea quadrisulcata (Maxim.) Franch. & Sav. Enchanter's nightshade IV, 2.8
**Jussiaea decurrens* (Walt.) DC. Primrose-willow, Water primrose IV, 1.17
J. repens L. Primrose-willow, Water primrose IV, 1.17
Ludwigia alternifolia L. Seedbox, Rattlebox IV, 1.16
Oenothera biennis L. Evening primrose IV, 1.14
O. tetragona Roth Sundrops IV, 1.15

53 *Araliaceae* (Ginseng family)

The members of the ginseng family, both woody and herbaceous, have mostly alternate compound leaves (though simple in English ivy, *Hedera helix*). The flowers, often unisexual, are small and borne in umbels which are paniculate or umbellate in a compound inflorescence. The ovary is below the other parts, and the styles are usually 5 (2–5). The fruit is a berry.

Aralia racemosa L. Spikenard IV, 2.33
Panax quinquefolium L. Ginseng IV, 2.34
P. trifolium L. Dwarf ginseng IV, 2.35

54 *Umbelliferae* (Parsley family)

These herbs of temperate regions usually have alternate or basal leaves with dilated and sheathing petioles. The flowers, small and usually borne in compound umbels (rarely in heads, as in *Eryngium*), have a reduced calyx, 5 petals, and 5 stamens. There are 2 styles, and the ovary is below the other flower parts (inferior); the fruit is 2-parted with 1 seed in each half. The family contains such vegetables as carrots, celery, and parsley, and also some poisonous plants.

Angelica venenosa (Greenway) Fernald Hairy angelica IV, 2.26
Bupleurum rotundifolium L. Hare's ear IV, 2.21
Cicuta maculata L. Water hemlock IV, 2.31
Conium maculatum L. Poison hemlock IV, 2.30
Daucus carota L. Wild carrot, Queen Anne's lace IV, 2.28
Erigenia bulbosa (Michx.) Nutt. Harbinger-of-spring IV, 2.32
Eryngium prostratum Nutt. Prostrate eryngo IV, 2.20
E. yuccifolium Michx. Rattlesnake-master VII, 2.6
**Osmorhiza claytoni* (Michx.) Clarke Hairy sweet cicely IV, 2.27
O. longistylis (Torr.) DC. Sweet cicely, Sweet anise, Anise-root IV, 2.27
Pastinaca sativa L. Wild parsnip IV, 2.22
Taenidia integerrima (L.) Drude Yellow pimpernel IV, 2.23
Thaspium barbinode (Michx.) Nutt. Meadow-parsnip IV, 2.24
**T. trifoliatum* (L.) Gray Purple meadow-parsnip IV, 2.25
**T. trifoliatum* var. *flavum* Blake Meadow-parsnip IV, 2.25

Torilis japonica (Houtt.) DC. Hedge parsley IV, 2.29
Zizia aptera (Gray) Fernald Golden Alexanders IV, 2.25
**Z. aurea* (L.) Koch Golden Alexanders IV, 2.25

55 *Pyrolaceae* (Wintergreen family)

Found in north temperate regions and related to the *Ericaceae* (no. 56), this family, with relatively few members, contains small evergreen plants and non-green saprophytes. The frequently pendent flowers have 5 sepals, 5 petals (separate or very slightly united), 10 stamens, and a single compound pistil.

Chimaphila maculata (L.) Pursh Spotted wintergreen, Striped pipsissiwa IV, 1.44
Monotropa hypopithys L. Pinesap VII, 3.3
M. uniflora L. Indian pipe VII, 3.2

FAMILIES HAVING PETALS AT LEAST PARTLY UNITED (NUMBERS 56–79)

Flowers are complete and radially symmetrical unless designated otherwise, and the ovary is above the attachment of other parts unless specified as being below or "inferior."

56 *Ericaceae* (Heath family)

This is a large family of chiefly woody plants including the mountain laurel, rhododendrons, azaleas, blueberries, and cranberries, all of which require acid soil. The calyx and corolla lobes are usually 5 each (rarely 4–7), and the stamens are as many or twice as many; the ovary is "superior" in some and "inferior" in some.

Epigaea repens L. Trailing arbutus IV, 1.99
Gaultheria procumbens L. Teaberry, Wintergreen, Mountain tea IV, 2.53

57 *Diapensiaceae* (Diapensia family)

This is a small family of low evergreen shrubs and herbs found principally in eastern North America. The flowers have 5 calyx

to the stigma. There are 2 ovaries but usually only 1 develops into a "pod" (actually a follicle); seeds are numerous and often bear tufts of hairs.

**Asclepias amplexicaulis* Sm. Blunt-leaved milkweed IV, 1.69
*A. *exaltata* L. Poke milkweed IV, 1.47
A. *incarnata* L. Swamp milkweed IV, 1.70
*A. *perennis* Walt. IV, 1.47
A. *purpurascens* L. Purple milkweed IV, 1.69
A. *quadrifolia* Jacq. Four-leaved milkweed IV, 1.103
*A. *syriaca* L. Common milkweed IV, 1.69
A. *tuberosa* L. Butterfly weed, Orange milkweed IV, 1.22
A. *variegata* L. White milkweed IV, 1.47
A. *viridiflora* Raf. Green milkweed IV, 1.104
**Gonolobus obliquus* (Jacq.) Schultes Angle-pod IV, 1.71
G. *shortii* Gray Angle-pod IV, 1.71

63 *Convolvulaceae* (Morning-glory family)

This family contains the sweet potato, some cultivated ornamental vines, several weeds, and the dodders, which are twining, leafless, non-green parasites. The corolla is usually funnel-shaped or trumpet-shaped and twisted in bud; there are 5 stamens and a single compound pistil with 1–4 stigmas.

**Convolvulus arvensis* L. Small bindweed IV, 1.48
*C. *sepium* L. Hedge bindweed IV, 1.49
C. *spithamaeus* L. Upright bindweed IV, 1.48
Ipomoea hederacea (L.) Jacq. Ivy-leaved morning-glory IV, 1.74
I. *pandurata* (L.) G.F.W. Mey. Wild potato vine IV, 1.49
I. *purpurea* (L.) Roth Common morning-glory IV, 1.73

64 *Polemoniaceae* (Phlox family)

This predominantly American family is chiefly herbaceous, bearing showy clusters of flowers, and includes several cultivated garden flowers. The united corolla is bell-shaped or more often tubular with spreading lobes; there are 5 stamens, 3 stigmas, and a 3-celled ovary which becomes a capsule in fruit.

**Phlox amoena* Sims Hairy phlox IV, 1.77
**P. amplifolia* Britt. Broad-leaved phlox IV, 1.80
**P. bifida* Beck Sand phlox IV, 1.76
P. carolina L. var. *triflora* (Michx.) Wherry Thick-leaf phlox IV, 1.78
P. divaricata L. Blue phlox, Wild sweet William IV, 1.79
**P. glaberrima* L. Smooth phlox IV, 1.78
P. maculata L. Meadow phlox IV, 1.80
**P. paniculata* L. Fall phlox, Veiny-leaved phlox, Panicled phlox IV, 1.80
P. pilosa L. Downy phlox, Prairie phlox IV, 1.77
**P. stolonifera* Sims Creeping phlox IV, 1.76
P. subulata L. Moss phlox, "Moss-pink" IV, 1.76
Polemonium reptans L. Jacob's-ladder, Greek valerian IV, 1.81

65 *Hydrophyllaceae* (Waterleaf family)

Cosmopolitan in distribution but most abundant in North America, the waterleaf family has flowers with calyx and corolla each 5-lobed, 5 stamens usually longer than the corolla, and a pistil with 2 styles and 2 stigmas.

Hydrophyllum appendiculatum Michx. Appendaged waterleaf, Lavender waterleaf IV, 1.83
H. canadense L. Broad-leaf waterleaf IV, 1.51
H. macrophyllum Nutt. Large-leaf waterleaf IV, 1.50
Phacelia bipinnatifida Michx. Purple phacelia IV, 1.82
P. purshii Buckl. Phacelia, Miami mist IV, 1.105

66 *Boraginaceae* (Borage family)

This large, chiefly herbaceous family is worldwide in distribution and is better represented in western United States than in the eastern states. Most of the plants are rough-hairy (though exceptional ones, such as *Mertensia*, are glabrous), with simple, alternate, usually entire-margined leaves. Flowers have a 5-lobed corolla with 5 stamens attached, and a deeply 4-lobed ovary which usually forms 4 nutlets in fruit.

Cynoglossum virginianum L. Wild comfrey, Hound's tongue IV, 1.106
Echium vulgare L. Blueweed, Viper's bugloss V, 3.31
Lithospermum canescens (Michx.) Lehm. Hoary puccoon IV, 1.23
Mertensia virginica (L.) Pers. Virginia bluebells, Virginia cowslip IV, 1.84
**Myosotis macrosperma* Engelm. White forget-me-not IV, 2.19
M. scorpioides L. Forget-me-not IV, 2.19
**M. verna* Nutt. White forget-me-not IV, 2.19

67 *Verbenaceae* (Verbena family)

This is a large family, both herbaceous and woody, with many more tropical than temperate species. Leaves are usually opposite (or whorled) and simple; small flowers are borne in spikes or compact headlike clusters. The corolla tube flares into 4 or 5 lobes, nearly radially symmetrical or slightly bilaterally symmetrical; the stamens are in 2 pairs; the ovary forms 2 or 4 nutlets in fruit but is not deeply 4-lobed.

Verbena canadensis L. Rose verbena IV, 1.75
**V. hastata* L. Blue vervain IV, 2.17
V. simplex Lehm. Narrow-leaved vervain IV, 2.17

68 *Labiatae* (Mint family)

Containing over 3,000 species and worldwide in both warm and temperate regions, the mint family is chiefly herbaceous, having opposite leaves and quadrangular stems, and is usually aromatic. The 5-lobed (occasionally 4-lobed) corolla is usually bilaterally symmetrical and 2-lipped but is nearly radially symmetrical in a few species. There are either 2 or 4 stamens, and the ovary is deeply 4-lobed, forming 4 nutlets in fruit.

The family is important as the source of many aromatic oils such as lavender, sage, rosemary, and mint, and several of the family, including thyme, savory, and basil, are used as culinary herbs. Many of the family are grown ornamentally.

Agastache nepetoides (L.) Ktze. Giant hyssop V, 2.35
Blephilia ciliata (L.) Benth. Downy wood-mint V, 2.26
**B. hirsuta* (Pursh) Benth. Hairy wood-mint V, 2.26
Collinsonia canadensis L. Horse-balm, Citronella V, 2.2
Cunila origanoides (L.) Britt. Dittany V, 2.28
Glechoma hederacea L. Ground-ivy V, 2.31
Hedeoma pulegioides (L.) Pers. American pennyroyal V, 2.29
Lamium amplexicaule L. Henbit, Dead-nettle V, 2.30
**L. purpureum* L. Purple dead-nettle V, 2.30
Meehania cordata (Nutt.) Britt. Meehania V, 2.18
**Mentha piperita* L. Peppermint IV, 2.18
M. spicata L. Spearmint IV, 2.18
**Monarda bradburiana* Beck White bergamot V, 2.12
**M. clinopodia* L. White bergamot V, 2.12
M. fistulosa L. Bergamot V, 2.11
M. russeliana Nutt. [*M. virgata*] White bergamot V, 2.12
Nepeta cataria L. Catnip V, 2.34
Physostegia virginiana (L.) Benth. False dragonhead, Obedient plant V, 2.20
Prunella vulgaris L. Heal-all, Self-heal V, 2.27
Pycnanthemum flexuosum (Walt.) BSP. [*P. tenuifolium*] Slender mountain-mint V, 2.37
**P. incanum* (L.) Michx. Hoary mountain-mint V, 2.36
P. pycnanthemoides (Leavenw.) Fernald Hoary mountain-mint V, 2.36
Salvia lyrata L. Lyre-leaved sage V, 2.25
**Scutellaria elliptica* Muhl. Hairy skullcap V, 2.23
S. incana Biehler Downy skullcap, Hoary skullcap V, 2.23
S. integrifolia L. Large-flowered skullcap V, 2.21
S. lateriflora L. Mad-dog skullcap V, 2.22
S. nervosa Pursh Veiny skullcap V, 2.24
**S. ovata* Hill Heart-leaved skullcap V, 2.23
**S. parvula* Michx. Small skullcap V, 2.24
**Stachys clingmanii* Small Clingman's hedge-nettle V, 2.32
S. riddellii House Riddell's hedge-nettle V, 2.32

S. tenuifolia Willd. Narrow-leaved hedge-nettle V, 2.33
Synandra hispidula (Michx.) Baill. Synandra V, 2.9
Teucrium canadense L. Germander, Wood-sage V, 3.33
Trichostema dichotomum L. Blue curls V, 3.32

69 *Solanaceae* (Nightshade family)

This large cosmopolitan family, with species most numerous in South America, contains food plants, drug plants, poisonous weeds, and ornamental flowers. Some examples are the potato, tomato, peppers, tobacco, petunia, and the source of belladonna and atropine. Most members of the family are herbaceous with alternate leaves, although some tropical species are woody. The flowers usually have a 5-lobed corolla, pleated in bud, with 5 stamens attached to the tube and alternating with the lobes. The fruit is either a berry or a capsule.

Datura stramonium L. Jimsonweed IV, 1.87
Nicandra physalodes (L.) Pers. Apple-of-Peru IV, 1.88

70 *Scrophulariaceae* (Figwort family)

The *Scrophulariaceae* comprise a large, predominantly herbaceous family found on every continent. Although the leaves may be opposite or whorled, they are most often alternate. The corolla is usually bilaterally symmetrical, but in some it is nearly radially symmetrical and either 5-lobed with 5 stamens or 4-lobed with 2 or 4 stamens. The corolla is often 2-lipped, usually with 4 stamens but with 2 in some and with a sterile fifth stamen in a few. The 2-lipped species with opposite leaves resemble the mint family, but all the *Scrophulariaceae* can be distinguished from the *Labiatae* by the fruit, which is a 2-celled, many-seeded capsule in contrast to the 4 nutlets of the mints. The family contains many garden ornamentals, including the snapdragon and the foxglove (*Digitalis*), which is also a drug source.

**Aureolaria flava* (L.) Farw. [*Gerardia flava*] Smooth false foxglove V, 3.5
*A. *laevigata* (Raf.) Raf. [*Gerardia laevigata*] Smooth false foxglove V, 3.5

**A. pectinata* (Nutt.) Pennell [*Gerardia pectinata*] Fernleaf false foxglove V, 3.6

A. pedicularia (L.) Raf. [*Gerardia pedicularia*] Fernleaf false foxglove V, 3.6

A. virginica (L.) Pennell [*Gerardia virginica*] False foxglove V, 3.5

Chelone glabra L. Turtlehead V, 2.10

Collinsia verna Nutt. Blue-eyed Mary V, 2.17

Dasistoma macrophylla (Nutt.) Raf. [*Seymeria macrophylla*] Mullein foxglove V, 3.7

Gerardia purpurea L. Purple gerardia V, 3.34

**G. tenuifolia* Vahl Slender gerardia V, 3.34

Linaria vulgaris Hill Butter-and-eggs V, 2.1

**Mimulus alatus* Ait. Monkey-flower V, 2.19

M. ringens L. Monkey-flower V, 2.19

Pedicularis canadensis L. Wood-betony, Lousewort V, 2.3

Penstemon brevisepalus Pennell Short-sepal beard-tongue V, 2.16

**P. canescens* Britt. Gray beard-tongue V, 2.16

P. digitalis Nutt. Foxglove beard-tongue V, 2.13

P. hirsutus (L.) Willd. Hairy beard-tongue V, 2.15

P. tenuiflorus Pennell Slender-flowered beard-tongue V, 2.14

Verbascum blattaria L. Moth mullein V, 3.8

**V. thapsus* L. Woolly mullein V, 3.8

Veronica officinalis L. Common speedwell V, 3.36

V. persica Poir. Bird's-eye V, 3.35

Veronicastrum virginicum (L.) Farw. Culver's root V, 3.37

71 *Orobanchaceae* (Broom-rape family)

This is a family of root parasites which lack chlorophyll. The leaves are reduced and scale-like; the flowers, having a 2-lipped corolla and 4 stamens, are similar in structure to those of the figwort family except for a 1-celled instead of a 2-celled ovary and fruit.

Conopholis americana (L.) Wallr. Squawroot, Cancer-root VII, 3.5

Epifagus virginiana (L.) Bart. Beech-drops VII, 3.4

72 *Acanthaceae* (Acanthus family)

The acanthus family has only a few herbaceous representatives in temperate United States although it is a large family of both herbaceous and woody species throughout the tropics. The leaves are opposite; the corolla is either 2-lipped or radially symmetrical and 5-lobed, and the 2 or 4 stamens are attached to it; the pistil has 2 stigmas and 2 cells in the ovary.

Justicia americana (L.) Vahl Water-willow V, 2.38
**Ruellia caroliniensis* (Walt.) Steud. Hairy ruellia IV, 1.85
*R. *humilis* Nutt. Sessile ruellia IV, 1.85
R. *strepens* L. Ruellia IV, 1.85

73 *Phrymaceae* (Lopseed family)

This family is composed of only 1 genus, which has a single species in eastern North America and a few species in eastern Asia.

Phryma leptostachya L. Lopseed V, 2.39

74 *Rubiaceae* (Madder family)

This is a large tropical family, predominantly woody, which includes coffee, quinine, and gardenias. The few representatives in temperate regions are mostly herbaceous. The leaves are simple, entire-margined, and opposite, or appear whorled when stipules are as large as the leaf blades. The corolla is 4- or 5-lobed (4-lobed in the species found in eastern United States), with stamens of the same number alternating with the corolla lobes. The ovary is beneath the attachment of the corolla tube.

**Diodia teres* Walt. Annual buttonweed, Poor Joe IV, 2.52
D. *virginiana* L. Buttonweed IV, 2.52
**Galium aparine* L. Bedstraw, Cleavers IV, 2.50
G. *concinnum* T. & G. Shining bedstraw IV, 2.50
Houstonia caerulea L. Bluets, Quaker-ladies IV, 1.86
*H. *canadensis* Willd. Fringed Houstonia IV, 2.51
H. *lanceolata* (Poir.) Britt. Houstonia IV, 2.51
*H. *longifolia* Gaertn. Long-leaved Houstonia IV, 2.51

**H. nigricans* (Lam.) Fernald Narrow-leaved Houstonia IV, 2.51
H. patens Ell. Small bluets, Star-violet IV, 2.64
**H. purpurea* L. Large Houstonia IV, 2.51
**H. serpyllifolia* Michx. Thyme-leaved bluets IV, 1.86
**H. tenuifolia* Nutt. Slender-leaved Houstonia IV, 2.51
Mitchella repens L. Partridge-berry IV, 1.52

75 *Caprifoliaceae* (Honeysuckle family)

Although a few members of the honeysuckle family are herbaceous, most are woody. The latter include many ornamental shrubs such as *Viburnum*, *Lonicera* (the honeysuckles), *Sambucus* (the elderberries), *Abelia*, and *Weigela*. The family is found principally in north temperate regions. The leaves are opposite; the flowers usually have 5 corolla lobes and 5 stamens, and are either radially or bilaterally symmetrical; the ovary is "inferior."

Triosteum angustifolium L. Yellow horse-gentian V, 3.9
T. aurantiacum Bickn. Horse-gentian V, 3.10
**T. perfoliatum* L. Horse-gentian V, 3.10

76 *Valerianaceae* (Valerian family)

The valerian family is a small group of mostly north-temperate herbaceous plants. They have opposite leaves and either radially or bilaterally symmetrical flowers with 5 corolla lobes, 1–4 stamens (most often 3), and an ovary below the corolla tube.

Valeriana pauciflora Michx. Valerian IV, 1.107
Valerianella intermedia Dyal and *V. patellaria* (Sulliv.) Wood Corn-salad, Lamb's-lettuce IV, 2.59

77 *Campanulaceae* (Bluebell family, Bellflower family)

The bluebell family is widely distributed in temperate and subtropical regions. Most members are herbaceous with alternate simple leaves. The flowers usually have a 5-lobed corolla and 5 stamens, and the ovary is below the attachment of the corolla.

Several genera are in ornamental cultivation, including 100 species in the genus *Campanula* alone.

Campanula americana L. Tall bellflower IV, 1.90
C. divaricata Michx. Southern harebell, Panicled bellflower IV, 2.46
Specularia perfoliata (L.) A. DC. Venus' looking-glass IV, 1.89

78 *Lobeliaceae* (Lobelia family)

[Ranked as a subfamily, *Lobelioideae*, under *Campanulaceae* by Fernald in *Gray's Manual of Botany*, Eighth Edition.]

This is a relatively small temperate and subtropical family, chiefly herbaceous but including a few shrubs. The 5-lobed corolla is 2-lipped; the 5 stamens are united into a tube around the style; and the ovary is below the attachment of the corolla. Several species of *Lobelia* are in ornamental cultivation.

Lobelia cardinalis L. Cardinal flower V, 2.4
L. inflata L. Indian tobacco V, 2.8
L. puberula Michx. Downy lobelia V, 2.6
L. siphilitica L. Great blue lobelia V, 2.5
L. spicata Lam. Pale spiked lobelia V, 2.7

79 *Compositae* (Composite family)

The family *Compositae* is the largest of all plant families and the most complex of all families of dicotyledons. It includes several edible vegetables, many noxious weeds, and many ornamental garden flowers, as well as interesting wild species.

The main distinguishing characteristics are: 1) composite flower-heads in which many small individual flowers are inserted on a common receptacle, subtended by an involucre; 2) corollas either tubular or strap-shaped, one kind or both in a single head; 3) union of anthers into a cylinder surrounding the style; and 4) a dry, single-seeded fruit produced beneath the attachment of other flower-parts.

Achillea millefolium L. Yarrow, Milfoil VI, 3.39
Actinomeris alternifolia (L.) DC. Wingstem, Yellow ironweed VI, 3.21

*Antennaria *plantaginifolia* (L.) Richard Pussy-toes VI, 1.1

A. *solitaria* Rydb. Pussy-toes VI, 1.1

Aster *cordifolius* L. Heart-leaved aster VI, 3.43

A. *divaricatus* L. White wood aster VI, 3.53

A. *infirmus* Michx. Cornel-leaf aster VI, 3.52

*A. *laevis* L. Smooth aster VI, 3.46

A. *lateriflorus* (L.) Britt. Calico aster VI, 3.51

*A. *linariifolius* L. Stiff-leaf aster VI, 3.48

*A. *lowrieanus* Porter Lowrie's aster VI, 3.43

*A. *macrophyllus* L. Large-leaf aster VI, 3.43

A. *novae-angliae* L. New England aster VI, 3.47

A. *oblongifolius* Nutt. Aromatic aster VI, 3.48

A. *patens* Ait. Spreading aster VI, 3.46

A. *pilosus* Willd. var. *demotus* Blake Frost-weed aster VI, 3.49

A. *prenanthoides* T. & G. Crooked-stem aster VI, 3.45

*A. *sagittifolius* Wedemeyer Arrow-leaf aster VI, 3.43

*A. *sericeus* Vent. Silky aster VI, 3.48

A. *shortii* Lindl. Short's aster VI, 3.42

A. *simplex* Willd. Panicled aster VI, 3.50

*A. *surculosus* Michx. Creeping aster VI, 3.48

*A. *umbellatus* Mill. Flat-topped aster VI, 3.52

A. *undulatus* L. Wavy-leaf aster VI, 3.44

*A. *vimineus* Lam. Small white aster VI, 3.51

Astranthium integrifolium (Michx.) Nutt. Western daisy VI, 3.38

Bidens aristosa (Michx.) Britt. Tickseed sunflower VI, 3.16

B. *cernua* L. Nodding bur-marigold, Sticktight VI, 3.15

*B. *coronata* (L.) Frisch Tickseed sunflower VI, 3.16

*B. *polylepis* Blake Tickseed sunflower VI, 3.16

Cacalia atriplicifolia L. Pale Indian-plantain VI, 1.3

Carduus nutans L. Nodding thistle, Musk thistle VI, 1.13

Centaurea maculosa Lam. Star thistle, Knapweed VI, 1.17

Chrysanthemum leucanthemum L. var. *pinnatifidum* Lecoq & Lamotte Ox-eye daisy, Field daisy VI, 3.37

Chrysopsis mariana (L.) Nutt. Maryland golden aster VI, 3.14
C. *nervosa* (Willd.) Fernald [C. *graminifolia*] Grass-leaved golden aster, Silkgrass VII, 2.7
Cichorium intybus L. Chicory VI, 2.1
**Cirsium altissimum* (L.) Spreng. Tall thistle VI, 1.15
C. *discolor* (Muhl.) Spreng. Field thistle VI, 1.15
C. *muticum* Michx. Swamp thistle VI, 1.16
C. *vulgare* (Savi) Tenore Common thistle, Bull thistle VI, 1.14
**Coreopsis auriculata* L. Lobed tickseed VI, 3.17
C. *major* Walt. Large coreopsis, Tickseed VI, 3.17
C. *tripteris* L. Tall coreopsis, Tickseed VI, 3.18
**Echinacea pallida* Nutt. Purple coneflower VI, 3.36
E. *purpurea* (L.) Moench Purple coneflower VI, 3.36
**Erigeron annuus* (L.) Pers. White-top VI, 3.41
E. *philadelphicus* L. Philadelphia fleabane VI, 3.41
E. *pulchellus* Michx. Robin's-plantain VI, 3.40
*E. *strigosus* Muhl. White-top VI, 3.41
Eupatorium coelestinum L. Mistflower VI, 1.8
E. *fistulosum* Barratt Joe-Pye weed VI, 1.9
*E. *incarnatum* Walt. Pink thoroughwort VI, 1.8
E. *perfoliatum* L. Boneset VI, 1.6
*E. *purpureum* L. Joe-Pye weed VI, 1.9
E. *rugosum* Houtt. White snakeroot VI, 1.4
E. *serotinum* Michx. Late thoroughwort VI, 1.5
E. *sessilifolium* L. Upland boneset VI, 1.7
Gnaphalium obtusifolium L. Everlasting, Cudweed, Catfoot VI, 1.2
*G. *purpureum* L. Purple cudweed VI, 1.2
Helenium autumnale L. Autumn sneezeweed, Yellow-headed sneezeweed VI, 3.19
H. *nudiflorum* Nutt. Purple-headed sneezeweed VI, 3.20
**Helianthus annuus* L. Annual sunflower p. 259
H. *decapetalus* L. Thin-leaved sunflower VI, 3.34
H. *divaricatus* L. Woodland sunflower VI, 3.32
*H. *hirsutus* Raf. Stiff-haired sunflower VI, 3.32
H. *microcephalus* T. & G. Small-headed sunflower, Small wood sunflower VI, 3.23

**H. mollis* Lam. Downy sunflower VI, 3.35
H. strumosus L. Rough-leaved sunflower VI, 3.33
H. tuberosus L. Jerusalem artichoke VI, 3.35
Heliopsis helianthoides (L.) Sweet False sunflower, Ox-eye VI, 3.31
Hieracium venosum L. Hawkweed, Rattlesnake-weed VI, 2.4
Krigia biflora (Walt.) Blake Dwarf dandelion, Cynthia VI, 2.3
*K. *dandelion* (L.) Nutt. Dwarf dandelion VI, 2.3
*K. *virginica* (L.) Willd. Dwarf dandelion VI, 2.3
**Liatris scariosa* Willd. Blazing star, Gayfeather VI, 1.11
L. *spicata* (L.) Willd. Blazing star, Gayfeather VI, 1.10
L. *squarrosa* L. Blazing star, Gayfeather VI, 1.11
**Onopordum* sp. Scotch thistle VI, 1.14
Polymnia uvedalia L. Yellow leaf-cup, Bear's foot VI, 3.28
Prenanthes altissima L. Rattlesnake-root, Tall white lettuce VI, 2.5
Ratibida pinnata (Vent.) Barnh. Prairie coneflower, Gray-headed coneflower VI, 3.27
Rudbeckia hirta L. Black-eyed Susan VI, 3.25
R. *laciniata* L. Wild goldengrow, Tall coneflower VI, 3.26
R. *triloba* L. Thin-leaved coneflower, Brown-eyed Susan VI, 3.24
Senecio aureus L. Golden ragwort VI, 3.12
S. *glabellus* Poir. Butterweed VI, 3.13
*S. *obovatus* Muhl. Round-leaved ragwort VI, 3.12
*S. *smallii* Britt. Small's ragwort VI, 3.12
Sericocarpus asteroides (L.) BSP. White-top aster VI, 3.54
*S. *linifolius* (L.) BSP. Narrow-leaved white-top aster VI, 3.54
**Silphium integrifolium* Michx. Rosinweed VI, 3.30
*S. *laciniatum* L. Compass plant VI, 3.30
S. *perfoliatum* L. Cup-plant, Indian cup VI, 3.29
*S. *terebinthinaceum* Jacq. Prairie dock VI, 3.30

S. *trifoliatum* L. Whorled rosinweed VI, 3.30
Solidago albopilosa Braun White-haired goldenrod, Rockhouse goldenrod VI, 3.8
S. *altissima* L. Tall goldenrod VI, 3.1
*S. *arguta* Ait. Cut-leaf goldenrod VI, 3.2
*S. *bicolor* L. White goldenrod, Silver-rod VI, 3.9
*S. *boottii* Hook. Boott's goldenrod VI, 3.2
S. *caesia* L. Wreath goldenrod, Blue-stemmed goldenrod VI, 3.6
*S. *canadensis* L. Canada goldenrod VI, 3.2
S. *erecta* Pursh Erect goldenrod, Slender goldenrod VI, 3.9
S. *flexicaulis* L. Broad-leaf goldenrod, Zigzag goldenrod VI, 3.7
*S. *gigantea* Ait. Great goldenrod VI, 3.2
S. *graminifolia* (L.) Salisb. Grass-leaved goldenrod, Bushy goldenrod VI, 3.11
*S. *hispida* Muhl. Hairy goldenrod VI, 3.9
S. *juncea* Ait. Early goldenrod VI, 3.2
*S. *nemoralis* Ait. Gray goldenrod, Old-field goldenrod VI, 3.2
*S. *odora* Ait. Sweet goldenrod VI, 3.2
S. *rugosa* Mill. var. *celtidifolia* (Small) Fernald Rough goldenrod VI, 3.4
S. *speciosa* Nutt. Showy goldenrod VI, 3.10
S. *sphacelata* Raf. False goldenrod VI, 3.5
S. *ulmifolia* Muhl. Elm-leaved goldenrod VI, 3.3
Taraxacum officinale Weber Dandelion VI, 2.2
Verbesina helianthoides Michx. Sunflower crownbeard VI, 3.22
Vernonia altissima Nutt. Ironweed VI, 1.12
*V. *fasciculata* Michx. Ironweed VI, 1.12
*V. *missurica* Raf. Ironweed VI, 1.12
*V. *noveboracensis* (L.) Michx. Ironweed VI, 1.12

SUGGESTED REFERENCES

For a more complete and technical treatment of species in the Kentucky flora the following standard botanical manuals are recommended:

Fernald, M. L. 1950. *Gray's Manual of Botany*, Eighth Edition. New York: American Book Company.

Gleason, H. A. 1952. *New Britton and Brown Illustrated Flora of the Northeastern United States and Adjacent Canada*. New York: New York Botanical Garden.

———, and Cronquist, A. 1963. *Manual of Vascular Plants of Northeastern United States and Adjacent Canada*. Princeton: D. Van Nostrand Company.

Wherry, E. T. 1948. *Guide to Eastern Ferns*, Second Edition. Philadelphia: University of Pennsylvania Press.

Several comprehensive, published floras of nearby states may also be helpful, although some species shown in them do not occur in Kentucky and some found in Kentucky do not occur in those states. The following are suggested:

Braun, E. L. 1967. *The Monocotyledoneae*. Vascular Flora of Ohio, Volume 1. Columbus: Ohio State University Press.

Deam, C. C. 1940. *Flora of Indiana*. Indianapolis: Indiana Department of Conservation, Division of Forestry.

Mohlenbrock, R. H. 1959. *A Flora of Southern Illinois*. Carbondale: Southern Illinois University Press.

Radford, A. E.; Ahles, H. E.; and Bell, C. R. 1964. *Manual of the Vascular Flora of the Carolinas*. Chapel Hill: University of North Carolina Press.

Strausbaugh, P. D., and Core, E. L. 1952–1964. *Flora of West Virginia*, Parts 1–4. Morgantown: West Virginia University Bulletin.

Index